THE WORK OF THE SPIRIT

THE WORK OF THE SPIRIT

Pneumatology and Pentecostalism

Edited by

Michael Welker

WILLIAM B. EERDMANS PUBLISHING COMPANY
GRAND RAPIDS, MICHIGAN / CAMBRIDGE, U.K.

Published 2006 by

Wm. B. Eerdmans Publishing Co.

2140 Oak Industrial Drive N.E., Grand Rapids, Michigan 49505 /

P.O. Box 163, Cambridge CB3 9PU U.K.

Printed in the United States of America

11 10 09 08 07 06   7 6 5 4 3 2 1

Library of Congress Cataloging-in-Publication Data

The work of the Spirit: pneumatology and Pentecostalism /
    edited by Michael Welker.
        p.   cm.
    Includes bibliographical references and index.
    ISBN-10: 0-8028-0387-3 / ISBN-13: 978-0-8028-0387-0 (pbk: alk. paper)
    1. Holy Spirit. 2. Pentecostalism.   I. Welker, Michael, 1947-

    BT121.3.W67   2006
    231'.3 — dc22

                                            2006027813

www.eerdmans.com

Contents

Acknowledgments

This book is the result of a consultation entitled "Pneumatology: Exploring the Work of the Spirit from Contemporary Perspectives," held in New York City in November 2004. It brought together international scholars in the areas of theology, biblical studies, religious history, anthropology, and natural sciences. The interdisciplinary discourse on the topic had a specific profile as scholars with Pentecostal and Charismatic religious backgrounds and scholars with Anglican, Reformed, Lutheran, Methodist, and Roman Catholic heritages entered into a dialogue with each other. The conference took place almost a century after the so-called "Azusa Street Revival" in Los Angeles, which is often regarded as the initial event in the amazing development and spreading of last century's Pentecostal and Charismatic movements — movements that now encompass more than one fourth of the two billion Christians in the world.

One of the main interests of the John Templeton Foundation is to support research on "spiritual realities." This is a very complicated area in which a myriad of vague notions have been propagated. They have often prevented serious academic discourse and have driven respected scholars away. The combination of a dialogue among different traditions of faith and a dialogue among different academic disciplines including the sciences and philosophy was meant to provide space for critical and self-critical reflection on "spiritual realities."

We thank the John Templeton Foundation for its generous support of the consultation and of this publication. We are particularly grateful to

ACKNOWLEDGMENTS

Dr. Mary Ann Meyers, who with great enthusiasm, kindness, and care planned and organized the meeting and the process of collecting and revising the contributions. We also thank Dr. Charles Harper for his constructive presence in the consultation, and Jennifer Hoffman, Alexander Massmann, and Tobias Hanel for assisting in the preparation of the volume.

MICHAEL WELKER

Introduction

MICHAEL WELKER

One easily runs into a "tower of Babel"–like constellation when one tries to deal with the notion of "the Spirit." Do we have as many different concepts and images of "the Spirit" as we have areas of knowledge, religions, and philosophies? Does every thinker, believer, or spiritually oriented group interested in this power create an individual notion of "the Spirit"? This book wants to show that "the Spirit" can be a nonelusive topic in communities determined to deal with academically accessible realities and to raise, to test, and to defend truth-claims.

In order to do so, it presents an encounter among three different traditions and groups of thinkers. One of these groups has dealt with "the Spirit" for many centuries (theologians and biblical scholars from the so-called mainline churches); the second group has reflected on churches and religious movements that center on "the Spirit" and its workings and have experienced an extremely strong resonance in the last century (theologians and historians which come out of or deal with the Pentecostal and Charismatic movements); the third group are scientifically and philosophically trained scholars who are familiar with nonreligious areas of knowledge and have standards to judge whether a concept of "the Spirit" can be convincing in their not necessarily religious environments.

Although the members of the consultation "Pnematology: Exploring the Work of the Spirit from Contemporary Perspectives" came from very different backgrounds, they were all willing to work together in a "truth-seeking community."

- The members of the first group did not simply want to affirm century-old teachings and dogmatic convictions. They offered fresh views on the biblical traditions and raised new questions about the personhood and the workings of the Spirit in creation and inside and outside of religious institutions.
- The scholars of the second group did not simply take the enormous resonance of the Pentecostal/Charismatic movement (whose more than 500,000,000 members now constitute one fourth of Christianity) as a proof of the truth of its experience and notions of "the Spirit." Rather, they critically reflected on the history, the theological grounds, and the future of this powerful movement.
- The third group compared theological and nontheological experiences, thoughts, and theories of the Spirit. It did so not by claiming a mediating or even superior perspective (i.e., scientists and philosophers tell conflicting theologians where the real truth is to be found). Rather, they identified phenomena at the boundaries and limits of conventional scientific and classical philosophical thinking, phenomena which could open one's eyes for the complex personality and reality of "the Spirit" witnessed to by very different faith traditions.

Part I

The biblical scholar James Dunn, who has written several important books on the Holy Spirit and its workings, highlights the many tensions inherent in observations of and reflections on the Spirit. Is the Spirit personal or impersonal, is it a divine or a human power, is it cosmologically or anthropologically relevant, does it operate in creation or salvation? Or is it both in some of these cases or in all of them? These are only a few of the many questions that have to be settled. Different contexts of observation and experience, Hellenistic, Jewish, and Christian conceptualizations, require nuanced answers. Dunn shows that from Old Testament witnesses onwards, "the Spirit" is in all cases connected with deep experiences, experiences of an awesome power. This awesome power can "rest" upon a single bearer of the Spirit, and it can be "poured out" upon many human beings.

With the notion of the exalted Jesus Christ "baptizing with the Spirit," the New Testament coined a fresh image that strengthened the hope for "a richer experience of God's vitalizing presence and activity" on earth. Jesus, "who had been inspired by the Spirit, had now become a dispenser of the Spirit." The early church witnessed to the fulfillment of this hope in its growth and mission within and beyond the realm of Judaism. Real spiritual experiences, ecstatic but not numinous, paved the way for the life and the spreading of the church. The real transformation in the image of Jesus Christ, becoming a member of the body of Christ was an experience of faith, and the resurrection as a "spiritual body," a body enlivened by the Holy Spirit, became the focus of Christian hope. Both discontinuity and continuity between the pre-Easter Jesus and the resurrected Christ remained most important. With this orientation the early church was able to "discern the spirits" in the midst of ecstatic experiences. For a dialogue between, and a mutual challenge of, classical academic theology and the new Pentecostal/Charismatic theology, it is crucial to acknowledge the ecstatic experience of the divine power of the Spirit and to recognize the importance of discerning the spirits. The ability to again connect both dimensions, Dunn concludes, "may be the key to Christianity's growth in the wider world and essential for its revitalization in the West."

Is the Spirit a person or an impersonal power? This is one of the basic questions raised by James Dunn. Bernd Oberdorfer shows that the concept of person was introduced for the Spirit in the fourth century in order to clarify the understanding of God. He cautions that in those days "person does not simply mean individuality with self-consciousness." The experience of Christians as a spiritual community and Christ's order, according to Matthew 28:19, to "baptize in the name of the Father and the Son and the Holy Spirit," recited in each baptism, forced Christian theology to develop a Trinitarian understanding of God and to seek an understanding of the Spirit's divine identity. Oberdorfer examines the most important steps in the history of theological thought that rose to these challenges. Drawing on insights of Wolfhart Pannenberg and Michael Welker, he comes to the conclusion that the Spirit should be understood in a complementary way as both a complex public person and the "dynamical 'field of power' *(Kraftfeld)* of the divinity." In these complementary perspectives a confusion of personhood with human personhood and the notion of a ubiquitous spirit without intentional structure can be avoided. The Spirit becomes present "where it wills" — and also in the perspective of being a field of power.

Offering "Trinitarian Prolegomena for a Pneumatological Theology of Religions," Veli-Matti Kärkkäinen ponders whether and in what way we can "speak of the presence of the Spirit in the world and among religions." He criticizes positions which try "to affirm a typically modernist idea of a 'rough parity' of all religions." Christian theology should honestly acknowledge that the doctrine of the Trinity is its structuring principle. He refers to three major Catholic voices — Raimundo Panikkar, Gavin D'Costa, and Jacques Dupuis — and to the Evangelical Mark Heim, who proposed an openly Trinitarian and pneumatological approach for interreligious encounters. Such an approach, he argues, permits us to establish a relation that affirms one's own faith-identity and yet remains open to mutual learning because of necessarily differentiated views of the Divine and the complex identity of the Spirit. Not a single idea or principle has to be defended, but rather we can explore a mutuality in our respect for the living God.

Further possibilities for interconfessional and even interreligious common grounds in the pneumatologically oriented discourse come into view when topics in the doctrine of creation are treated from a pneumatological perspective. Lyle Dabney ponders whether the Spirit — when Genesis 1 witnesses to the "Spirit moving over the face of the waters" — is "the breath of God that gives breath to all creation, which is the possibility of God for the world and the possibility of the world for God, a relationship that even permits the speaking . . . and the hearing" of the divine Word and the human words. Dabney sees the Spirit as the divine power which enables creatures to bend their lives to a common purpose and yet live in distinct social existences. The Spirit ennobles creatures to an emergent co-creativity: "For in the Spirit and through the Word God brings us into being as God's own image in the world, a being which is itself a bearer of God's Word in the Spirit. . . . As creatures of Word and Spirit, therefore, we are made to take part in God's speaking of the Word of creation in the Spirit."

Having insisted on the ecstatic character of the experience of the Spirit (James Dunn) on the one hand and on the workings of the Spirit in very basic interactions in creation (Lyle Dabney) on the other, one must clarify a bifurcation or a polarization in the understanding of the workings of the Spirit. This task is fulfilled by Kathryn Tanner, who asks whether the Spirit works immediately "in exceptional events . . . upon the interior depth of individual persons," or whether the Spirit works gradually in ordinary life — "historical process, mediation, publicity. . . ." Tanner observes a potentially dangerous "will to power" in appeals to the direct working of the Spirit on individual persons. Such appeals can serve as "an attack on religious authorities," who can indeed be guided by more profound and truthful spiritual and theological insights or by a religiously coded self-righteousness and stubbornness.

Tanner warns against strong appeals to the direct and immediate working of the Spirit. They can easily turn into an indirect "attack on the authority of all communally or socially validated forms of intellectual, religious, or moral achievement that take their rise from long, slow processes of training and learning." Here the Spirit as patient "teacher," guiding the community into a common and shared cognition of truth, comes into view. The acknowledgment of the Spirit's workings in patient processes and institutionalized forms does not question the "appreciation for the surprise of the new." It only questions a notion that sees a spirit as outdoing all other authorities by mere appeals to its immediate presence in the interior of individual lives. It pleads for shared experiences of the Spirit, which do not dismiss the need for a common discernment of the spirits.

Part II

Frank Macchia shows that "a crisis experience called the 'baptism in the Holy Spirit'" became the hallmark of the Pentecostal movement. The interpretations of this experience, however, differ between the different strands of this movement. This constellation, Macchia argues, creates dynamics that challenge Pentecostals to develop and expand their own understanding of Spirit baptism and at the same time contribute to an ecumenical pneumatology, which would be seminal for other church families. He warns against "the displacement of Spirit baptism, the 'crown jewel' of Christian experience." The experience of empowerment for witness takes on different forms, the new beginnings of Christian life will be seen in more or less spectacular and dramatic ways, but the concentration on the initiation of Christian life by the Spirit and its workings should not be lost. The concentration on this charismatic event, however, should not blur or even dismiss the Spirit's sanctifying and soteriological work within human lives, which cannot be separated from God's self-disclosure in Jesus Christ, the Spirit Baptizer.

Macchia assumes that the emphasis on the spectacular spiritual power and the often strong connection of Spirit baptism and speaking in tongues may have led to a narrow understanding of sanctification and to an abstraction from the biblical insight that the Spirit transforms in sanctification into the image of Christ. He proposes an ecumenical discourse on ecclesiological, Trinitarian, and eschatological issues in which the "baptizing in the Spirit" should play a major role: "Spirit baptism points to redemption through Christ as substantially pneumatological and eschatological."

The complex history of the Pentecostal/Charismatic movement and the reasons "why the revival flourished" are dealt with in the chapter presented by Grant Wacker. He argues that the Pentecostal movement was able to "hold two seemingly incompatible impulses in productive tension": the ecstatic experience of an otherworldly power and a this-worldly practicality. Pentecostal spirituality and church practice responded to the longing to be touched by God and to fascination by the experience of the numinous. Moreover, it encouraged entrepreneurship in organizing successful worships and in engaging the media and politics by impressive religious rhetoric. Wacker recalls powerful lives and careers in the service of the movement, "gifted with many of those elusive talents that (make) a person truly and inexplicably charismatic." He identifies the "working DNA" of successful religious movements in their combination of "untidiness, distinctiveness, and normalcy," in their attempt "to make the fragile, flickering candle of life burn a bit brighter and a bit longer."

Whereas Grant Wacker reflects on the history and the success story of the Charismatic/Pentecostal movement, Margaret Poloma analyzes the current situation and elements of decision and crisis. She focuses on the Assemblies of God, the second largest Pentecostal denomination in the U.S. and — with a membership of over 50,000,000 globally — the largest single Pentecostal body. This chapter diagnoses a tension between the need for periodic revivals in order to strengthen Pentecostal identity and the tendency particularly among white American Pentecostals to downplay or even tame revivals in order to seek acceptance by post-Enlightenment Evangelical and secular communities. What Tanner regards as an evolutionary progress and maturation in religious life — that is, downplaying or even avoiding "controversial issues that come with 'dynamic filling' and 'empowerment'" — is seen as a potential crisis by Poloma. The appeal to a "transforming experience with God" (J. D. Johns) and the embrace of a worldview that welcomes such experience are crucial to sustain the core identity of the Pentecostal movement. Subtle yet mighty tensions between

Pentecostal, Fundamentalist, and Evangelical worldviews, which usually escape general public and academic attention, have to be observed and reflected more thoroughly. Margaret Poloma asks whether we have to face an "erosion of a distinct Pentecostal identity" or whether this identity and its attraction will migrate to "immigrant churches" that do not fear a premodern worldview, but are open to "signs and wonders from on high."

Part III

John Polkinghorne, particle physicist and Anglican priest, proposes an understanding of the Spirit and its workings that is not only compatible with biblical witnesses and insights but also with the account of the cosmic process and the evolution of terrestrial life given by contemporary natural sciences. The discovery of widespread intrinsic (!) unpredictability in nature in the twentieth century, the discovery of the "chaos theory," and the study of the behavior of complex systems solicited new reflections on the interplay of "Chance and Necessity" (Monod) in cosmological and world-historical processes. Necessity in this context, however, is not any lawful regularity of the world as such: "the given physical fabric of the cosmos had to be 'fine-tuned' if there was to be any possibility of carbon-based life developing anywhere at all within it." And "chance" is not a "cosmic lottery" of erratic instances but rather the contingent particularities which, in their interplay with fine-tuned necessity, make the evolutionary process fertile. Supporting Kathryn Tanner's arguing for a bivalent working of the Spirit and drawing on theological observations of the Orthodox theologian Vladimir Lossky, Polkinghorne proposes an understanding of the secret and hidden presence of the Spirit in natural and historical processes. The hidden working of the Spirit in the world's unfolding history through the input of pure information "would constitute a pneumatological account of continuous creation, divine participation in the evolving fruitfulness of the world, exercised with covert reticence within the open grain of nature."

Coming from the Pentecostal tradition and deeply interested in an ecumenically and academically open Pentecostal theology, Amos Yong reconstructs the basic outlines of Philip Clayton's complex theory of emergence, which he regards as a promising philosophical bridge theory between the sciences and theology. He sees, however, the need to supplement this theory theologically. In a bold move, he wants to enrich this theory of emergence by insights gained from a pneumatological reading of the biblical creation accounts and the Psalms. Like Lyle Dabney he argues that God's creativity has to be understood as originating in the divine Word and Spirit and having not only ontological but also "epistemological and linguistic implications, thus providing for the possibility of thought . . . and of language." The creation narratives speak indeed of an emergent co-creativity of the creatures. Since they do not think in one-to-one correlations, but in one-to-many correlations (God and the cosmological, biological, cultural creatures), they are not afraid to blur the difference between the creative God and the co-creative creatures. Neither are they pressed towards an either-or in terms of "creation and evolution."

There are differences of intensity in this co-creativity that, in Yong's view, might be expressed theoretically with the help of Clayton's metaphysical theory of emergence. Yong sees the academic risks involved in his bringing together of ancient narratives and postmodern philosophical and interdisciplinary theorizing. He argues that overt theological problems with Clayton's metaphysics of emergence should invite us to take this risk. "A pneumatologically informed metaphysics . . . requires us to hold the immanent and transcendent aspects of divine presence and activity together, regardless of how tempted we are to privilege one over the other." With regard to pneumatology, he sees the potential to express both the purposeful person-character and the emergent field-character of the Spirit (cf. Oberdorfer).

The chapter written by Donald York, professor of astronomy and astrophysics, grew out of direct dialogue with his wife Anna, a pastor, and also of an indirect dialogue with their Pentecostal background. This contribution asks a question which is most important for "truth-seeking communities." What is at work when geniuses make discoveries that change the world of science forever, such as Galileo's insight that the earth moves around the sun (1610), or Kant's correct theory about the Milky Way (1755), even when the experimental demonstration occurs only centuries later (1838 and 1921)? What guides progress in truth-seeking communities and encourages us to make truth-claims, although full evidence is still lacking? How can we be so bold as to speak of our "worldviews" and, for instance, of true cosmological knowledge, when we have to admit "that we know only 5% of the universe and that 95% of it is 'dark', or a mystery, even to the greatest minds who are working on the problem"? Is a guiding and encouraging power at work that gives both the boldness and the patience in the individual and in the common search for truth? Donald and Anna York see the Spirit at work in this process and the Wisdom either identical with the Spirit or given by it. They describe the Wisdom with the help of Proverbs and other Wisdom traditions and identify its qualities as "knowledge, discernment, truth, and beneficial results."

Michael Welker, theologian and philosopher, contrasts the powerful concept of the spirit first proposed by Aristotle in book XII of his *Metaphysics* and the concept of the Spirit witnessed to by the biblical traditions. He shows that the philosophical concept which shaped occidental thinking in epistemology, anthropology, and diverse cultural and social theories is fundamentally different from the Holy Spirit in Jewish and Christian religious thinking. The philosophical spirit is self-referential and full of certainty. The Spirit of the biblical traditions, the "Spirit of truth," bears witness to Christ and to God the Creator and does not speak on its own authority (cf. John 15:26). This difference has far-reaching consequences.

Both in academic and religious processes an understanding of the working of the Spirit as a truth-revealing power is required. This understanding has to acknowledge the Spirit's empathetic and context-sensitive presence. It is also a poly-contextual and polyphonic presence. Emergent processes have to be grasped in order to appreciate the Spirit's working. A different excitement and awe from the excitement generated by individual and bodily mediated spectacular experiences come into view, an excitement that necessarily goes hand in hand with the need for the "discernment of the spirits." Although the ancient symbols of "pouring" and "Spirit baptism" are adequate for the power envisioned and its working, a new sensitivity for the hiddenness of the Spirit in creation, for its patient working as a comforting, guiding, teaching, and truth-revealing power, can and should be raised by a multidisciplinary inquiry. It is in "truth-seeking communities"[1] — both in academic and religious contexts — that the excitement resulting from the experience of the Spirit has to be complemented by the discernment of the spirits.

---

1. In other constellations of discourse about the Spirit, the working of the Spirit in justice- and healing-seeking communities would also come to the fore.

I. Reconceiving the Spirit, Its Personhood and Its Workings

Towards the Spirit of Christ: The Emergence of the Distinctive Features of Christian Pneumatology

JAMES D. G. DUNN

Introduction

The emergence of Christianity is marked by a number of significant developments in pneumatology — so much so that it becomes a question whether emerging Christianity brought these developments in its train, or whether these developments were among the major factors calling Christianity into existence in its distinctive claims and as a distinctive religious movement within the first-century eastern Mediterranean world.

Of course, developmental hypotheses in regard to the Spirit have been meat and drink to generations of scholarship. As we shall see in the next section, the tensions between spirit cosmically conceived and spirit anthropologically conceived, the continuities and discontinuities between divine spirit and human spirit, between creation and salvation, have been present from the first. And within that overarching schema, the recognition of a developing conceptuality of divine spirit within the early Judeo-Christian tradition is, of course, nothing new. I think, in particular, of a growing sense of the Spirit as a *moral* force, often linked with the increasing use of the attribute *holy* spirit.[1] Or of the sense of the Spirit as a personal rather than an impersonal power.[2] But these are not particularly

---

1. The epithet "holy" is attached to s/Spirit only at a relatively late date in early Jewish literature — Ps. 51:11; Isa. 63:11; Wis. 9:17; Sus. 1:45; 2 Esdr. 14:22 — but is a regular feature of the New Testament writings.

2. R. Bultmann, *Theology of the New Testament*, vol. 1 (London: SCM, 1952), famously

linked to the emergence of Christianity, or are more coincidental with the emergence of Christianity than distinctive or causative of it.

Nor am I thinking of the kind of questions which have largely dominated the last century's discussion of the conceptualization of the Spirit or of the Spirit's role. Can we distinguish a Hellenistic conceptualization of the Spirit from a Jewish one? The perception of such a distinction was what marked the beginning of twentieth-century debate on the subject — Hermann Gunkel pressing behind the idealistic concept of divine spirit to the more primitive concept of prophetic inspiration and miracle-working power.[3] So the question of development could be posed in terms of some kind of transition from Jewish to Greek categories. That remains a major issue within the larger discussion,[4] but it has become much less clear in its implications for the beginnings of Christianity, since the influence of Greek conceptualities upon the language used by the first Christians predates the emergence of Christianity by a century or two, and since the major influence of middle Platonism on Christian theology postdates the emergence of Christianity by a century or two.

Gunkel's focus on the charismatic Spirit (to use later shorthand) also led to the Charisma/Amt debate regarding Christianity's origins.[5] Did Christianity begin as a charismatic movement, with church order and office to be regarded as a secondary, "routinizing" or "institutionalizing" activity, designed to control and regularize the unpredictability of Spirit manifestation?[6] On a broader church front, the emergence of Pentecostal-

---

summed the differences in early Christian conceptions of the Spirit in the contrast between "animistic thinking," where the *pneuma* "is conceived as an independent agent, a personal power which like a demon can fall upon a man and take possession of him," and "dynamistic thinking," where *pneuma* "appears as an impersonal force which fills a man like a fluid, so to say" (p. 155).

3. H. Gunkel, *Die Wirkungen des Heiligen Geistes nach der populären Anschauung der apostolischen Zeit und der Lehre des Apostels Paulus* (Göttingen: Vandenhoeck, 1888).

4. Still largely determining the analyses of E. Schweizer, *"pneuma," Theological Dictionary of the New Testament* (Grand Rapids: Eerdmans, 1964-1976), 6:396-451; F. W. Horn, *Das Angeld des Geistes: Studien zur paulinischen Pneumatologie* (Forschungen zur Religion und Literatur des Alten und Neuen Testaments 154; Göttingen: Vandenhoeck, 1992).

5. R. Sohm, *Kirchenrecht*, vol. 1 (1892; München/Leipzig: Duncker & Humblot, 1923); A. Harnack, *The Constitution and Law of the Church in the First Two Centuries* (London: Williams & Norgate, 1910).

6. The debate rumbled through the twentieth century, with major contributions from E. Schweizer, *Church Order in the New Testament* (London: SCM, 1961); E. Käsemann,

ism posed a different set of developmental questions for our understanding of Christianity's beginnings — particularly as to whether we have to distinguish a prophetic Spirit from a salvific Spirit, with the implication that Christianity's emergence was marked by some kind of tension between the two or, alternatively, of transition in conceptuality from one to the other.[7] This too remains a frontline issue within Pentecostally influenced scholarship, with wider ramifications for Christian theology and the churches.

What I have in mind, however, are other developments that, surprisingly, have been given little attention hitherto. But first, a reminder of what the first Christians could take for granted so far as a more widespread understanding of the Spirit within their native Judaism was concerned.[8]

The Spirit in Early Jewish Thought

From earliest Hebrew thought the term *ruach* had various meanings, all more or less equally prominent. (1) *Wind,* an invisible, mysterious, powerful force,[9] regularly with the notion of strength or violence present.[10]

"Ministry and Community in the New Testament," *Essays on New Testament Themes* (London: SCM, 1964), pp. 63-94; H. von Campenhausen, *Ecclesiastical Authority and Spiritual Power in the Church of the First Three Centuries* (1953; London: A. & C. Black, 1969); see also my *Jesus and the Spirit* (London: SCM, 1975; Grand Rapids: Eerdmans, 1997), chs. 8-9. The influence of Max Weber's theory of the charismatic prophet and the routinizing of charisma are evident; see further M. Y. MacDonald, *The Pauline Churches: A Socio-historical Study of Institutionalization in the Pauline and Deutero-Pauline Writings* (Society for New Testament Studies Monograph Series 60; Cambridge: Cambridge University Press, 1988).

7. Particularly R. P. Menzies, *The Development of Early Christian Pneumatology with Special Reference to Luke-Acts* (Journal for the Study of the New Testament — Supplement Series 54; Sheffield: Sheffield Academic, 1991), and M. Turner, *Power from on High: The Spirit in Israel's Witness in Luke-Acts* (Sheffield: Sheffield Academic, 1996), in interaction with my *Baptism in the Holy Spirit: A Re-examination of the New Testament Teaching on the Gift of the Spirit in Relation to Pentecostalism Today* (London: SCM, 1970).

8. I have inserted the following section into the paper prepared for the Symposium at the request of the Symposium's participants, drawing principally on the first two sections of my article, "Spirit, Holy Spirit," *New Bible Dictionary* (ed. D. R. W. Wood; Leicester: Inter-Varsity, [3]1996): 1125-27.

9. Gen. 8:1; Exod. 10:13, 19; Num. 11:31; 1 Kgs. 18:45; Prov. 25:23; Jer. 10:13; Hos. 13:15; Jon. 4:8.

10. Exod. 14:21; 1 Kgs. 19:11; Pss. 48:7; 55:8; Isa. 7:2; Ezek. 27:26; Jon. 1:4.

(2) *Breath* (i.e., air on a small scale), or *spirit*,[11] the same mysterious force seen as the life and vitality of human life. It can be disturbed or activated in a particular direction,[12] can be impaired or diminished[13] and revive again.[14] That is, the dynamic life-force which constitutes a person can be low (it disappears at death), or there can be a sudden surge of vital power. (3) *Divine power*, where *ruach* is used to describe occasions when individuals seemed to be carried out of themselves — not just a surge of vitality, but a supernatural force taking possession. So particularly with the early charismatic leaders[15] and the early prophets; it was the divine *ruach* that induced ecstasy and prophetic speech.[16]

The overlap of these meanings is most clearly seen in Ezekiel's vision of the valley of dry bones, where *ruach* can be translated with equal effect as "wind," "breath," or "spirit" (Ezek. 37:9). And how should we translate *ruach* in Genesis 1:2? It is this continuum of meaning which explains why initially there was no clear sense of distinction between the divine *ruach* and the anthropological *ruach*; it was the divine *ruach* which gave life to the human created (Gen. 2:7). The wordplay is still active in the New Testament writings, particularly John 3:8 and 20:22. And the assumption remains that *ruach* is the dimension of human existence in and through which God is encountered (particularly Rom. 8:16), leaving various passages where it remains unclear whether divine Spirit or human spirit is in view.[17]

Similarly, there was no initial distinction between the different phenomena of inspiration: a *ruach* from God could be for evil as well as for good.[18] Only later does a clear distinction open up between divine spirit and demonic spirit, with the latter frequently referred to in the Jewish pseudepigrapha and the Gospels and Acts, but the former, the (Holy) Spirit of God, dominating earliest Christian usage. We may be able to detect a similar hesitancy lest the Spirit's inspiration be always understood in

11. Gen. 6:17; 7:15, 22; Pss. 31:5; 32:2; Eccl. 3:19, 21; Jer. 10:14; 51:17; Ezek. 11:5.
12. Gen. 41:8; Num. 5:14, 30; Judg. 8:3; 1 Kgs. 21:5; 1 Chron. 5:26; Job 21:4; Prov. 29:11; Jer. 51:17; Dan. 2:1, 3.
13. Josh. 5:1; 1 Kgs. 10:5; Ps. 143:7; Isa. 19:3.
14. Gen. 45:27; Judg. 15:19; 1 Sam. 30:12.
15. Judg. 3:10; 6:34; 11:29; 13:25; 14:6, 19; 15:14-15; 1 Sam. 11:6.
16. Num. 24:2; 1 Sam. 10:6, 10; 19:20, 23-24.
17. As in Luke 1:80; 1 Cor. 14:32; Jas. 4:5.
18. Judg. 9:23; 1 Sam. 16:14-16; 1 Kgs. 22:19-23.

terms of ecstatic inspiration, as in earliest prophecy as attested by 1 Samuel 10:5-6 and 19:20-24. This could be an explanation of the striking reluctance of the classical (eighth- and seventh-century) writing prophets to attribute their inspiration to the Spirit, preferring to attribute it to the word of God (Jer. 20:9; Amos 3:8) and the hand of God (Isa. 8:11; Jer. 15:17). In the exilic and postexilic literature the role of the divine *ruach* as inspirer of prophecy comes back into prominence (Neh. 9:20, 30; Zech. 7:12). And it is this understanding of the Spirit which became dominant in the rabbinic Judaism that emerged with Christianity from first-century Second Temple Judaism and which provides the Pentecostal view of the Spirit with its strongest argument.

Even this brief survey of usage makes it clear that the concept *ruach* was from the beginning an existential term. At its heart was the *experience* of a mysterious, awesome power — the mighty invisible force of the wind, the mystery of vitality, the otherly power that transforms — all *ruach*, all manifestations of divine energy. The same association of the divine *ruach* with numinous experience is implicit in the fact that *ruach* denotes the cosmic and inescapable presence of God in Psalm 139:7. It was hope for a far richer experience of God's vitalizing presence and activity within Israel that lay at the heart of the prophets' expectation for the age to come (Ezek. 36:26-27; 37). And it is here that we find most of the significant and too little emphasized developments that marked out emerging Christianity as claiming, or as shaped by new insights into God's way of dealing with his people through his Spirit.

The Expectation of a Spirit-Bestowing Figure

So far as we can tell, *there was no expectation of a messianic figure bestowing the Spirit in pre-Christian Judaism.*

The expectation of a Spirit-bestowal ushering in or characterizing the age to come is well attested in Jewish scripture. In addition to Ezekiel 36:26-27 just noted, I need mention only familiar texts like Isaiah 44:3, God's promise to Israel — "I will pour out my spirit on your descendants"; Ezekiel 39:29 — God looks to Israel's return from exile, "when I pour out my spirit upon the house of Israel"; and Joel 2:28-29 — God promises, "I will pour out my spirit on all flesh." So the thought of an outpouring of the divine spirit was hardly new to Christianity. On the contrary, it was the belief that such promises had been fulfilled which contributed to the earliest Christian movement's cutting edge.[19]

Likewise, we are familiar with expectation of a messianic figure, that is, of an *anointed* figure, that is, of a *Spirit*-anointed figure. Most obvious here can be cited the two famous Isaiah passages: Isaiah 11:2 — "the spirit of the Lord will rest upon him [that is, the branch from the stump of Jesse], the spirit of wisdom and understanding, etc."; and Isaiah 61:1 — "The Spirit of the Lord is upon me, because the Lord has anointed me; he has sent me to bring good news to the oppressed, etc." So neither was thought of a Spirit-anointed figure inaugurating the age to come strange to Jewish ears. Of course, once again, it was Christianity's claim, or even Jesus' own claim,[20] that this expectation had already been fulfilled in Jesus which gave the movement he called into existence its initial impetus. But that did not constitute a development in the understanding of the Spirit and how the Spirit operates.

The somewhat surprising fact, then, is that *the expectation attributed to John the Baptist is, so far as we can tell, without precedent in Second Temple Judaism.* For the varied traditions of the Baptist's preaching are agreed. According to Q,[21] John proclaimed, "I baptize you with water, but one who is more powerful than I is coming; he will baptize you with holy spirit and fire" (Matt. 3:11/Luke 3:16). According to Mark, similarly: "I baptize you with water, but he will baptize you with holy spirit" (Mark 1:8). According to the Fourth Evangelist, John testified: "He who sent me to baptize in water, he told me, 'The one on whom you see the spirit descending and remaining, he it is who baptizes in holy spirit'" (John 1:33).

Here indeed is a striking feature: of only two items on which the diverse Gospel traditions regarding the Baptist's preaching agree, one is the Baptist's prediction that the one to come would "baptize in holy spirit." The image used, "baptize," was obviously drawn by the Baptist from his single most distinguishing feature: he was "the one who baptizes *(ho baptizōn)*" (Mark 6:14, 24), "the Baptist *(ho Baptistēs)*" (Mark 6:25; 8:28), a title that can only have meaning if his baptizing activity marked him out as quite different from other preachers and movements of the time.[22] So it is

19. Thus the claim and character of the Acts of the Apostles, starting with the account of Pentecost (Acts 2).

20. See details in my *Jesus Remembered* (Grand Rapids: Eerdmans, 2003), pp. 655-66.

21. "Q" is the generally accepted designation of the non-Markan sayings source on which Matthew and Luke seem to have been able to draw.

22. See further *Jesus Remembered*, pp. 355-57.

understandable that the Baptist should coin a fresh image and usage in characterizing the figure whom he anticipated as likewise "baptizing."

The imagery is *consistent* with the other water imagery used in the prophetic passages already cited, but otherwise it is without precedent. But the really surprising thing is that the Baptist looked for the outpouring of the Spirit to come through the expected intermediary. There is no precedent for that in the literature of Second Temple Judaism known to us.[23] It is just possible that when the Baptist spoke of "the one to come" he had *God* in mind. In which case his expectation would *not* be new — the hoped-for outpouring of the Spirit either attributed explicitly to God (as in the passages cited above) or being expressed in the form of a "divine passive" (the Spirit would be poured out). But it is very unlikely that the Baptist had God in mind, since he talks of untying the coming one's sandals, and it is hard to imagine the Baptist so trivializing the relation between God and a human being.[24]

Nor can we derive the Baptist's expectation as a retrogression from subsequent Christian belief regarding Jesus. For the belief that Jesus bestowed the Spirit of Pentecost (see below) meshes at best awkwardly and uncomfortably with the other imagery used by the Baptist. The Baptist's expectation of a baptism in holy spirit and fire is best understood as the Baptist's own version of the expectation of an end-time tribulation, the "birth pangs" of the new age — a baptism of judgment, a purgative or destructive plunging into the river of fiery breath flowing from the divine throne.[25] And whereas that fits well with the Q version of the Baptist's preaching, as a preacher of imminent judgment, the account of Pentecost, regarded as the fulfillment of the Baptist's expectation (Acts 1:5; 11:16), lacks all note of judgment and purgation. So it makes best sense of the data to conclude that the expectation of an eschatological redeemer himself "baptizing" in Spirit was *the Baptist's own coinage.*[26]

It is interesting to note that the actual image coined by the Baptist was not much taken up in earliest Christianity. Apart from Acts 1:5 and

---

23. I discussed this point in an early article — "Spirit-and-Fire Baptism," *Novum Testamentum* 14 (1972): 81-92, reprinted in my *The Christ and the Spirit,* vol. 2: *Pneumatology* (Grand Rapids: Eerdmans, 1998), pp. 93-102.

24. See again *Jesus Remembered,* p. 369.

25. *Jesus Remembered,* pp. 364-69.

26. See further "The Birth of a Metaphor — Baptized in Spirit," *Expository Times* 89 (1977-78): 134-38, 173-75, reprinted in *Pneumatology,* pp. 103-17.

11:16, only 1 Corinthians 12:13 really calls for notice ("in one Spirit we were all baptized into one body"). And subsequently the image of "baptizing in Spirit" was largely subsumed within orthodox theology of baptism, and the image of Christ as dispenser of Spirit was caught up in the confusion of the Filioque dispute (whether the Spirit "proceeds" from "the Father" only, or from "the Father and the Son"). It is only really in twentieth-century Pentecostalism that the theme and the attendant Christology have revived. Which is a pity, since the lack of attention given to the Baptist's breakthrough has diminished and hidden its significance from view. The real significance of the Baptist's prediction and the Christian claim to its fulfillment in Jesus the Christ becomes apparent in the second point of development in earliest Christian understanding of the Spirit to which I call attention.

The Exalted Jesus as Bestower of the Divine Spirit

One of the most striking of early formulations involving the gift of the Spirit is the attribution of the gift to Jesus, the exalted Christ. It comes in the course of the Pentecost-day sermon set by Luke on the lips of Peter (Acts 2:14-39). The sermon starts by identifying the Pentecost experience, particularly the ecstatic praise and/or proclamation ("the mighty deeds of God") in tongues (2:11), as the fulfillment of the Joel prophecy — the effect of the pouring out of the Spirit "in the last days" (2:16-18).[27] But it builds up to the further claim that Pentecost is the result of Jesus being exalted to the right hand of God, in accord with Psalm 110:1, "The Lord said to my Lord, 'Sit at my right hand until I put your enemies under your feet'" (Acts 2:34-36).[28] The linking thought is that Jesus, having been exalted to God's right hand as Lord and Christ, had received the promise of the Holy Spirit from the Father, and had poured out what the audience were seeing and hearing with their own eyes and ears (2:33). The striking thing is that *it was the exalted Christ, not God himself, who had poured out the end-time Spirit.*

This claim has not been given sufficient attention in inquiries into

27. It is something of a curiosity that "in the last days" is Luke's or his source's modification of the Joel text.

28. Ps. 110:1 is one of the foundation texts in the development of earliest Christology; see, e.g., my *The Theology of Paul the Apostle* (Grand Rapids: Eerdmans/Edinburgh: T&T Clark, 1998), pp. 246-49, with further bibliography in n. 58.

the beginnings of distinctively Christian theology. There are several possible reasons.

One is that the claim does not seem to have been made much of during the first generation of Christianity. In Paul it is always God who is described as the one who gives the Spirit.[29] When Ephesians takes up the Pentecost theme, it is only in terms of the exalted Christ giving gifts, ministry gifts to humans (Eph. 4:8), not the Spirit as such. And even if Luke was drawing on very early kerygmatic material in his crafting of the sermon of Acts 2:14-39, he too does not make much of the claim, beyond the assertion that Pentecost was the fulfillment of the Baptist's expectation of one to come who would baptize in Holy Spirit (Acts 1:5; 11:16).[30] It is the Fourth Evangelist who makes more of the claim. It is possible to read John 3:34 as speaking about *Jesus* giving the Spirit: "He whom God sent speaks the words of God, for he gives the Spirit without measure."[31] And it is John who represents Jesus himself as saying, "When the Counsellor comes, whom *I will send* to you from the Father, the Spirit of truth who comes/proceeds from the Father" (John 15:26). But, as already indicated, any distinctive role for the exalted Christ in the giving of the Spirit becomes lost, on the one hand, in the theology of baptism (and confirmation) as the means of conveying the Spirit, and on the other hand in the subsequent disputes as to whether the Spirit proceeds from the Father only (as in Eastern Christianity) or from the Father and the Son (as in Western Christianity).

A possible second reason why the affirmation of Jesus as the one who poured out the Spirit at Pentecost has been so neglected is that the focus in the earliest explosion of christological reflection was on the relation between Jesus and God, not on Jesus' relation to the Spirit (but I will say more on this anon). As with the later confessional debates of the fourth century, the primary concern was to clarify how the Son related to the Father, with the relationship of the Spirit more in the nature of a tidying-up operation in order to secure a rounded Trinitarian doctrine. What is too

29. 1 Cor. 2:12; 2 Cor. 1:21-22; 5:5; Gal. 3:5; 4:6; Eph. 1:17; 1 Thess. 4:8; cf. the "divine passives" of Rom. 5:5 and 1 Cor. 12:13.

30. Lukan specialists note that Acts is characterized by an "absentee Christology," Christ seemingly inactive in heaven awaiting his return as judge (10:42; 17:31), and present in the "now" time more through his "name" (particularly Acts 3–4) than anything else.

31. Brief discussion in R. E. Brown, *The Gospel according to John* (Anchor Bible 29; New York: Doubleday, 1966), pp. 161-62; G. M. Burge, *The Anointed Community: The Holy Spirit in the Johannine Tradition* (Grand Rapids: Eerdmans, 1987), pp. 81-84.

little appreciated, however, is how quickly the former reflection developed and how deeply it transformed Jewish monotheism into early Christian monotheism.[32] I need refer only to the astonishing assertions of the first Christian theologian, Paul, in 1 Corinthians 8:4-6 and Philippians 2:10-11.[33] In the former, the basic and central Jewish credo, the *Shema*, "The LORD our *God* is one LORD" (Deut. 6:4), is redefined in a mind-blowing way: "For us there is one *God*, the Father . . . and one *Lord*, Jesus Christ" (1 Cor. 8:6). In the latter, one of the most unyieldingly monotheistic passages of Second Isaiah (Isa. 45:23 — "I am God, and there is no other. . . . To me every knee shall bow, every tongue shall swear") is referred to the exalted Christ: "*At the name of Jesus* every knee shall bow . . . and every tongue confess that Jesus Christ is Lord, to the glory of the Father" (Phil. 2:10-11). When such theological transformations were in train so quickly, it is perhaps hardly surprising that the further claim that the exalted Christ was now also the source of the eschatological Spirit gained little attention.

There is a third possible reason why the thought of the exalted Christ as giver of the Spirit did not make much headway in the earliest christological reflections. Speculation within Second Temple Judaism was already familiar with the thought of exalted humans sharing in divine functions. The suggestion that fabled heroes of the past, like Adam and Abel, Enoch and Melchizedek, were already glorious heavenly beings sitting on thrones and ready to take part in the final judgment, is one which we meet in several writings of the period.[34] Possibly then, the attribution of the Spirit to the exalted Christ was not regarded as something very distinctive, simply the Lord God sharing another of his functions with the Lord Christ. The Baptist's expectation of the coming one as baptizer in the Spirit might not have seemed to require a radical redefinition or reattribution of *divine* functions.

But none of this is quite satisfactory. For where *God* was so uniformly understood to be the one who gives the Spirit, the reattribution of the gift of the Spirit to *Christ* was a significant development, much more so

32. Often quoted is the observation of M. Hengel, *The Son of God* (London: SCM, 1976), "that more happened in this period of less than two decades than in the whole of the next seven centuries, up to the time when the doctrine of the early church was completed" (2).

33. See further, e.g., my *Theology of Paul*, pp. 253, 251; and more broadly, L. Hurtado, *Lord Jesus Christ: Devotion to Jesus in Earliest Christianity* (Grand Rapids: Eerdmans, 2003).

34. *Testament of Abraham* 11 and 13; *Jubilees* 4:22-23; *1 Enoch* 12–16; *2 Enoch* 22:8; 11QMelchizedek 13–14.

than the thought of exalted humans sharing in final judgment (cf. 1 Cor. 6:2). It is, after all, *the Spirit of God* that we are talking about. And for the giving of *God's* Spirit to be attributed to *Christ* is a major development.[35] Perhaps we should see here an early forerunner of the Filioque controversy, where there was some hesitation in eliding the distinctive role of God the Father in relation to the Spirit. From the perspective of Eastern Orthodoxy, to portray the Son as also the source of the Spirit is to compromise the Father as the source of deity within the unity of the Godhead.[36] So, analogously, at the beginnings of Christianity, it might have been instinctively perceived that to attribute other divine functions to the exalted Christ need not compromise the divine unity in any serious degree. But to attribute *the Spirit of God* to the exalted Christ was another matter. Yet this appears to be what Peter's Pentecost sermon does, and subsequently also the Fourth Evangelist in his own way. If so, the development in Christian theology, and from a very early date is significant.

The sensitivities and hesitations which may be evident in all this help highlight a closely related development in early Christian talk of the Spirit.

The Spirit of Christ

The question of how Jesus was seen to relate to the Spirit at the beginnings of Christianity is not simply a matter of taking seriously two neglected but unprecedented claims — on the one hand, the Baptist's expectation of one to come who would baptize in Spirit, and, on the other, the understanding of Peter's Pentecost sermon that the divine Spirit of Pentecost had been poured forth by the exalted Christ. For the explosive force within Christianity's emerging distinctiveness was the conviction that something had happened to Jesus, that the Messiah, prophet and teacher of Nazareth, had been raised from the dead and exalted to God's right hand. And at the heart of that conviction was the perception that this transition, as we might say, from prophet to Lord, involved *a transition in Jesus' relation with the Spirit of God.* In a word, the one who had been *in-*

35. See particularly M. Turner, "The Spirit of Christ and 'Divine' Christology," in J. B. Green and M. Turner (eds.), *Jesus of Nazareth: Lord and Christ,* I. H. Marshall FS (Grand Rapids: Eerdmans, 1994), pp. 413-36.

36. Extensive discussion is found in Y. Congar, *I Believe in the Holy Spirit,* vol. 3: *The River of Life Flows in the East and in the West* (London: Geoffrey Chapman, 1983).

spired by the Spirit had now become *dispenser of* the Spirit. Three aspects call for attention.

(a) First, I have previously tried to call attention (without much success!) to a curious feature in talk of Jesus' resurrection in relation to the Spirit. I detect a certain sense of awkwardness in such talk, or, to be more precise, in Paul's talk of Jesus' resurrection in relation to the Spirit.[37] On the face of it, the matter ought to be straightforward. In his major treatment of Jesus' resurrection (1 Cor. 15), Paul clearly understands Jesus' resurrection to be the precedent and pattern for the general resurrection at the end of the age. Christ's resurrection is the "firstfruits" of the eschatological resurrection, that is, the first sheaf of the harvest of the dead (15:23). The resurrection of the dead will be the image of his resurrection (15:47-49).[38] But the final resurrection will be effected by the agency of God's Spirit: the resurrected body will be a *sōma pneumatikon,* a body enlivened by the divine Spirit (15:44); the gift of the Spirit itself is the first installment and guarantee *(arrabōn)* of the resurrection of the body (2 Cor. 5:5); God will give life to our mortal bodies through the Spirit that dwells in us (Rom. 8:11). So it would follow naturally, would it not, that if the Spirit was the effective force in the *final* resurrection, then we could have expected Paul to speak of the Spirit equally as the effective force in the *first* resurrection, the archetypal resurrection of Christ. But this is where the surprise comes in, the awkwardness of which I spoke. For Paul seems to hesitate to do just that. Indeed, *Paul seems to go out of his way* to avoid saying just that, *to avoid attributing Jesus' resurrection to the agency of the Spirit.*

I am thinking particularly of three Romans texts. In Romans 1:4 Paul speaks of Jesus' resurrection "according to the Spirit of holiness," where the prepositional phrase is notoriously obscure; in what sense was Jesus resurrection "according to the Holy Spirit"? In Romans 6:4 Paul seems to avoid any reference to the Spirit in saying "that as Christ was raised from the dead through the *glory* of the Father, so also we should walk in *newness of life*." And in Romans 8:11, where it would have been much simpler to say, "the Spirit that gave life to Jesus will give life to you," Paul's syntax becomes surprisingly roundabout: "If the Spirit of him who raised Jesus from the

---

37. *Christology in the Making* (London: SCM/Grand Rapids: Eerdmans, ²1989), p. 144.

38. This is part of a larger motif in Paul, wherein the process of salvation is understood as a process of becoming conformed to Christ's death until the climax of sharing in his resurrection, i.e., of experiencing a resurrection like his (Rom. 6:5; 2 Cor. 4:16–5:5; Phil. 3:10-11, 21).

dead dwells in you, he who raised Christ Jesus from the dead will also give life to your mortal bodies through his Spirit that dwells in you."

Perhaps I am being oversensitive here. But I still do find it curious that Paul should apparently have shied away from the straightforward assertion: "God raised Jesus by/through the Spirit." Could it be, I find myself asking, that Paul already perceived a transition in the relationship between Christ and the Spirit which made him hesitate to ascribe Jesus' resurrection to the Spirit? To speak of Jesus of Nazareth as a man inspired by the Spirit was one thing. But to attribute Jesus' transition to resurrected and exalted Lordship likewise to the Spirit may have ceased to be appropriate in the light of that exaltation. Jesus, as Lord and dispenser of the Spirit, could not have his transition to Lordship attributed to the Spirit.

(b) There is a second curious feature, a similar failure of what might have been expected to transpire. I refer to the way in which in early Christian thought Jesus was seen to have absorbed the roles typically attributed in Second Temple Judaism to such figures as Wisdom/Sophia and Word/ Logos. As is familiar to students working in this area, passages like 1 Corinthians 8:6 and Colossians 1:15-17 seem to attribute to Christ the role in creation previously attributed to divine Wisdom.[39] And all Christians are well aware of how the prologue to the Fourth Gospel identifies Jesus as the divine Word/Logos become flesh (John 1:1-14). In both cases Jesus seems so to absorb the roles of Wisdom and Word as to leave no role for Sophia and Logos apart from Christ.

Now we know that in early Judaism such language functioned as a way of speaking about God in his interaction with his cosmos and his people.[40] In speaking of divine Wisdom, the Jewish sage was affirming the wisdom of God's creative, revelatory, and redemptive actions. To speak of the divine Word was to affirm the rationality and coherence of God's activity. Talk of Wisdom and Word affirmed the *immanence* of God without detracting from God's *transcendence.* So *to identify Jesus as divine Wisdom and Word was in effect to identify Jesus as God's self-revelation, God imma-*

39. See my *Christology,* ch. 6.

40. The claim as worded here is somewhat controversial: there is ongoing disagreement as to whether Wisdom/Word are divine beings distinct from God, divine hypostases, or more like personifications of divine attributes and activities (see again my *Christology,* chs. 6-7). Nevertheless, however we conceptualize Wisdom and Word, it remains true that they functioned in Second Temple Judaism as means of asserting the nearness of the transcendent God.

nent. The same is true, *mutatis mutandis,* with other terms like the name of God, and the glory of God.

The point is that in early Judaism the Spirit of God was another way of speaking of God's presence and activity within history. As the psalmist asked, "Where can I go from your spirit? Or where can I flee from your presence?" (Ps. 139:7). As Wisdom and Word are sometimes effectively synonyms, variant ways of affirming God's immanence, so also Spirit can function as a synonym for Wisdom or Word, making the same affirmation.[41] So if we find the early Christians in effect identifying Jesus with or as divine Wisdom and Word, why do we not find in early Christianity a similar willingness to identify Jesus with divine Spirit? If Jesus was seen to absorb so completely the functions of Wisdom and Spirit, why was he not seen to absorb the function of Spirit?

The only answer I can suggest is that Spirit was instinctively understood to manifest God in a distinctive way, not simply as an alternative to other ways of speaking of God immanent. Part of that would be a recognition that Sophia and Logos could be much more easily depicted in personal terms, whereas Spirit was much more understood in impersonal terms as life-force. Whatever the reason, the transition in Jesus' relationship with the Spirit took a different turn, not that of a straightforward identification with or absorption of its role, but as a continuing interaction, involving some measure of identification of role (1 Cor. 15:45),[42] but also some sense of the exalted Christ having become positioned as it were between God and Spirit. *Whereas Wisdom and Word could be wholly identified with or as Christ, the Spirit remained distinct from Christ.* In other words, in the hesitations and awkwardnesses of even such very early attempts to appreciate the full significance of Christ, we may see the factors and tensions which in due course resulted in a Trinitarian restatement of the doctrine of God by Christians.

(c) I should perhaps just add the further feature to which I drew attention in my earlier work in this area — the way in which the Spirit quickly became known as "the Spirit of Christ," "the Spirit of God's Son,"

41. Details are found in my *Christology,* pp. 134-35, 219, 317 no. 31.

42. 1 Cor. 15:45 is a text with which I have long wrestled — "1 Corinthians 15:45 — Last Adam, Life-giving Spirit," in B. Lindars and S. S. Smalley (eds.), *Christ and Spirit in the New Testament,* C. F. D. Moule FS (Cambridge: Cambridge University Press, 1973), pp. 127-41, reprinted in my *The Christ and the Spirit,* vol. 1: *Christology* (Grand Rapids: Eerdmans, 1998), pp. 154-66; also *Christology,* pp. 145-46; also *Theology of Paul,* pp. 241-42, 260-62.

"the Spirit of Jesus Christ" (Rom. 8:9; Gal. 4:6; Phil. 1:19).[43] This was evidently a way of holding together the pre-Easter Jesus and the post-Easter Christ. For the Spirit of God's Son is precisely the Spirit who expresses the *abba*-prayer of Jesus' ministry, whose presence in the believer constitutes the believer's own sonship and participation in Christ's sonship (Rom. 8:14-17; Gal. 4:6), and whose function is to transform believers more and more into the image of Christ, that they might become more and more conformed to the image of his sonship (Rom. 8:29; 2 Cor. 3:18). So to be transformed by the Spirit of the Son is not simply another way of talking about hope of resurrection, about being conformed to the resurrected body of Christ. What was evidently in Paul's mind is rather a process of becoming like Jesus during his mission on earth. *The Spirit is the Spirit of Christ's sonship, not just of his Lordship.* If there is anything in this, it suggests that the Spirit was a vital factor in the early church's recognition that *the earthly Jesus was still important for theology and discipleship* and that the exaltation of Christ to God's right hand should not be allowed to blot out all else as no longer of significance. Of course, the fact that the tradition contained in the Synoptic Gospels remained so important makes the same point.

All in all, then, such early statements regarding the Spirit become crucial clues as to why Christian theology developed in the way that it did. Indeed, such statements, and the insights or instincts they expressed, probably contributed decisive impulses to the development of the distinctively Christian understanding of God. For it soon became apparent that Christianity could not be content to understand Christ as a glorified man, an apotheosis; that Christianity could not be content with a conclusion to the effect that God's immanent activity was wholly absorbed by and limited to Christ; that Christianity could not be content with an exalted Christ who was not also and at the same time the Jesus of Nazareth who died on the cross. At each point it was early Christianity's instinctive feel for pneumatology that helped, perhaps decisively helped, to prevent such narrowing of perspective and to maintain the breadth and strength of subsequent Christology.

43. *Christology,* pp. 143, 145.

JAMES D. G. DUNN

The Spirit of Gentile Mission

So far I have focused only on the pneumatological impact on the development of early Christian understanding of Christ and his significance, or, alternatively expressed, the christological impact on the traditional understanding of God's Spirit within Second Temple Judaism. But there is, if anything, a still more dramatic development in earliest Christianity which has to be attributed in some sense to the Spirit, or perhaps more accurately, a development given its dramatic effect by being attributed to the Spirit. I refer to the outreach within the very early Christian mission beyond the bounds of Palestine and beyond the bounds of Judaism — a development that ultimately transformed a messianic renewal movement within Judaism into the separate religion of Christianity that has determined so much of Western history and culture.

The central fact here is that *this development was understood to be the direct result of the activity of the Spirit.* It was because the Spirit was seen to have been poured out on Gentiles, freely and fully, and without any expectation of these Gentiles becoming proselytes, that the emergent Christian movement found that it could not be contained within even the diversity of Second Temple Judaism and set out on the road that resulted in Christianity becoming a predominantly Gentile religion.

There are two accounts of this decisive development. Luke's account in the Acts of the Apostles 10–11 is clearest. Peter, the leading apostle within the infant church, was persuaded by a vision to respond favorably to the invitation of a God-fearing Gentile centurion, one Cornelius, to come and preach the gospel in Cornelius's house. When Peter did so, he found that the Spirit anticipated the climax of his sermon. Before he had finished preaching, the Spirit was poured out on the Gentile audience (10:44-48; 11:15-18). Peter and the Jewish believers who had accompanied him had no choice but to agree that God had accepted Cornelius and his friends, even though they remained uncircumcised, and that they should be baptized forthwith in full recognition of their acceptance (10:47; 11:17). Later on, in Acts 15, it is Peter's testimony to the fact that God had thus shown his acceptance of uncircumcised Gentiles "by giving them the Holy Spirit, just as he did to us" (15:8), that persuades the council in Jerusalem that circumcision should *not* be required of future Gentile converts — a decision that ensured in effect that the new movement would not be simply a movement to win proselytes to Judaism.

Paul's account of the matter is less explicit, but just as telling in its effect. At a meeting in Jerusalem at which the demand was made that Gentile believers must be circumcised (probably Paul's account of the same Jerusalem council), it was Paul's advocacy that carried the day. Paul was able to testify that God had been working through his Gentile mission just as effectively as he had through Peter's Jewish mission. God's "grace," through Paul, was drawing Gentiles into the movement, to belief in Christ, without awaiting their being circumcised (Gal. 2:7-9). Lack of circumcision had been proved to be no bar to the grace of God, so that there was no justification or need to require those who already were rejoicing in the grace of God to accept circumcision now (2:3-6).[44] "Grace," we should observe, is a term almost synonymous with "Spirit" in Paul's letters.[45] The outcome was essentially as in Acts 15: the believing Jews were so impressed by the testimony, and by the clear evidence of divine grace, of God's acceptance of uncircumcised Gentiles that they acceded to Paul's argument and gave full recognition to his Gentile mission (2:9).

The points to be noted here are twofold. First, we should note that Second Temple Judaism was not an evangelistic religion. Proselytes and sympathetic God-fearers were more than welcome, but there is little evidence of evangelistic outreach.[46] This is understandable, since Judaism was an ethnic religion, the religion of those who lived in or came from Judea. But this means that the sect of the Nazarenes was distinctive within Second Temple Judaism, more or less from the start, by virtue of its evangelistic drive. That too is attributed to the Spirit at the beginning of the Acts — "you will receive power when the Holy Spirit has come upon you; and you will be my witnesses in Jerusalem, in all Judea and Samaria, and to the ends of the earth" (Acts 1:8). The testimony here is not one we should ignore or play down. It attests the very early conviction that the compulsion which drove the first Christian evangelists to preach the gospel to non-Jews,

---

44. The experience of the Galatians was obviously regarded by Paul as characteristic for Gentile acceptance of the gospel: they had received the Spirit not by doing what the law demanded but by hearing the gospel with faith (Gal. 3:1-5).

45. Bultmann, *Theology,* 1:290-91; my *Theology of Paul,* pp. 319-23. In Luke's account of the larger "breakthrough" to Gentiles in Antioch, he also expresses the decisive evidence of God's approval in terms of "grace" (Acts 11:23).

46. S. McKnight, *A Light Among Gentiles: Jewish Missionary Activity in the Second Temple Period* (Minneapolis: Fortress, 1991); M. Goodman, *Mission and Conversion: Proselytizing in the Religious History of the Roman Empire* (Oxford: Clarendon, 1994).

without expecting them to become proselytes, was *a compulsion from the Spirit of God.*

Second, it should also be noted that the eschatological outpouring of the Spirit within Second Temple Judaism was most typically expected as *only for Israel* (or the remnant).[47] Consequently there would presumably have been little expectation among the first Christian evangelists and missionaries that the Gentiles would be granted the Spirit. Alternatively, if they thought of Gentiles coming into this eschatological blessing, it would presumably have been as part of some hope that in the last days Gentiles would flood in to Zion to acknowledge Yahweh to be God — what is frequently described as "the eschatological pilgrimage of the Gentiles."[48] If so, the Spirit's outpouring on them could have been anticipated as, at best, a *corollary* to their eschatological pilgrimage, that is, to their becoming proselytes.

The historical circumstances that we have to envisage, therefore, seem to be somewhat in the following order. Jewish believers in Messiah Jesus, in proclaiming their faith outside Palestine, presumably in the local synagogues, found to their surprise that Gentile adherents and sympathizers who attended the synagogue were receiving the Spirit as fully and as freely as the full-born Jews and proselytes. Whether willingly or not, they were forced by what they saw with their own eyes to conclude that Gentiles while still in their uncircumcised state had been granted a blessing hitherto assumed to be more or less the sole prerogative of Israel. Only such an astonishing, unprecedented sequence of happenings could have driven otherwise orthodox Jews to conclude that God's acceptance of Gentiles no longer awaited their becoming proselytes. And that conclusion was forced upon them *by the action of the Spirit.*

Here is the precedent *par excellence* for innovation in the affairs of humankind with God. The tradition (of God's special favor for Israel) had been established for centuries; but now within a few weeks, in a short sequence of events, that tradition was broken through and declared *passe.* The conviction that Israel was God's peculiar possession and that the gift

47. The nearest we have to such expectation is Joel 2:28-32, but this seems to be a variation of the more typical expectation that when God pours his Spirit upon the people of God, Gentiles will be attracted to Zion and become part of the eschatological community. See the thesis of F. Philip, "'Apostle to the Gentiles': The Origins of Pauline Pneumatology" (Ph.D. dissertation, Durham University, 2003).

48. See details in my *Jesus Remembered,* pp. 394-95.

of the Spirit was an eschatological blessing which would further and finally demonstrate God's special care and favor for Israel had been axiomatic for generations of Israel. But now the Spirit had demonstrated, apparently beyond question, that the axiom could no longer be maintained and had to be revised. Truly, the Spirit is a power that shakes the foundations and shatters old moulds, a perennial challenge and rebuke to all narrow factionalism and mere traditionalism.

The Spirit as Experienced

Thus far I have been content to observe the ways in which talk of the Spirit contributed to several radical developments in earliest Christian understanding, both of Christ, and of the mission to which those who named themselves by the name of Christ believed themselves called. Some of this was a matter of theological reflection, particularly on the relationship between the Spirit and Christ. But a crucial element in other cases was the perceived intervention of the Spirit — the Spirit of Pentecost, the Spirit of adoption, the Spirit "falling upon" uncircumcised Gentiles, in spite of centuries-old tradition and expectation. In each case, not just theological *reflection* was involved, but spiritual *experience*. In the crucial developments which shaped the distinctiveness of Christian pneumatology it is important to observe that the Spirit *(ruach, pneuma)* was still understood as an *existential* term, expressive of life-transforming experiences.

Typical of earliest Christianity is the question put by Paul to the Galatians: "Did you receive the Spirit by doing the works of the law or by hearing with faith?" (Gal. 3:2). Notice how *the question assumes that the receiving of the Spirit was something perceptible;* reception of the Spirit was an *event* that Paul was confident they could recall in their experience; it was the experience that marked the beginning of their lives as Christians. Similarly, the question put by Paul to the Ephesian "disciples" in Acts 19:2: "Did you receive the Holy Spirit when you became believers?" The question expects an answer: they should *know* whether they have received the Spirit; and not as a deduction from some other act, but as a matter of direct experience. I like to quote Lesslie Newbigin's observation at this point: Paul's "modern successors are more inclined to ask either, 'Did you believe exactly what we teach?' or 'Were the hands that were laid on you our hands?' and — if the answer is satisfactory — to assure the converts that they have received the Holy Spirit even if they don't know it. There is a world of difference between these two attitudes."[49] There is indeed!

The degree to which such experience sparked off new theological insights, challenged and reshaped old traditional perspectives needs to be given fresh attention, not least because of the tremendous repercussions that made Christianity what it is and that reverberate down to the present day. The experience of Pentecost transformed the Baptist's expectation from one of harrowing judgment to one of empowering for mission. The experience of uncircumcised Gentiles receiving the Spirit while still uncircumcised transformed a messianic Jewish sect into a predominantly Gentile religion. And, as I have suggested elsewhere, experience may have played a greater part in the development of the understanding of God as Trinity than we have allowed for, since it is the same *Spirit* that cries *"Abba, Father"* and *"Jesus is Lord"* (Rom. 8:15-16; 1 Cor. 12:3).[50]

Now we know that, properly speaking, there is no such thing as wholly "raw experience." What we experience is in large part determined by our inherited culture and upbringing. How many Protestants have experienced visions of the Virgin Mary? We know that the channels of our perception, the filters which process raw data in our seeing and hearing, our conceptualization and verbalization, all shape what we perceive and conceptualize and articulate. So what we are speaking about in each case is experiences *which were attributed to the Spirit.* None of the experiences mentioned above came neatly labeled "from or of the Holy Spirit." In each case we have to speak of *interpreted* experience. In each case, we have to speak of a moment of insight or of revelation: "This must be the Spirit of God." In the words of Peter's Pentecost sermon, "This is what was spoken through the prophet" (Acts 2:16). The point is well illustrated by what Peter says later in the same sermon: the exalted Christ "has poured out this which you see and hear" (2:33). In so saying, Peter in effect *identifies the Spirit with the phenomena* observable by the crowd (what you see and hear).

What was it, then, that caused them to make this interpretation? How could they be so certain that what they were experiencing was the Spirit of God? Two points call for comment here.

One is the uncomfortable fact that many of these initial experiences

---

49. L. Newbigin, *The Household of God* (London: SCM, 1953), p. 95.
50. *Theology of Paul*, p. 264.

which so shaped Christian mission and theology were what can appropriately be described as "ecstatic" — a discomfort that, as I already suggested, may have been experienced by the eighth- and seventh-century writing prophets. Certainly "ecstatic" must be deemed an appropriate description of the experience of Pentecost and of the similar experience of the centurion Cornelius in Acts 10–11. In the former case the noise was sufficient to bring together a large crowd, according to Luke's account (Acts 2:6), "what you see and hear" (2:33); and in the latter, the visible impact on Cornelius and his friends was sufficient to persuade skeptical Jewish believers that God had indeed accepted them (10:45-46; 11:15-18). As I have noted elsewhere,[51] Luke's account of earliest Christian beginnings seems to be "enthusiastic" in character, that is, to share some of the features of prophetic and ecstatic movements down through the history of Christianity — Montanists, Messalians, radical Reformers, the French Prophets of Wesley's time, and so on. And presumably when Paul spoke of the grace of God that was so visible and self-evidently of God as to convince him and others that Gentiles had indeed received the Spirit, what he was remembering and reporting were charismatic eruptions and the like, understood as manifestations of the Spirit and grace of God (Gal. 2:7-9; 3:2-5; 1 Cor. 1:5, 7).[52]

For many this is a disturbing conclusion. The very features of primitive or raw spirituality, which the church has regarded with deep suspicion and usually dismissed out of hand for most of its history, were the features that occasioned the astonishing developments that made Christianity what it is and what it believes! *Christianity began as an enthusiastic sect!* However, this should not be a matter for embarrassment among Christians and theologians. It simply underlines that when we speak of the Spirit of God we are speaking of an unpredictable power that impacts the lives of (ordinary) believers in unexpected ways, usually enlivening and even transforming their worship and commitment. This is actually good news, and not simply for Pentecostals, but for all who are concerned for the future of Christianity and its mission, for all who have found worship a matter of rote repetition or have experienced theology as only for the archivist or pedant. But ecumenically, it does mean that the traditional churches need to be more open to the still growing third or charismatic di-

---

51. *Unity and Diversity in the New Testament* (London: SCM, ²1990), pp. 174-84.

52. We may compare Acts 2:12-13 on the one hand with 1 Cor. 14:23 and on the other with Eph. 5:18.

mension of Christianity, and theologically, dogmaticians need to integrate the *experienced* Spirit more fully into their systems.

The second point is the importance of *"discerning the spirits,"* of checking and evaluating claims to Spirit experience.[53] This is a task that the enthusiast can too easily ignore, so confident is he or she that what has been experienced is of the Spirit; an enthusiast is usually also a fundamentalist, at least in the sense that the significance of the experience is regarded as clear-cut and beyond dispute. But Paul clearly saw the need for such discernment in all cases of claimed inspiration: prophecy should go hand in hand with discernment (1 Cor. 12:10); others should evaluate a prophecy when it was given (14:29); "do not despise prophecy, but test everything" (1 Thess. 5:20-21). His criteria for discernment are most clearly laid out in 1 Corinthians 12–14: confession of Jesus as Lord (12:3); love (13); community benefit/upbuilding (14:3-5, 12, 17, 26).[54] The most sophisticated criterion of all, presumably, was Paul's identification of the Spirit as the Spirit of Christ, the Spirit that reproduced the same sense of sonship as had characterized Jesus' own mission (Rom. 8:15-16; Gal. 4:6), the Spirit that produced the fruit of Christ-like character (Gal. 5:22-23), the Spirit that shaped the believer to become more and more like Christ (2 Cor. 3:18).[55]

It is at this point that we may see how the more theologically and pastorally astute Paul went beyond the enthusiastic Luke and safeguarded Luke's portrayal of Christianity's beginnings from becoming the only model for church renewal. For his own part, Paul had no hesitation in calling to mind the enthusiastic manifestations of the Spirit, the miracles worked among the Galatians (Gal. 3:5), "the signs and wonders" (a favorite Lukan phrase) wrought regularly in his mission (Rom. 15:19). But it is probably significant that when he recalled the work of the Spirit, which constituted the proof positive that God was calling for and richly blessing the Gentile mission, he spoke then not of miracles and signs and wonders, but of *the grace of God* working through him (Gal. 2:7-9). For "grace" was itself a word that Paul found it necessary to coin afresh in order to describe the wonder of what he and others were experiencing.[56] As such it epito-

---

53. To beat another old drum — "Discernment of Spirits — A Neglected Gift," in W. Harrington, ed., *Witness to the Spirit: Essays on Revelation, Spirit, Redemption* (Dublin: Irish Biblical Association, 1979), pp. 79-96, reprinted in *Pneumatology*, pp. 311-28.

54. See further my *Jesus and the Spirit*, pp. 293-97.

55. *Jesus and the Spirit*, pp. 318-22; *Unity and Diversity*, pp. 190-95.

56. See again *Theology of Paul*, pp. 319-23.

mized the effect of the Spirit on their lives, not in terms of power or of ecstatic worship, but in terms of *a wholly generous acceptance and enabling by
God.* For Paul *charisma* never amounted to anything unless it expressed
the *charis,* the grace of God manifested most clearly in Christ.

To gain a proper balance, to maintain a healthy tension between
Luke's presentation of the Spirit and Paul's has to be one of the continuous
and ongoing tasks of any church or theology.

Conclusion

In this paper I have reviewed a number of features of talk about the Spirit
in our earliest Christian sources — all of them either surprising for their
time, or largely neglected by subsequent Christian reflection on the Spirit,
or both.

The interplay of Christ and the Spirit in the texts considered has
been particularly intriguing: (1) the conviction that Jesus was not only inspired by the Spirit, but was also, on being exalted to God's right hand,
given authority to bestow the Spirit; (2) the instinct that Jesus' resurrection
should not be attributed to the Spirit and that the exalted Christ was
somehow Lord of the Spirit of God; (3) the sense that Jesus did not absorb
the role of the Spirit and that *there was still a role for the Spirit not restricted
to Christ,* and yet the Spirit was to be recognized now as *the Spirit of Jesus,*
as the Spirit bearing and generating the character of Christ. In the light of
all this, it must be judged unfortunate that the subsequent development in
Christian understanding of God did not integrate the Spirit more fully
into that developing understanding, and that in the full Trinitarian understanding of God, the Spirit was something of an afterthought.

Most significant for the development of Christianity itself, as a Jewish messianic movement that became a world religion in its own right, was
the impact of spiritual experience identified as experience of God's Spirit:
(4) experience shared by Gentiles without their first having to become
Jews; (5) experiences that, in character and evaluation, would probably
have been an embarrassment to subsequent generations of the church;
(6) experiences that need to be discerned and evaluated as to their source
and significance for the community's benefit; (7) and yet experiences that
have a powerfully generative and attractive effect and that may be the key
to Christianity's growth in the wider world and essential for its revitaliza-

tion in the West. A church that seeks to restrict and control the Spirit, as too dangerous and unpredictable, may be safe, but it has signed its own death warrant. A church that seeks to follow where the Spirit leads will have to expect the unexpected and be prepared to be shaken to its core. But that's life, the life of the Spirit.

The Holy Spirit — A Person?
Reflection on the Spirit's Trinitarian Identity

BERND OBERDORFER

Is the Holy Spirit a person? "Strange question," some might answer, "of course it is. Doesn't the classical Trinitarian dogma speak of 'one divine essence in three *persons*'? And the Spirit is obviously one of them!" But others might doubt this, and common sense is on their side. "If you personalize the Spirit," they might say, "you will get a ghost." That means that if we simply analogize the Holy Spirit to a human person, we will arrive at the concept of an invisible entity, appearing here and there, "wherever it wants to" (John 3:8), doing strange things in supernatural ways. How should we come to believe that this is the shape of God's presence in the world, as Holy Scripture puts it?

In fact, the question of the Spirit's 'personality' is a very complex one. Historically we should ask how and in what sense the concept of *person* was introduced into the fourth-century discussions of the Trinitarian being of God — and how and in what sense the term was used for the *Spirit's* identity. We will see that there were strong reservations about the use of the term for the distinct Trinitarian *hypostaseis* (modes of being) in general, and that it was enormously difficult to integrate the Holy Spirit into a model of 'personal identity' which was developed with reference to the Father and the Son. Further, we have to consider the meaning of *person* itself. *Person,* in the fourth century, did not mean the same as it means in the modern age, and we need to reflect on the relevance that shift bears on the use of the term in Trinitarian theology. But, even more importantly, today as well as in ancient times, *person* does not simply mean *indi-*

viduality with self-consciousness. The concept of person essentially implies the dimension of the social resonance in the many different spheres of private and public life. Personality is more than hermetic, isolated individuality, more than I actually know of myself, more than I can consciously display of myself. To put it simply: The way people see me is part of my personality. Thus, the question of whether and how we can call the Holy Spirit a *person* cannot be solved by asking whether and how the Holy Spirit can be described in analogy to a self-conscious individual. In the biblical witnesses, however, one of the crucial characteristics of the Spirit is to produce a sphere of public resonance of Christ and his manifestation of God. Thus, to call the Holy Spirit a person (or — as Michael Welker put it[1] — a "public person"), could help to develop a more adequate concept of person in general. Yet, even with such an elaborated concept of person we will have to ask whether or not the use of the term *person* makes a full understanding of the biblical witnesses more difficult and, consequently, of the Trinitarian identity of the Holy Spirit. In any case, as I would like to outline at the end of the paper, personal and nonpersonal conceptions of the Spirit's very being should complement and explain one another.

The Development of the Trinitarian Terminology — and the Holy Spirit

It is extremely important to see that the Trinitarian question arose from the problem of *Christology.*[2] If Jesus Christ fully manifests and represents God's eternal will, and if his destiny is decisive for the eternal destination of humankind, then it is of the greatest soteriological relevance that there is no ontological and epistemological difference between him and God. In a very early text, we read in 2 *Clement* 1:1: "We must think about Christ the same way we think about God." This became, so to speak, the headline to the dis-

---

1. See his *Gottes Geist: Theologie des Heiligen Geistes* (Neukirchen-Vluyn: Neukirchener, 1992), pp. 259-313; ET: *God the Spirit* (Minneapolis: Fortress, 1994), pp. 279-341.

2. For the development of Trinitarian theology in the early church, see my *Filioque* (Göttingen: Vandenhoeck & Ruprecht, 2001), pp. 37-128, and my article, "Trinität. III: Dogmengeschichtlich, 1. Alte Kirche," in H. D. Betz (ed.), *Religion in Geschichte und Gegenwart: Handwörterbuch für Theologie und Religionswissenschaft* (4th ed.; Tübingen: Mohr Siebeck), 8:602-8.

cussions of the following centuries. The question of the Son's relation to the Father with reference to their common divine character was the catalyst for theological reflections, eventually resulting in the Trinitarian dogma. Not coincidentally, the *homoousios* formula of the Nicene Synod of 325 was used only to define the eternal being of the *Son*. In short, the Trinitarian question was — for the time being — hardly more than a *binitarian* question.

Two factors in particular left the question open to an 'expansion' to trinitarianism. First of all, the Christians' strong consciousness of being a *spiritual* community, a community constituted by the Holy Spirit. Secondly — and most influentially — Christ's command to "baptize in the name of the Father and the Son and the Holy Spirit" (Matt. 28:19), which was the liturgical formula recited in every ceremony of baptism. Interestingly, in the Creed of the Nicene Synod the Holy Spirit is simply named without any explication. But the fact that it had to be named at least shows that integrating the Spirit into the understanding of the eternal being of God has always been a challenge. Only when, more than thirty years later, some bishops in Libya publicly contested the full Godhead of the Spirit, was theology forced to reflect explicitly on that question. Quite characteristically, the arguments for the *Spirit's* full Godhead then were analogous to the arguments brought forward in favor of the *Son's*: if the Spirit is only a power of God and not God himself in the full sense, then we cannot be certain that we really encounter *God* in the preaching of the gospel and in the sacraments, and we will not have the certainty that the God who displays himself in the revelation of Christ (communicated to us "in the power of the Spirit") is identical with God's very being.

Historically thus the Trinitarian question emerged from a binitarian focus. Consequently, the categories of Trinitarian theology were developed by reflecting on the Father-Son relation, and the Holy Spirit had to be integrated into this model in a second step. To put it in a formal and abstract way, the question to be solved was: how can we articulate real distinctions within the Godhead and nevertheless maintain its undivided unity? There are two aspects to this question. First of all, what *categories* can we use to distinguish a plurality of real 'entities' within the one God? Secondly, how can we describe these different 'entities' in their respective 'individuality'? That means: What *is* the Father, what *is* the Son, what *is* the Holy Spirit, and what are their respective relations?

The discussions of the fourth century concentrated on the first aspect, resulting in the famous 'Cappadocian' formula *mia ousia* — *treis hypostaseis*.

This formula, taken as such, does not display its origin in the reflection on the distinction of the Father and the Son. The term *hypostasis* (*subsistentia,* mode of being) is neutral and technical, which does not show any preference for a specific model to describe the 'individuality' of Father, Son, or Spirit. But if we take a closer look at the attempts to define the distinctions between these three *hypostaseis,* we can clearly see that it was the Father-Son model which was decisive. The differentiation of the *hypostaseis* was based upon the concept of *origin,* which obviously emerged from the semantics of the relationship between Father and Son. So as the 'individuality' of the Son was defined by his 'eternal generation' *(gennēsis),* the 'individuality' of the Spirit also had to be derived from its origin in the Father. Yet it is significant that the Greek church fathers came up only with the colorless term *ekporeusis* (*processio,* a going forth). While it is biblical (John 15:26), it does not say anything specific about the Spirit's mode of being. According to the Greek theologians, it is enough to know that the Spirit proceeds from the Father *in a different way* than the Son does. The concrete mode of this *different way* remains *arrētos* (unexpressed, even inexpressible); it must not (and need not) be described. In the Greek writings, only a few ideas can be found about the identity of the Spirit in its relation to the Father and the Son, about the Spirit's 'function' in relation to the Father and the Son, and about its relevance for the divinity of God. According to Gregory of Nazianzus, for example, the Holy Spirit is a divine *hypostasis* because it ascribes holiness and a spiritual character to God ("God is holy," "God is spirit") and thus also to the Father and the Son. Gregory also says that the Spirit's function in relation to the Son is to 'give light' upon the Son *(ekphanēsis)*: the Son 'shines' through the light of the Spirit. But these ideas remain consciously vague and restrictive, due to the apophatic limits of our theological knowledge.

The Latin reaction to the term *hypostasis* was quite reserved. Its possible translation *substantia* seemed to lead to the assumption of *three substances,* which would multiply the one divine substance (or essence) and thus result in tritheism. Long before, in the beginning of the third century, Tertullian had already introduced the term *persona* as a category to distinguish the three divine 'entities' *(una substantia — tres personae),*[3] albeit

---

3. He referred to the use of the term *persona* in the Latin grammar, which speaks of the *triplex natura personarum:* the person who speaks ("I"), the person spoken to ("You"), and the person spoken of ("He or She"). Cf. R. Spaemann, *Personen* (Stuttgart: Klett, 1996), p. 31.

without developing a consistent theory. The Latin fathers of the fourth century, particularly Augustine, adopted the term *persona* when they tried to unfold the Trinitarian dogma. For the Greeks, however, this concept had a *modalistic* touch. The original meaning of *persona* is that of a 'mask' or 'role' in a theatre, and so the use of the word would possibly imply that God's real face is hidden behind different masks which he changes from time to time. Unlike what we would expect, the distrust of the word *persona* was not caused by the suspicion of tritheism (three *persons* in the sense of three *individuals*) but rather by the fear that *persona* was not able to express *real distinctions* within the one divine essence.

Clearly, the Latin fathers did not refer to the meaning 'mask' when they used the term *persona* to distinguish the three real divine 'entities.'[4] In a more general sense, *persona* in postclassical Latin could simply mean 'someone,' 'subject of (legal) responsibility,' 'point of reference' for ascriptions *(Zuschreibungen)*. Thus, in its original theological use, the term did not mean much more than *hypostasis*. Moreover, even in that weakened sense, Augustine was very cautious to use the word anyway. "Dictum est tamen tres personae," he wrote in his *De Trinitate* (V/9,10), "non ut illud diceretur sed ne taceretur." He explicitly refused to refer to any *special* meaning of the word, but accepted its use only for lack of better alternatives.

Nevertheless, the word was born and took on a life of its own. Its close relationship to human individuality entailed specific dynamics. While Augustine was far from precisely defining *persona*, Boethius, most influentially, stated: "persona est rationalis naturae individua substantia," which was fundamental not only for the history of the concept of *person* in

---

4. Spaemann rightly remarks (cf. *Personen*, p. 31) that the meaning 'mask' or 'role' entails an element of self-distance and self-identification (distance from the role as well as 'living the role') and an element of social acceptance which were important to the history of the anthropological use of the term 'person' because they made it clear that to call someone a person is not the same as to ascribe some 'objective' attributes to an entity. A human being *is* not simply a person in the same sense he or she *is* an entity walking on two legs. "Here we already find a structural element of our modern concept of person, the element of nonidentity" (ibid., trans. B.O.). But at any rate, Spaemann himself adds that for the ancient philosophers *persona* remained a "secondary identity and thus also a weaker identity than the natural one" (ibid., trans. B.O.). Evidently, this is the crucial problem when the term is transferred into a Trinitarian context. The distinction between (Trinitarian) person and (divine) essence is different from the distinction between mask and masked 'real' nature or between role and role player.

general⁵ but also for Trinitarian reflection in scholastic theology. Yet, as we will see, the problem was always — the Spirit.

Augustine, however, developed a second model of distinguishing the three divine 'entities' which was more important to him than the *persona* model, namely the model of *relation*. Strictly speaking, the identity of the trinitarian 'entities' is based only upon their respective relations. To understand this, we have to consider the Aristotelian logics and ontology of *substantia* and *accidens* which was the philosophical framework of this concept. The problem was that, on the one hand, the Trinitarian 'persons' could not be distinguished by *substantia,* while, on the other hand, their different identity could not be taken as a mere *accidens.* In the first case, it was the one essence of God that had to be safeguarded; in the second case, the fact that the difference in identity was at the heart of God's real essence. Augustine focused on the logical category of *relation* because this enabled him to establish a real (i.e., substantial, not accidental) differentiation in God without jettisoning the undivided unity of the divine essence.

Interestingly, Augustine did not regard *any* relations between the trinitarian 'persons' as significant for their respective identity. He privileged instead the category of *origin.* This indicates that he — as well as the Greeks — developed this model out of the Father-Son relation. As far as the Holy Spirit was concerned, however, there was an important difference from the Greek model. Whereas the Greeks could feel the Spirit's identity was sufficiently described by its procession out of the Father, in the Augustinian model there had to be a relation — that is, a relation of origin — between the Spirit and the Son as well in order to designate their real difference. Because in the history of revelation the Holy Spirit is the Spirit of the Father and the Son, and since it is sent to the disciples and the church from the Father and the Son, Augustine concluded that the Spirit's eternal being is defined by its procession out of the Father and the Son *(ex Patre Filioque).*

Nota bene: Augustine did not have a relational concept of 'person' in general — which would mean that personhood develops in relations — but instead he used the word *persona* as a simple term to indicate the fact of three 'someones' in God. The respective identity of these 'someones,' then, he did not describe by unfolding a concept of 'person' but with reference to their respective relations of origin. Not before the High Middle Ages do we find a relational concept of person. Thomas Aquinas combined

5. See Spaemann, *Personen,* pp. 32-36.

the Boethian idea of *individua substantia* with the Augustinian category of *relatio* and gave a concise definition of Trinitarian personhood as being *relatio subsistens* (*SummaTheologica* q. 29,4).

As to the Holy Spirit, in some respects the concept of relation hindered Augustine from developing a 'personalistic' understanding of its identity. If the Holy Spirit is the Spirit of the Father and the Son and if it proceeds from the Father and the Son, he concluded that it is the link between the Father and the Son. Its identity is defined by being their hypostasized community. We might say the Spirit is their 'community in person.' But that would be a metaphorical (and somewhat paradoxical) use of the term 'person' (at least if strongly linked to any commonsense image of 'individuality'). Besides which, we might as well say that the Spirit is the '*sphere* of the community' of the Father and the Son and thus use 'nonpersonal' terminology. This shift to nonpersonal language, quite surprisingly, is implied as well in the terminology of *love* which Augustine adopts, calling the Spirit the 'bond of love' or even the 'mutual love' of the Father and the Son, the love with which they love each other. Ultimately, it is fairly difficult to regard the act of love between two persons itself as being a person.

It has often been remarked that these 'nonpersonal' definitions in a way conceal the Spirit's identity. This is partly true. On the other hand, however, they might help to avoid a reductionist ('personalistic') concept of the Holy Spirit as well as a reductionist ('individualistic') concept of person.

The Concept of Person and the Mutual Relations of Its Anthropological and Its Trinitarian Use

If we had to write a history of the concept of person in the sense of human personhood and thereby to investigate the impact of Christian theology on that history, we certainly would have to consider, apart from the Trinitarian dogma, the christological dogma with its formula 'one person in two natures.' It is a difficult (and quite subtle) question as to whether the christological use of 'persona' is consistent with its Trinitarian use.[6]

6. Cf., e.g., G. Essen, *Die Freiheit Jesu: Der neuchalkedonische Enhypostasiebegriff im Horizont neuzeitlicher Subjekt- und Personphilosophie* (Regensburg: Pustet, 2001). It is re-

But we do not have to follow this path. For our purposes, it is sufficient to remark that the focus on *Christ's* 'personality,' in the long run, supported a more 'personalistic' understanding of the Trinitarian distinctions.[7]

In some respects, however, a tension arose between this model of three *persons* and the most influential model derived from Augustine's famous analogy of the divine Trinity and the elementary modes of (human) mind, *memoria — intellectus — voluntas* or *mens — notitia — amor*. This model almost necessarily evokes the image of a self-conscious individual — Augustine himself encouraged this by declaring the *individual mind* to be *imago Dei*, that is, *imago Trinitatis*, and rejecting any 'social' concept of the Trinity — and it was exactly this image which was adopted in modern philosophical theology (e.g., Leibniz, Lessing[8]) as the only possible way to make rational sense of the doctrine of the Trinity. Interestingly, it was in this period that God finally — as Tillich put it with slight irony — "became a person," whereas the patristic fathers (in order to avoid any modalist touch) had reserved the term 'persona' only to designate the Trinitarian *hypostases* (plural).

Thus, in the modern age, there was a twofold use of the term 'person' with reference to God: On the one hand, there is the theistic model of *God* as a 'person,' of a 'personal God' with consciousness, perhaps self-awareness, and will. On the other hand, we have the model of the *three* Trinitarian 'persons.' In Enlightenment philosophy and theology, the latter was widely criticized (insofar as it was an element of the so-called 'immanent Trinity') in the name of the first, which seemed to be able to save the rational plausibility of the Christian doctrine of God. But the theistic model of a 'personal and conscious God' was destroyed by the criticism of Kant and, particularly, Fichte. Fichte showed that consciousness and will

---

markable that in the Trinitarian debate, *persona* is a term for *distinction*, whereas in the christological debate, it is a term for *unity*.

7. *Nota bene:* This does not necessarily imply a reductionist model of personhood as such. On the contrary, the need to integrate the two 'natures' required an 'element of non-identity' as well. The person of Christ is neither simply identical with his divine 'nature' nor with his human 'nature.'

8. See, e.g., G. E. Lessing, "Des Andreas Wissowatius Einwürfe wider die Dreieinigkeit," in idem, *Werke*, ed. H. G. Göpfert, vol. 7 (München: Hanser, 1976; reprint Darmstadt: Wissenschaftliche Buchgesellschaft, 1996), pp. 198-225, and para. 73 of his "Erziehung des Menschengeschlechts," in idem, *Werke*, vol. 8 (München: Hanser, 1979; reprint Darmstadt, 1996), pp. 489-510, 505-6.

can only be ascribed to *finite* entities, implying thereby that speaking of a personal God makes God finite.

In nineteenth- and twentieth-century theology, we see several ways of dealing with this critique. One of them was to separate the person model from its theistic implications. God was still regarded as 'person' or 'personality' *(Persönlichkeit)*, but in a nontheistic, nonspeculative way, for example, by declaring God to be the 'Thou' that speaks to our heart and within our conscience. We can call this the 'personalistic' way of reasoning. Another way was to establish a speculative model of God as 'absolute spirit' which evolves and realizes itself within history. This Hegelian model could be understood as a rational reconstruction of the Trinitarian model based upon the idea of God as *summus spiritus,* but leaving behind any 'individualistic' implications with which this traditional model could possibly be associated. Thus, in this model, the concept of 'person' did not play a major role. By contrast, a third model focused on the concept of God's 'personality,' yet developing it in a Trinitarian way (as pursued, e.g., by Isaak August Dorner). Not surprisingly, Dorner preferred the term 'hypostases' (modes of being, *Seinsweisen*) to the term 'persons' to designate the three divine 'entities.'

But in *none* of these models, as can be clearly seen, does the idea of the 'three persons' have any relevance. This also applies to the beginning of the 'Trinitarian renaissance' in the twentieth century. Karl Barth grounded the doctrine of the Trinity in his analysis of God's self-revelation. The triune God is the unity of the Revealer, the act of revelation, and the effect of revelation *(Offenbarer, Offenbarung, Offenbarsein)*. The doctrine of the Trinity has the function of designating the identity and sovereignty of God in every aspect of his self-revelation ("God is only recognized by God"). Whereas Christ represents the 'objectivity' of this self-revelation, the Spirit represents its subjective dimension, that is, making people understand and believe in the reality of God's self-revelation which they would not have been able to understand and accept based on their own efforts. It is evident that this emphasis on epistemology must have led Barth to give preference to the language of *Seinsweisen* rather than to the semantics of persons.[9]

Another great innovator of twentieth-century Trinitarian thought,

9. See particularly *Kirchliche Dogmatik* I/1 (Zürich: Theologischer Verlag, 1932). Cf. my *Filioque* (Göttingen: Vandenhoeck & Ruprecht, 2001), pp. 354-71; M. Murrmann-Kahl, *"Mysterium Trinitatis"?* (Berlin/New York: Walter de Gruyter, 1997), pp. 17-100.

BERND OBERDORFER

Karl Rahner, explicitly stated that the meaning of 'person' in modern culture makes it almost impossible to use the term for Trinitarian distinctions any longer. Because modernity understands a person as an individual 'center of action' *(Aktzentrum),* according to Rahner, speaking of 'three divine persons' will almost necessarily lead to a tritheistic misunderstanding of God's triune being.[10]

It was Wolfhart Pannenberg who came to defend the Trinitarian use of 'person' with explicit reference to a modern understanding of 'person.' For, according to modern philosophical anthropology, personhood is not an isolated, immutable entity but rather comes into being, develops, and is formed by a social context. Persons exist only in relations, and their personality is not independent of these relations. Pannenberg states that exactly the same situation applies to the Trinitarian persons. They are defined by their relations to each other. More radically than tradition has done, Pannenberg links the concept of person to the concept of relation, and unlike tradition, Pannenberg refuses to give preference to the relations of *origin* as the only relations relevant to the very being of a Trinitarian person. The Son, for example, is not only defined by being generated out of the Father, but also by being illuminated by the Spirit. Again, the very being of the Father depends on his being acknowledged by the Son through the Spirit. Further, the identity of the Spirit is defined not only by its procession out of the Father (and — as in the Western tradition — of the Son) but also by its active relations to the Father and the Son. In short, the Trinity is a network of concrete relations which make the Trinitarian persons what they are.

What follows from this for the understanding of the Holy Spirit?

The Holy Spirit — A Person or a Field of Power?

It is interesting that Pannenberg accentuates the Spirit's personhood but at the same time adopts a nonpersonal conception of the 'field' from physics in order to designate (or, to put it more carefully, to illustrate) the Spirit's identity. How do these go together?

---

10. See his most influential study, "Der dreifaltige Gott als transzendenter Urgrund der Heilsgeschichte," in J. Feiner and M. Löhrer (eds.), *Mysterium Salutis,* vol. 2 (Einsiedeln et al., 1967), pp. 317-401. Cf. my *Filioque,* pp. 371-88.

The concept of person must be freed from its restriction to conscious, self-aware individuality. A person, as argued above, originates in manifold — active as well as passive — interactions with the person's social environment. Thus, in order to find out who the Spirit is, we have to investigate its manifold interactions with the Father and the Son. For this purpose, Pannenberg refers to the Augustinian tradition considering the Spirit to be the community or the "bond of unity" between the Father and the Son. To put it more precisely, the Spirit, going forth from the Father to the Son and recirculating to the Father, mutually reveals to them their respective identities and thus constitutes their community, even their unity which is a unity of irreducibly distinct 'entities.' By revealing their *difference* to the Father and the Son, the Spirit reveals to them their *unity*. Because this eternal revelation reveals more than just something which exists independently of this revelation, we can say that the Spirit *constitutes* both the differentiation and the unity of the Father and the Son, and so the Spirit *is* the reality of their difference as well as of their unity. In other words, they would not be different, and they would not be one, without the Spirit.

Yet again, we may ask why we should call the unity-in-difference of two persons a person. When speaking of a person we expect a specific entity to behave in a particular way *(Verhaltenserwartung)*, and we ascribe to this entity an essential capability both of perceiving, acting, and reacting as well as of having intentions (where all of these concepts are understood in a broad sense). By expecting this entity to 'behave' specifically within its concrete and manifold social context, we identify it. A person is not an isolated, eternal substance, but rather is defined by the way the person and his or her environment interact, both in active and passive ways. A person is formed by the way he or she perceives and forms the 'world' *and* by the way this 'world' perceives and influences him or her.[11]

As to the 'personality' of the Holy Spirit, we then should ask what its distinctive and indispensable contribution to the very being of the Father and the Son consists of. Further, we should also consider the impact of the Father and the Son on the Spirit's very being. In short, we have to reflect on

---

11. This view of personality is strongly influenced by crucial insights of Schleiermacher. See particularly his *Versuch einer Theorie des geselligen Betragens* and his lectures in *Philosophical Ethics*. Cf. my "'Umrisse der Persönlichkeit': Personalität beim jungen Schleiermacher — Ein Beitrag zur gegenwärtigen ethischen Diskussion," in *Evangelische Theologie* 60 (2000): 9-24.

no less than the whole range of its active and passive relations to and from the Father and the Son. This implies a critique of the (Western and Eastern!) tradition, which was content to define the Spirit's identity only by its origination out of the Father (or of the Father and the Son). It also implies a critique of the Augustinian tradition of the Spirit as *vinculum unitatis*. This tradition obviously is able to ascribe to the Spirit an *active* contribution to the being of the Father and the Son. However, it overemphasizes their *similarity*, and it can hardly show that the Spirit's relation to the Father is different from its relation to the Son. So without neglecting the truth entailed in the doctrine of the *vinculum unitatis*, we need to ask: what does the Spirit in particular *give* to the Father, and what in particular does it *give* to the Son? Michael Welker, as previously mentioned, called the Spirit a "public person" in a non-self-referential sense. That is to say, the Spirit is the "public person" *of Christ;* it is the sphere of Christ's resonance. The Spirit's identity, thus, is not defined by its reflection on itself, but rather by its reference to Christ. Welker speaks of the Spirit's essential 'selflessness' *(Selbstlosigkeit)* or 'self-withdrawal' *(Selbstzurücknahme).* The Spirit is what it is not by revealing itself but by revealing Christ. Unfolding this idea in a Trinitarian way, we can say that the Spirit is itself by revealing Christ as the Son and — in doing so — revealing God as the Father as well. This applies not only to the 'economic' but also to the 'immanent' Trinity: the Spirit (to use the Cappadocian concept of *ekphanēsis*) 'gives light' upon the Son in order to make him 'shine' *for the Father,* as well as revealing the Father as Father *to the Son.* Thus, the Spirit opens up the Son to the Father and the Father to the Son, and so the Spirit brings them together, revealing to them their close relationship, their intimate community, and even unity-in-difference. In this sense, the Spirit is the 'spirit' or 'aura' or 'atmosphere' of this community, the sphere within which this community is being realized.

Speaking of 'sphere,' we come to the point where personal and nonpersonal aspects of the conception of the Holy Spirit meet. It was again Wolfhart Pannenberg's[12] observation that in the early church, there was a kind of 'spiritualization' of the Spirit not appropriate to the particularly Old Testament understanding of the Spirit as the dynamic 'field of power' *(Kraftfeld)* of divinity. Historically, this 'spiritualization' (which resulted in a consciousness/self-awareness model of God) was almost inevitable be-

---

12. To the following, see his *Systematische Theologie,* vol. 1 (Göttingen: Vandenhoeck & Ruprecht, 1988), pp. 414-16.

cause the only alternative available was the Stoic model of the Spirit as a very fine material substance present all over creation. This model was unacceptable because it would have made the Spirit a part of the material world. Modern physics, however, according to Pannenberg, provides a new understanding of a 'field of power' which does not necessarily imply materialistic consequences. Modern *field theories* "no longer conceive of field phenomena as material substances, but as autonomous as over against the material world and defined only by their relations to space or space time."[13] Pannenberg therefore says "that the biblical claims about the Spirit of God are much closer to the modern idea of a universal field of power (which Michael Faraday was the first to develop), in relation to which all material, corporeal entities can be regarded as secondary manifestations, than the classical idea of God as *Nous*."[14] Based on this, Pannenberg restates the doctrine of the divine essence in its relation to the Trinitarian persons. If the divine essence is being described as the 'field of power' of the 'Spirit of Love,' then divinity need no longer be thought of as a subject (as is the case in the *Nous* model). "Divinity, conceived as a field, can be understood as manifesting itself in all three Trinitarian persons equally."[15] The Holy Spirit *as a person*, then, *is* this field of divine love and power, seen from the perspective of autonomy from the persons of the Father and the Son, meaning the Holy Spirit is the mode in which the Father and the Son experience their community. The Holy Spirit is the objectification of their community. "Because both of them [Father and Son] — albeit in different ways — are confronted with the common essence of divinity in the form of the Spirit, they are linked to each other by the unity of the Spirit."[16]

According to this model, however, the Spirit as a person would not simply coincide with the divine essence. The Spirit, in other words, would have to have its own relation to the divine essence. So we can say that the Spirit recognizes itself as being the divine "Spirit of Love" only in the mir-

13. See Pannenberg, *Systematische Theologie,* 1:414 (trans. B.O.).
14. Ibid. — Whether this is an appropriate understanding of the *field theory* in terms of physics may be (and has been) doubted. Critics in particular object to the claim that the field is autonomous from the material world. Although this quite obviously qualifies the use of the model as a means to illustrate the plausibility of the Christian concept of Trinity in dialogue with modern scientific worldviews, it does not necessarily make the consistency of Pannenberg's conception of the doctrine of Trinity itself collapse.
15. See Pannenberg, *Systematische Theologie,* 1:415.
16. Ibid.

ror of the community of the Father and the Son. It *needs* this mirror to recognize divinity.

This concept can be identified as a very subtle and complex reformulation of the Anselmian axiom "In Deo omnia sunt unum ubi non obviat aliqua relationis oppositio." Unlike in Anselm, the 'relations' are not restricted here to the category of origin. Additionally, the *unum* is now defined as a pneumatical 'field of power' rather than as *summus spiritus* (in the sense of consciousness or self-awareness). Considering this, it is a question of perspective and context as to whether we speak of the Spirit in personal or nonpersonal terms. Both are possible, and both are necessary. At any rate, both ways qualify and challenge each other. The nonpersonal field metaphor recalls that a person cannot be simply understood in analogy to conscious, self-aware individuality. Using personal language also reminds us that understanding the Spirit as 'field' must mean more than a simple ubiquity. It implies at least an intentional structure, because the Spirit appears "wherever it *wants* to."

The Presence of the Spirit

The doctrine of the Trinity confronts us with the meaning of the revelation of God's creative, saving, and redeeming work towards and within the world in terms of our understanding of God's very being. Our notion of God is constituted by that revelation. But it is also supposed to return to it. Every explication of the triune being of God has to be scrutinized as to whether and how it fosters our understanding of God's work itself. To follow this hermeneutical circle is essential to prevent the doctrine of the Trinity from becoming mere pointless speculation about a reality beyond our knowledge, as Kant put it. Thus, the question I would like to focus on at the end of this chapter is whether the very being of the Holy Spirit can be conceived of in terms of personal and nonpersonal metaphors. If so, what does it mean that the Spirit's trinitarian being may be described as both *the realization and the reality* of the unity-in-difference of the Father and the Son, that is, the realizing 'person' and the realized 'sphere' of their unity-in-difference? What does this contribute to understanding the presence of the Spirit in the world and its function within the history of salvation? Tackling this question might also be relevant to promoting theological dialogue between the 'historic mainline' churches with their elaborate doctrinal and liturgical traditions and the powerfully emerging Pentecostal churches with their emphasis on the experience of the Spirit.

Let us look first at the Spirit's role within the 'story' of Christ's work of salvation. The crucial disclosure of Christ's relation to God and at the same time the starting point of his messianic way, of course, is his baptism, when the heavens are opened and the voice from above calls him "my beloved Son," thus identifying the speaker as the loving Father. Interestingly, this happens only after the Spirit has come down upon Christ. What is of great significance as well is that for the time being it happens in an intimate scene between the two of them ("*You* are my beloved Son!"). So we can rightly say that it is the Spirit who discloses the Father to the Son and the Son to the Father and, by doing so, not only displays but even brings about their community. But it is also the Spirit who opens heaven to earth, overcoming the distance between the sphere where God dwells and the sphere of human life. There is no 'Shekinah' without the Spirit. Not coincidentally, then, it is only after the Spirit's coming upon him that Christ sets out to preach the gospel, to share and renew the lives of the outcasts, to heal the diseases of the sick and disabled. If it is true that the focus of Christ's gospel is to reveal God's presence as the loving Father and that the focus of Christ's 'Sonship' is to *be* this presence, and if it is also true that this can happen only 'in the power of the Spirit' as both realization and reality of the Father's and the Son's community, then we are entitled to say that it is the Spirit who 'dis-closes' (literally) the close relationship of the Father and the Son to humankind in an epistemological and ontological sense, that is, by *revealing* that relationship to humankind and *integrating* humankind into that relationship, letting human beings participate in their community.

In a very complex way, the cross then is the crisis *and* the confirmation of the unity-in-difference between the Father and the Son. On the one hand, the cross displays the abyss of differentiation as well as the abyss of 'undifferentiation'; on the other hand, it displays the endurance of this relation even in the deep loneliness of the alleged blasphemist sentenced to death. The German theologian Hans-Georg Geyer once said that the cross visualized the breathtaking possibility of God's retreat from relationality into pure substantiality.[17] Given that the Spirit is the warrant of God's

---

17. H.-G. Geyer: "Anfänge zum Begriff der Versöhnung," in *Evangelische Theologie* 38 (1978): 235-51.

relationality, we might as well say — and perhaps more accurately — that the cross visualizes the possibility of the Spirit's retreat from Jesus and thus the end of Jesus' communion with the Father, which means the end of God's embracing presence in the world, the end of God's accessibility. Jesus and God would be differentiated then, and God would be undifferentiated, both a horrible and a hopeless vision. Jesus experiences this vision of the absent Spirit, he faces the abyss — but he overcomes it by trusting the Father. He experiences the ontological loneliness of a world deserted by God's caring community ("My God, my God, why have you forsaken me?" Mark 15:34). But he does not try desperately to hold onto the Spirit's presence either. He lets go of the Spirit. He returns it to — none other than the Father! "Father, into your hands I commend my spirit!" (Luke 23:46). So by letting go of the Spirit, he confirms his trust in the Father's caring Fatherhood, in the perseverance of their community. Thus, amidst the abyss of differentiation, he trusts in the reality of their unity. Amidst the experience of God's radical alienation, he keeps his hope of God's presence.

The resurrection is in a sense the Spirit's *return* to the Son, the Father's confirmation of his unity with the Son, which — as it turns now out — was not erased but rather intensified by the experience of radical differentiation. No alienation, the resurrection unveils, is deep enough to sever the Father's unity with the Son.[18] But resurrection is not a mere return to 'business as usual,' as if nothing had happened.[19] The cross is not an accident which is simply undone by resurrection without leaving any traces and scars. Just as the risen Christ displays the wounds the nails of the cross have caused, so his unity with the Father is shaped by the experience of the cross as well. Because this unity is realized by and hypostatized in the Spirit, the same goes for our understanding of the Spirit. The Son is the Son only 'in the power of the Spirit,' but he is the Son only in that he lets go of the Spirit, trusting in its return. Paradoxically spoken, on the cross the Spirit is present only in the mode of its absence and is active only in the

---

18. In this respect, the resurrection also confirms Jesus' concern with the outcasts and his community with them.

19. This has often been emphasized by M. Welker. Cf. "Auferstehung," in *Glaube und Lernen* 9 (1994): 39-49; *Was geht vor beim Abendmahl?* (Stuttgart: Quell, 1999), pp. 22-31; ET: *What Happens in Holy Communion?* (Grand Rapids: Eerdmans, 2000), pp. 10-19, esp. 14-15. See also my "'Was sucht ihr den Lebendigen bei den Toten?' Überlegungen zur Realität der Auferstehung in Auseinandersetzung mit Gerd Lüdemann," in *Kerygma und Dogma* 46 (2000): 225-40.

mode of its passivity. The Spirit lets go of the Son as well. The cross, thus, not only marks the Son's difference from the Father, but also his distinction from the Spirit as being the warrant and sphere of their community. He is in radical need of the Spirit. The resurrection then, conversely, reveals the Spirit under the aspect of its intentional activity. Far from simply resuscitating a dead body, it renews the community of the Father and the Son, thus definitively ratifying the Father's declaration after Jesus' baptism. Yet resurrection also shows that the cross is an essential part of the drama of God's unity. In other words, the absence of the Spirit on the cross is a dimension of its presence, an aspect of its identity. The radical differentiation has turned out to be essential to God's being-in-communion itself. The unity which the Spirit provides *and is* is a unity-*in-difference* in a very radical sense.

What does this Trinitarian concept of the Spirit as realization and reality of the unity-in-difference of the Father and the Son mean for our understanding of salvation? It hardly need be mentioned that, according to the New Testament, the mission of the apostles, the spreading of the gospel, and the emergence of the church as the congregation of believers in Christ were effects and results of the activity of the Spirit and thus fruits and even forms of its presence. The very existence of the church was seen as 'absolutely dependent' on the coming of the Spirit. This is completely consistent with our observation that, in Jesus' baptism, the Spirit transcended the gap between heaven and earth, dis-closing the community of the Father and the Son, opening it up for others to join or, more precisely, to be integrated into.

The Gospel of John in particular reflects on how the Spirit's post-Easter presence is related to the Father and the Son. Interestingly, it gives three different expressions of the origin of this presence. First, Jesus announces that the Father will "send" the Spirit "in my name" (John 14:26), then he says that he himself will "send" it "from the Father" (John 15:26), and finally he states that the Spirit itself will "come" to "glorify" the Son (John 16:13-14).[20] The Spirit, as can be clearly seen, does not act on its own account, but reveals itself only by revealing the Son and his unity-in-difference with the Father. It is not a merely passive 'sphere of influence' of their powerful presence either. The Spirit's active work reveals "Jesus as being the Christ, the Son of God" (John 20:31) and makes people believe in this lifesaving truth. Moreover, John's gospel leaves no doubt that the

---

20. Cf. my *Filioque* (Göttingen: Vandenhoeck & Ruprecht, 2001), pp. 42-44.

Spirit's coming presupposes, and is only possible after, Christ's 'exaltation,' which means the coherent unity of crucifixion, resurrection, and return to the Father. "Unless I leave, the Paraclete will not come to you. Once I have left, however, I will send him to you" (John 16:7). The Spirit is thus destined to let people participate in the community of the Father and the Son, a community shaped by the experience of the abyss of differentiation and alienation and of having overcome it, albeit — this is important — without amnesia. If precisely these concrete dynamics of differentiation and unification display the very being of God, and if the Holy Spirit is both realizing 'person' and 'sphere' of reality of precisely this community-in-difference of the Father and the Son in God's self, and if it is this Spirit who both reveals this community and is the 'sphere' of its presence in the world, letting people share this communicating community, then the emerging spiritual community, which is the church, must receive its character and its identity from this very Spirit from which and in which it lives.

Of the manifold implications this has for the understanding of the church I can name only a few. To begin with, the Spirit's presence is not a matter of availability — be it natural or supernatural. If the Son could only hope to keep his community with the loving Father by trustfully letting go of the Spirit of this community, then the same goes for the church. The *promise* of the Spirit's presence does not imply the guarantee of its permanent accessibility. This does not mean, however, that the presence of the Spirit becomes a kind of ghostly phenomenon, incomprehensible, unpredictable, and shapeless. Quite to the contrary, it is because we *recognize* the Spirit as the Spirit of Christ's community-in-difference with the Father that we *know* it will only be present if — and that we will only experience this community if — we do not hold onto it. It is precisely *this* Spirit, it is exactly *this* community that we are entitled to hope for. "Do not quench (or limit) the Spirit," Paul writes (1 Thess. 5:19), and that is what we would do if we did not let go of it. Paradoxically, we would then miss the Spirit's very identity.

Moreover, if the Spirit's identity is shaped by the dynamics of differentiation and unification, this must be significant for the being of the church as well. The Spirit does not form a community of triumph without scars, but rather a community of transformation, of forgiveness, of the healing of memories — yet without these narratives of transformation falling into oblivion, leaving space only for the enthusiasm of present experiences of being saved (or of being *safe*). The church is a community in which the memories of transformation are shared. The presence and deliberate cultivation of these memories not only creates a fundamental solidarity among the current members of the church, but also motivates their deep solidarity with all those still 'outside.' As the Spirit integrates the radical alienation, that is, the cross, into the very being of God, there is no alienation in the world that could definitively separate from the church as being *creatura Spiritus*. The dynamics of the Spirit thus transcend the boundaries of any given church.

But again these dynamics do not simply create a 'success story.' The 'power' of the Spirit is 'beyond measure' not merely in the sense of quantity, but also (and even more appropriately so) in the sense of quality. As Christ let go of the Spirit, consenting to the Father's will, so, too, the Spirit let go of Christ, abstaining from using its power in a direct way. It did not enforce the community of the Father and the Son. It did not suspend the 'drama' of this community. It remained patient. It let it happen. The Spirit's power thus encloses the experience of powerlessness, which also goes for the Spirit's presence in the church. The Spirit is a transforming, community-forming power, but a power which does not impose itself without considering the characteristics, the limits, even the idiosyncrasies of human life. Instead it fulfills its transforming work by objectifying itself, giving itself into the hands of human beings and their limited, fragile forces. It was, once more, Paul who emphasized this dialectical character of the Spirit's work: "We do have this treasure but in earthen vessels" (2 Cor. 4:7), and again, "When I am weak, then I am strong" (2 Cor. 12:10). Not coincidentally, it was Paul who spoke of the "sighs without words" with which the Spirit intercedes for us before God (Rom. 8:26).

If the dialectics of power and powerlessness, of activity and letting go, are crucial to our understanding of the Spirit's reality, then — and this is my final point — how can we apply it to the distinction of the personal and nonpersonal aspects of its being with which we started? At first sight, it might seem appropriate to describe the powerful activity in terms of personal intentionality, whereas the passivity of emerging processes should fit better to nonpersonal metaphors. But on closer examination, this concept does not work properly. On the one hand, the intentional structure of personality not only implies powerful activity but also deliberate self-withdrawal *(Selbstzurücknahme)*.[21] On the other hand, the con-

21. Cf. Michael Welker, *Gottes Geist*, passim.

cept of 'sphere' or 'field' does not at all exclude activity (field of *power*!) — albeit the nonpersonal term may well be adequate after all to express the Spirit's self-withdrawal by giving itself into the hands of humans. From this perspective it becomes evident once again that we need personal and nonpersonal metaphors to complement and explain one another.

"How to Speak of the Spirit among Religions": Trinitarian Prolegomena for a Pneumatological Theology of Religions

VELI-MATTI KÄRKKÄINEN

Introduction

> *To me, mindfulness is very much like the Holy Spirit. Both are agents of healing. When you have mindfulness, you have love and understanding, you see more deeply, you can heal the wounds in your own mind. . . . Mindfulness helps us touch nirvana, and the Holy Spirit offers us a door to the Trinity.*
>
> THICH NHAT HANH[1]

> *[P]rovisionally, at least, the Holy Spirit could be discerned to be present and active even in Buddhist rituals opposing the world's forces of destruction insofar as the biblical fruits of the Spirit, for example, could be detected.*
>
> AMOS YONG[2]

To speak of the presence of the Spirit in the world and among religions is a notoriously challenging task. While most everybody agrees that the pres-

---

1. T. Nhat Hanh, *Living Buddha, Living Christ* (New York: Riverhead Books, 1994), pp. 14, 20.

2. A. Yong, "Does the Wind Blow the Middle Way? Pneumatology and the Buddhist-Christian Dialogue" (unpublished manuscript, 2004), p. 266.

ence of the Holy Spirit is not limited to the sphere of the Christian church, nothing like unanimity exists concerning the nature and efficacy, if any, of the activity of the Spirit. Take the examples above. How do we know whether the claims of the Vietnamese-American Buddhist Thich Nhat Hanh and Malaysian-American Christian Amos Yong can be substantiated in the grammar of these respective faiths? And if for a moment we agree their statements are valid, what then are the implications for faith and interfaith dialogue?

The purpose of the present chapter is to make a contribution to the continuing discussion of the role of the Spirit in the world, especially among religions, by setting forth some Trinitarian "rules" — better to say guidelines — for speaking about the Spirit. In other words, I argue that the proper context for advancing a pneumatological theology of religions is a healthy trinitarian framework. Having recently finished the monograph *Trinity and Religious Pluralism: The Doctrine of the Trinity in Christian Theology of Religions*,[3] I have felt the need to continue the reflection on the theology of religions from a pneumatological perspective. It seems to me too often that pneumatological approaches to religions suffer from an inadequate Trinitarian framework, which results in a disconnection between the Spirit and Christ and/or the Spirit and the Creator; these disconnections, in turn, lead to the separation between the Spirit and the church and the Spirit and the kingdom. A healthy Trinitarian theology, my essay argues, is the best safeguard against lacunae such as those.

Before engaging the task, however, one needs to stop and ask the obvious question: Can one — or in what sense can one — speak of the presence of the Spirit among religions? One needs not only to ask this question but the even more foundational one: How can we speak of the Spirit in the world in the first place? In other words: Not only is it highly challenging to address the topic of the Spirit in relation to other religions; the whole task of speaking of the Spirit in the world seems to encounter numerous problems. Should we focus on the "hidden" or "veiled" presence of the Spirit in the world, or, as John Polkinghorne puts it,[4] on the Spirit's "exuberance often exhibited in contemporary charismatic experience"? Or, to use Kathryn Tanner's terminology: Should we speak of the "immediate," direct and instantaneous or the "gradual," "human and fully fallible" mediated

---

3. (Aldershot: Ashgate, 2004).

4. J. Polkinghorne, "The Hidden Spirit and the Cosmos," p. 170 herein.

presence of the Spirit?[5] The New Testament theologian James D. G. Dunn adds many more challenges such as the pneumatological discourse either cosmically or anthropologically conceived, pneumatology stressing either the continuity or discontinuity between the divine and human spirit, and so on.[6] With reference to Vladimir Lossky of the Christian East, Polkinghorne reminds us: "The Holy Spirit, as person, remains unmanifested, hidden, concealing Himself in His very appearing."[7] This prompts the obvious question: How can we even begin to give any kinds of "guidelines" for discerning the presence of the Spirit in the world? In the symposium discussion we came to the conclusion that while any talk about the Spirit — of God — needs to be approached with great care and humility, it is still the task of theologians to try to set forth some guidelines to make our human speech about the divine more appropriate.[8]

In the first part of my presentation, I will set the stage for a Trinitarian approach to the question of Christianity's relation to other religions. This orientation calls for remarks on three interrelated topics: Where are we in the theology of religions discourse? Where are we in the talk about the Trinity? And, in what ways, if any, have these two coalesced? In the second part, I will map out key tasks and challenges that lie before us on the way to reflecting theologically on the role of the Spirit among religions. My approach is thus more methodological, a kind of prolegomenon, the implications of which need to be taken up and tested in an actual interreligious dialogue. Yet, going beyond the mere prolegomenon — and in order to make my discussion more concrete and specific — in the sec-

---

5. K. Tanner, "Workings of the Spirit: Simplicity or Complexity?" p. 87 herein.

6. J. D. G. Dunn, "Towards the Spirit of Christ: The Emergence of the Distinctive Features of Christian Pneumatology," herein.

7. V. Lossky, *The Mystical Theology of the Eastern Church* (Cambridge: James Clarke, 1957, p. 160), quoted in Polkinghorne, "The Hidden Spirit and Cosmos," p. 171.

8. D. L. Dabney ("The Nature of the Spirit: Creation as a Premonition of God," p. 71 herein) remarks that in the contemporary postmodern context, talk about God takes place through the lenses of pneumatology in that it addresses first the question of human identity. If I correctly understand Dabney's approach, this does not mean a return to the old idea of Classical Liberalism, so aptly caricatured by K. Barth, that to speak of God one needs to speak loudly of the human person. Dabney's program has to do with his desire to qualify and supplement (but of course not to leave behind) the older theological methods in either Catholicism, which begins with the first article (of the creed, i.e., with God and creation), or Protestantism, with the second article (Christ and redemption), in favor of a turn to the third article, thus the Spirit.

ond part I will also reflect on the meaning of these Trinitarian rules for Islam-Christian encounter based on a long-term dialogue between the Roman Catholic Church (in France) and Muslims.[9] Significantly enough, that dialogue took a Trinitarian approach and also addressed the role of the Spirit in relation to the Islamic faith. Tentatively, therefore, it provides an opportunity to test the Trinitarian guidelines presented here.

Major Turns in the Theology of Religions

Christian theology of religions has taken several significant turns despite its relatively short history.[10] Here I am concerned only with one particular turn in its history. Let me call it a movement from christocentric to theocentric to pneumatocentric approaches, and finally toward Trinitarian approaches. As long as Christian theology was based on a more or less exclusivist standpoint, the point of departure for the theology of religions discourse was the finality of Christ.[11] A turn to theocentrism seemed to give more space for opening up to other religions; in that phase, the Trinity was nothing more than an obstacle for the dialogue, especially with monotheistic faiths such as Judaism and Islam. Soon, among theologians from across the ecumenical spectrum (from Eastern Orthodoxy to Roman Catholicism to Protestantism of various sorts), a turn to the 'Spirit' was en-

9. For details, see my *Trinity and Religious Pluralism,* ch. 10. Since the late 1970s, there has been a theological and pastoral dialogue in France between the Roman Catholic Church and a significantly large Islamic community. Full documentation (in French) of the dialogue facilitated by the Secretariat for Relations with Islam (*Secrétariat pour les Relations avec l'Islam;* hereafter S.R.I.) can be found in R. Jukko, *Trinitarian Theology in Christian-Muslim Encounters: Theological Foundations of the Work of the French Catholic Church's Secretariat for Relations with Islam* (Helsinki: Luther-Agricola Gesellschaft, 2001).

10. I am not, of course, suggesting that the *question* of the theology of religions — Christianity's relation to other religions — is a new one. It is not. (For a detailed biblical and historical review, see further my book *An Introduction to the Theology of Religions: Biblical, Historical, and Contemporary Perspectives* [Downers Grove, Ill.: InterVarsity Press, 2003], parts II-III). My remark here refers to the fact that as a *separate* theological discipline, theology of religions is a fairly new development, stemming from somewhere in the 1950s or so.

11. I am making vast generalizations here. Christocentrism (or, to be more precise, Christocentrisms) is in itself a diverse approach, from a traditional Protestant exclusivistic stance to a postconciliar official Catholic inclusivism to the moderate pluralism of some Catholic thinkers, such as the early P. Knitter.

thusiastically initiated.[12] The turn to pneumatology seemed to promise a lot. After all, does the Spirit not speak for universality while Christ speaks for particularity? Pneumatology also seemed to connect with the strongly pneumatological and spiritualistic orientations of other religions, especially in the East.

The latest phase of the theology of religions discourse is the turn to the Trinity.[13] Before looking at this latest phase, a few summary comments concerning the current stage of Trinitarian discourse are in order.

Trinitarian Discourse in Contemporary Theology

Schematically, one may outline the emerging theological consensus about the Trinity in the following way: First, the doctrine of the Trinity is the structuring principle of Christian theology rather than an appendix to Christian talk about God. Thus, to identify the God of the Bible one needs to refer to the triune God: Father, Son, and Spirit.

Second, making the Trinity the beginning and structuring principle of Christian theology and the doctrine of God means that to speak of God means to speak of Jesus Christ who reveals the Father in the power of the Spirit. Third, the knowledge of the Christian God — Father, Son, and Spirit — can be possible only through God's self-revelation in the Son. Rather than being an exercise in speculative theology, the Trinity is a datum of revelation.[14] Therefore, fourth, history matters! The biblical God — Father, Son, and Spirit — cannot be understood as an abstraction apart from the events of history. The coming of Jesus, the incarnation, and the resurrection from the dead by the Father through the Spirit are historical

12. See, e.g., A. Yong, "The Turn to Pneumatology in Christian Theology of Religions: Conduit or Detour?" *Journal of Ecumenical Studies* 35 (1998): 437-54. This turn to the Spirit reflects the wider pneumatological renaissance in theology. See further my *Pneumatology: The Holy Spirit in Ecumenical, International, and Contextual Perspective* (Grand Rapids: Baker Academic, 2002), ch. 1.

13. See my *Trinity and Religious Pluralism*, pp. 1-12.

14. This much has to be said, even though the consensus among students of the Bible recognizes that there is no doctrine of the Trinity in the Bible, not even in the New Testament. However, there is a Trinitarian structure to the biblical salvation history, to the coming of God's kingdom, inaugurated by Jesus Christ in the power of the Spirit. Dunn's essay ("Towards the Spirit of Christ") carefully traces the beginnings of the Trinitarianism in the New Testament with reference to the Spirit-Christ relationship.

claims. Fifth, while not all contemporary theologians are 'Social Trinitarians,' a strong consensus understands the Christian God as a divine communion.[15] This is the theological conclusion from the biblical idea that God is love.

One might assume that these perspectives would be enthusiastically applied to the question of Christianity's relation to other religions. In general, this has not been the case until very recently.

Trinity and Religions at a Meeting Place: A History of Research

The pioneer in the field was the Catholic, Asian-American scholar of religion Raimundo Panikkar. In his small, yet highly significant book *The Trinity and the Religious Experience of Man* (1973),[16] Panikkar argued for the viability of a Trinitarian approach based on the groundbreaking idea that not only do all religions reflect a Trinitarian substructure, but that there is a Trinitarian structure to reality.[17] While departing from his Christian faith, he ends up constructing a highly idiosyncratic view of the Trinity.[18] What bothers me in Panikkar's proposal, among other things, is the divorce between Christ and history on the one hand and, consequently, between the Spirit and Christ on the other.[19]

The next major study on the topic did not appear until 2000, titled *The Meeting of Religions and the Trinity,* by the Catholic Gavin D'Costa[20] from England. D'Costa's contribution to my agenda is threefold. Having first shown the fallacy of pluralistic approaches, both Christian and among

---

15. B. Oberdorfer, "The Holy Spirit — A Person? Reflection on the Spirit's Trinitarian Identity," pp. 17-46 herein, speaks of the personhood as constituted socially; thus *"person* does not simply mean *individuality with self-consciousness"* (pp. 27-28). On p. 36 he says: "Persons only exist in relations, and their personality is not independent of these relations."

16. (Maryknoll, N.Y.: Orbis/London: Darton, Longman & Todd, 1973); this book is also titled *The Trinity and the World Religions.*

17. Panikkar's term of choice for describing this is *cosmotheandrism.*

18. For Panikkar, the Father is the kenotic "Nothing," the Absolute Nameless; the Son is God; and the Spirit is "immanence" and mediator who, like Hinduism's divine *Sakti,* penetrates everything and manifests the divine.

19. See further my *Trinity and Religious Pluralism,* pp. 128-33 especially.

20. (Maryknoll, N.Y.: Orbis, 2000). For an exposition and critical assessment, see my *Trinity and Religious Pluralism,* ch. 4.

other religions, D'Costa works hard to argue that because of the presence in the world of the Spirit of God, "there too is the ambiguous presence of the triune God, the church, and the kingdom" (p. 11).[21] In other words, the Spirit's presence in the world is not only integrally Trinitarian but also ecclesiological, which in turn is related to the coming of the kingdom. This means that D'Costa wants to keep together Spirit, Trinity, church, and kingdom in a way only few contemporary theologians are willing to do outside of exclusivistic approaches to religions. Thirdly, D'Costa argues that while religions as such are not salvific,[22] we Christians can — and should — learn a lot through "the Holy Spirit's invitation to relational engagement." My sympathies in general go with D'Costa's approach, even though, ironically, I find the grounds for his proposal less than convincing and not winning ecumenical support.[23]

Another Catholic theologian, the veteran theologian of religions Jacques Dupuis, in his magnum opus *Toward a Christian Theology of Religious Pluralism* (1997),[24] had already made a lasting contribution to the topic of the Trinity and religions. Echoing the typical recent turn in this field, in his later work Dupuis shifted emphasis from Christ to the Spirit and the Trinity.[25] What makes me somewhat critical of Dupuis's approach is his tendency to downplay the integral relation of the Spirit to the church and, consequently, the relation of the kingdom to the church.

The most significant Trinitarian theology of religions outside Catho-

---

21. It would be an interesting topic to consider how D'Costa's view of the "ambiguous" presence of God through the Spirit in the world is related to Polkinghorne's idea of the "veiled" presence of the Spirit on the one hand, and Tanner's concept of a "mediated" presence on the other.

22. There is heavy debate among Catholic theologians as to the right reading of Vatican II concerning this question. Knitter argues for a pluralistic reading of Vatican II, while D'Costa argues, alongside the current magisterial opinion, for an inclusivist interpretation.

23. On the one hand D'Costa bases his proposal on a selective reading of the biblical data, especially on the Paraclete passages of John 14 and 16, and, on the other hand, on Vatican II and subsequent papal pronouncements on religions. I think much better biblical grounds can be found to support the integral relationship between Spirit and church. In addition, to non-Catholics reference to a particular church's teaching documents hardly wins much hearing. See further my *Trinity and Religious Pluralism*, pp. 76-79.

24. (Maryknoll, N.Y.: Orbis, 1997). For an exposition and critical assessment, see my *Trinity and Religious Pluralism*, ch. 3.

25. It is noteworthy that the first major contribution by Dupuis was Christocentric: *Jesus Christ at the Encounter of World Religions* (Maryknoll, N.Y.: Orbis, 1991).

lic theology comes from the hand of S. Mark Heim, who originally comes
from Evangelicalism. His book *The Depths of the Riches: A Trinitarian Theology of Religious Ends* (2001)[26] is perhaps the 'most pluralistic' theology of
religions yet to appear: on the basis of the diversity in the triune God,
Heim advances the thesis that not only are religions different, but they also
have different, God-willed 'ends' in terms of salvation goals. While I ap-
plaud Heim's sincere effort to construct a new way of looking at other religions through the lens of the Christian doctrine of the Trinity, I find both
the methodology and main results of his proposal wanting.[27] Furthermore, curiously enough, Heim is almost silent about the role of the Spirit
in his theological construction.

The most recent contribution to a distinctively pneumatological theology of religions with a view to the importance of the Trinity is offered by
Amos Yong, a Pentecostal, in his *Beyond the Impasse: Toward a Pneumatological Theology of Religions.*[28] He sets forth three "axioms" for the development of a pneumatological theology of religions in a trinitarian
framework: first, God is universally present and active in the Spirit; second, God's Spirit is the life-breath of the *imago Dei* in every human being
and the presupposition of all human relationships and communities; and
third, the religions of the world, like all else that exists, are providentially
sustained by the Spirit of God for divine purposes. Now these axioms are
hardly debatable. Yet they beg for further elucidation and clarification. It is
not self-evident how "trinitarian" they are; what is distinctively Trinitarian
about these claims? There are other proposals,[29] yet for the purposes of

26. (Grand Rapids: Eerdmans, 2001). For an exposition and critical assessment, see
my *Trinity and Religious Pluralism,* ch. 9. Even with all the criticism against his proposal, I
also think that Heim has significantly advanced the discussion. He avoids the typical fallacy
of a "rough parity" pluralism by insisting on real differences among religions and being bold
about setting forth a proposal of his own. Panikkar is another pluralist whose proposal genuinely values difference even though he envisions a future "convergence" of religions.

27. For the critique, see my *Trinity and Religious Pluralism,* pp. 143-51 especially.

28. (Grand Rapids: Baker Academic, 2003). For the contribution of K. Rahner,
W. Pannenberg, and the Evangelical-Charismatic theologian C. Pinnock, see my *Trinity and
Religious Pluralism.*

29. Mention should still be made of another significant study that deals with our
topic, idiosyncratic as it is in its approach and bordering on a "universal theology," namely,
the book by the senior religious scholar N. Smart (in collaboration with his student, the
Eastern Orthodox S. Konstantine) titled *Christian Systematic Theology in a World Context*
(Minneapolis: Fortress, 1991). My reading of that book leaves me wondering if it goes be-

this presentation the ones I have mentioned seem to be the most pregnant theologically.

In the second part of the presentation — in a critical dialogue with theologians mentioned so far, yet also going beyond their work — I will reflect on the topic of speaking about the Spirit among religions in a Trinitarian context. I will also reflect on the implications for Christian-Muslim encounter.

Trinity as the Way to Distinguish the Christian God among Gods

No less a theological giant than Karl Barth made this programmatic statement:

> The doctrine of the Trinity is what basically distinguishes the Christian doctrine of God as Christian, and therefore what already distinguishes the Christian concept of revelation as Christian, in contrast to all other possible doctrines of God or concepts of revelation.[30]

In other words, Trinity is not an appendix to the notion of 'One God'; rather, the 'name'[31] of the biblical God is Father, Son, and Spirit. It is not possible to speak of Father as 'God' as if Son and Spirit were not needed to consider God. The Father's relation to Son and Spirit is foundational for the identity of the Father.[32] This also means that the understand-

---

yond the contours of a specifically *Christian* theology of religions in that Smart and Konstantine build their "trinitarian" doctrine on a mixture of religious traditions which does not easily commend itself to more typical Trinitarian approaches.

30. K. Barth, *Church Dogmatics,* I/1, ed. T. F. Torrance and G. Bromiley (Edinburgh: T & T Clark, 1956), p. 301. Materially the same is argued in R. W. Jenson, *The Triune Identity: God According to the Gospel* (Philadelphia: Fortress, 1982), p. ix: "The doctrine of the Trinity comprises . . . the Christian faith's repertoire of ways of *identifying* its God, to say *which* of the many candidates for godhead we mean when we say, for example, 'God is loving'" (italics in the original).

31. When saying this, I am not necessarily convinced that Jenson's idea of Father, Son, and Spirit as "proper name" in the New Testament as Yahweh was in the Old Testament is the best way of putting it.

32. See further R. W. Jenson, *The Triune Identity,* pp. 51, 73. When insisting on the necessity of holding on to the Trinitarian identification of the Christian God, I am not at the

ing of God becomes relational, indeed "the triune identities are *relations*" and therefore, to quote R. W. Jenson:

> What there is to being God the Father is being addressed as "Father" by the Son, Jesus; what there is to being God the Spirit is being the spirit of this communication. *In that* Jesus cries, "Father, into your hands . . ." and *in that* he who says this will be the final event, *there is* the Father. *In that* Jesus gives his spirit, and *in that* this gift will constitute the final community, *there is* the Spirit.[33]

Consequently, Trinity introduces not only relationality (communion) into the life of God, a topic I will take up in what follows, but also history and time. God's relation — reaching out — to the world in incarnation, salvation, and consummation is not something external to the divine life. "Rather, God's involvement in the course of the world affairs is so intimate that the character of divinity itself is shaped by it."[34]

While there is of course no reason to limit the knowledge of God to the particularity of Jesus of Nazareth, it also is true, to quote Heim, that "the Trinity is unavoidably Christocentric."[35] It is one of the tendencies of (pneumatological) theologies of religions to seek release from the contours of history, and (as they believe) of particularity.[36] It is an under-

---

same time denying the importance of establishing some commonality between the Christian God and the gods of other religions or, as it has been put in classical theology, the God of the philosophers. Pannenberg has seen this clearly. While he insists on the uniqueness of the triune God, based on the biblical revelation as it interprets salvation history, he also insists on the correlation between general god-talk and talk about the distinctively Christian Trinitarian God. Taking his cue from the fact that in the Bible the term *god* not only serves as a proper name *(Yahweh)* but also as a general designation *(Elohim)*, he argues that specifically Christian God-talk makes sense only in connection with terms for species. Therefore, to make God-talk intelligible, both in Christian theology and in relation to especially the Jewish faith, but also other (theistic) faiths, Christian theology should not cut off ties to philosophical and religious discourse. This also guards Christian Trinitarian talk from "involuntarily regressing to a situation of a plurality of gods in which Christian talk about God has reference to the specific biblical God as one God among others." W. Pannenberg, *Systematic Theology*, vol. 1, trans. G. Bromiley (Grand Rapids: Eerdmans, 1991), p. 69.

33. Jenson, *The Triune Identity*, p. 175 (italics in the original).

34. T. Peters, *God — The World's Future: Systematic Theology for a Postmodern Era* (Minneapolis: Fortress, 1992), p. 108.

35. Heim, *The Depth of the Riches*, p. 135.

36. I understand thinkers such as Panikkar as advocating a Christology "from above"

standable, yet theologically highly problematic road.[37] In terms of interfaith dialogue it means that to bracket out Trinity for the sake of dialogue when talking to, say, Muslims, is a strategy which creates more problems than it solves.

Regarding the Islamic faith, the most obvious question is of course whether Yahweh, the Father of Jesus Christ, is the same God as Allah, as the Qur'an claims (Sura 29:46). Things get complicated when the Trinity is introduced to the picture. For Muslims, the Christian doctrine of the Trinity is a distortion (Sura 5:73 among others), a form of tritheism, making Christians not true monotheists but rather "associators" (those who have committed the sin of *shirk,* associating other deities with God).[38] In my reading, the Muslim-Catholic dialogue in France left the question of identity open — wisely so. However, they were quick to affirm that dialogue between Muslims and Christians "takes place between believers, between religious men and women who seek God in their own tradition," and that "both Christians and Muslims are believers in the creator God, and they speak to this one God and seek him."[39]

Coming back to the Spirit, one could ask in light of this: Does this mean to diminish the role of the Spirit — or to try to limit the cosmic sphere of the Spirit? On the contrary, to quote the Catholic pneumatologist Kilian McDonnell, O.S.B.: "To do pneumatology is to insist that the Spirit is equal to the Father and to the Son."[40] According to the New

---

rather than "from below" since he first constructs a "Christic" principle apart from historical contours and only then reads it back, if at all, into the person of Christ. This is materially what he is saying in his often quoted dictum: "Jesus is Christ but Christ is not Jesus." Methodologically, it is of course ironic that a contemporary theologian and scholar of *religions* such as Panikkar could be found guilty of championing a "from above" approach.

37. Smart and Konstantine (*Christian Systematic Theology,* p. 177) seem to insist on not ignoring history since "the Divine occurs as transcendent in the midst of history," yet they do so in a way that eschews the particularity of Christian theology (with its claim to Jesus' incarnation).

38. See further my *Trinity and Religious Pluralism,* pp. 156-58.

39. Jukko, *Trinitarian Theology in Muslim-Christian Encounters,* p. 89; see also p. 84. I criticized the Catholic Dupuis — in his explicitly Trinitarian theology of religions! — for too easily establishing the identity between the Muslim and Christian God (*Trinity and Religious Pluralism,* pp. 63-64; see also p. 53).

40. K. McDonnell, O.S.B., "Pneumatology Overview," in *CTSA Proceedings* 51 (1996): 189. For a more accessible source, see McDonnell, "Theological Presuppositions in Our Preaching about the Spirit," *Theological Studies* 59 (1998): 219-35.

Testament testimony, "the Spirit is not less important for understanding who God is and what God does than the saving work of Christ."[41] Let me take a closer look at the implications of the way we speak of the presence and ministry of the Spirit in the world.

The Trinitarian Presence of the Spirit in the World

There is an ancient rule — pejoratively labeled the "Augustinian rule of thumb"[42] — according to which the inner works of the Trinity are separable and the outward works inseparable. Notwithstanding the contemporary critique of the rule,[43] it still serves as a guiding principle when speaking about the role of the Spirit in the world, even among religions. In order to refer to the presence of the Spirit, whether as the life-principle, the divine breath of all living creatures, a (soteriological) 'gift,' or as the agent of eschatological transformation,[44] one needs to speak of the Spirit of

41. McDonnell, "Pneumatology," p. 189. It is of course ironic that while in Christian theology in general pneumatology has suffered from a secondary place in relation to Christology, in the *theology of religions* the opposite has been the case lately. For an interesting way to discuss this relationship in a Trinitarian framework, see further McDonnell, "Pneumatology," pp. 190-92; and "Theological Presuppositions," pp. 221-23, especially. McDonnell calls Christ the "what" (the content of the gospel and thus of Christian preaching) and the Spirit the "how," the total horizon within which theological reflection and preaching take place. In other words, after Pentecost, the apostles where not sent out to preach about the Spirit but rather about Christ — in the power of the Spirit.

42. The rule was in effect well before Augustine; what Augustine did was to highlight the second part of the rule (the indivisibility of the outward works of the Trinity); by doing so, he also echoed the teaching of the Cappadocians in the East.

43. Among others, K. Rahner, R. W. Jenson, and the late Catholic C. Mowry LaCugna have expressed severe critique towards the rule. E.g., Jenson's main reason for the critique is that the idea of the indivisibility of outer works is being understood in terms of the creative and saving works being *indifferently* the work of each person rather than in terms of being the joint work of Father, Son, and Spirit. This critique, however, is hardly convincing. Why should one understand (the second part of) Augustine's rule in this way? Ironically, it was used by the Cappadocians to establish the unity of the godhead in terms of the unity of operation.

44. An urgent task for contemporary pneumatology with significant implications for the theology of religions is to establish the continuity of the work of the Spirit from creation to new creation. W. Pannenberg has done some important groundwork here. See further my "The Working of the Spirit of God in Creation and in the People of God: The Pneumatology of Wolfhart Pannenberg," *Pneuma* 26, no. 1 (Fall 2004): 17-35. See also Yong, *Beyond the Im-*

Yahweh, the Spirit of the God of Jesus Christ. Pneumatological discourse unrelated to the Father and Son may seem to promise more, yet it begins to lose its contours and often ends up being nothing other than another way to affirm a typically modernist idea of a 'rough parity' of all religions.

The Trinity serves here as elsewhere in a criteriological function. As Dupuis notes, the Trinity helps us avoid three typical, interrelated errors. The first error puts Christ and God in opposition as if one could choose *either* a 'theocentric' *or* 'christocentric' option. The second error that the Trinity helps us avoid is either 'regnocentrism' (the idea of the kingdom of God at the center) or 'soteriocentrism' (salvation, rather than a Savior, at the center) as the focus at the expense of Christology, as for example Knitter seems to be doing.

The third error is to champion that kind of pneumatological approach that tends to diminish the role of Jesus Christ as more limited than that of the Spirit. Indeed, the basic fallacy of the first wave of pneumatological approaches to the theology of religions was the desire to make the Spirit an itinerant preacher who only occasionally joined forces with the other Trinitarian members. The Augustinian rule is no good news to that kind of pneumatological theology of religions that seeks release for the Spirit from the confines of the Father-Spirit and Son-Spirit relationship. It is of course true that while Jesus Christ[45] represents particularity, the Spirit represents universality,[46] yet this is true only in a healthy Trinitarian context. The freedom of the Spirit cannot be set in opposition to the person and ministry of Jesus Christ, any more than that of the Son to the Father.[47]

---

passe, pp. 36-42. This seems to be the goal of the project by Dabney ("The Nature of the Spirit," p. 12) as well: "Such a theology encompasses both creation and redemption from a perspective of creation and new creation."

45. For pluralists such as Panikkar, only "Jesus" (of Nazareth) denotes particularity; "Christ" for Panikkar means a "Christic" principle, freed from the confines of historical contours, thus making it possible to identify more than one C/christ. "Jesus is Christ, but Christ is not [merely or not even primarily] Jesus." Here the Christic principle basically serves the same kind of "freeing" function that for some other theologians the Spirit does in relation to Jesus/Father.

46. In what follows, I will come back to take another look at the widely used concepts of "universal" and "particular" in the sphere of the theology of religions.

47. One way, it is popular in both patristic theology (Irenaeus, *Adversus Haereses* 4.4) and current theology (e.g., Yong, *Beyond the Impasse*, pp. 43-44) to speak of the Son and Spirit as the "two hands" of God. While it makes the point, it also supports the kind of subordina-

All of this requires some answer to the all-important question for our purposes: how do we establish the Spirit-Christ/Christ-Spirit relationship? This, in turn, will affect how we conceive of the relationship between the church and Spirit, and consequently, church and kingdom. Let's take one topic at a time.

Pneumatology and Christology as One Divine Economy

In the New Testament, Son and Spirit presuppose each other.[48] The role of the Spirit comes to focus in that Jesus was related to the Spirit,[49] and the Spirit is the Spirit of Christ.[50] A Trinitarian "Spirit-Christology"[51] "shows

---

tionism which contemporary Trinitarian theology wants to avoid (C. Mowry LaCugna, *God for Us: The Trinity and Christian Life* [San Francisco: HarperSanFrancisco, 1991], pp. 24-29, named this tendency "orthodox subordinationism"!). I find the approach of Pannenberg healthier — and more biblical — in that there are mutually dependent relationships among Father, Son, and Spirit. E.g., the Father cannot be the Father without the Son, who humbly differentiates himself from the Father, thus acknowledging the Lordship of the Father of the kingdom.

48. One of the reasons why the approach of writers such as Smart and Konstantine to *Christian* theology of religions does not commend itself to me is the superficial handling of biblical materials concerning the historical Jesus and its relation to the question of the relation of Jesus/Christ to Spirit. They simply ignore historical questions and, somewhat like Panikkar, feel free to propose a new construal of Spirit and Christ without much support from anywhere. Consequently, it seems to me the authors too easily find parallels between Christian Trinity and, say, *sat-cit-ānanda* (being, consciousness, and bliss) of the Advaita Vedanta tradition or the Hindu vision of three deities, *Brahma, Shiva, Vishnu.* I don't of course find the search for these parallels problematic in any way; what I am saying here is that one cannot too easily assume them.

49. Well aware of the fact that a strand of "historical Jesus scholarship" (e.g., J. D. Crossan) has been reluctant to make much of the connection of the (eschatological) Spirit to Jesus of Nazareth, I can safely go with the majority of contemporary biblical scholars who argue that it is absolutely integral to the identity and mission of Jesus to be conscious of the presence of God's Spirit in his life (N. T. Wright, J. D. G. Dunn, et al.).

50. For details, see Dunn "Towards the Spirit of Christ," pp. 9-13 especially. I am of course aware of the diversity of New Testament theologies of the Spirit. This diversity, in my understanding, however, does not in any way negate my basic argumentation here. See further my *Pneumatology,* pp. 28-36.

51. My quotation marks indicate that what I am saying here does not necessarily entail subscription to any particular kind of Spirit-Christology or to a Spirit-Christology at all (understood in the technical sense of the word).

the influence of the Holy Spirit throughout the earthly life of Jesus, from his conception through the power of the Spirit (see Lk 1:35) to his resurrection at the hands of God by the power of the same Spirit (see Rom 8:11)."[52] In other words, Jesus is both the giver[53] and receiver of the Spirit. The Spirit's role, on the other hand, is to help us turn to Christ and by doing so to the Father.[54]

Wherever the Spirit inspires the knowledge of God, be it within the sphere of the church or outside, salvation brought about by the Spirit is referred to the saving work of Christ, his incarnation, death, and resurrection. As Dupuis says, there are not "two distinct channels [i.e., that of the Son and the Spirit] through which God's saving presence reaches out to people in distinct economies of salvation,"[55] but one. Considering the relationship between Christ and the Spirit mutually presupposing does not in any way deny the universal, cosmic sphere of the ministry of the Spirit. Rather, it is a question of being able to recognize which Spirit, whose Spirit.

The integral relationship between Jesus Christ and the Spirit also introduces the cross into the equation, another topic routinely eschewed in the theology of religions for the sake of not blocking dialogue, as many believe.[56] With reference to Moltmann's theology of the cross, my former student at Fuller, Eugen Matei, puts it succinctly: "The cross, therefore, where God *himself* was in Christ (2 Cor. 5:19), is the place where God represents and reveals himself, and even more than that, it is the place where he identifies and defines himself."[57] In other words, the cross is not some-

---

52. Dupuis, *Toward a Christian Theology*, 206. So also Pannenberg, *Systematic Theology*, 3:16-17: "The christological constitution and the pneumatological constitution do not exclude one another but belong together because the Spirit and the Son mutually indwell one another as Trinitarian persons."

53. Dunn ("Towards the Spirit of Christ," pp. 10-13 herein) shows convincingly that in the earliest Christian pneumatology it was the Exalted Christ who was the giver of the Spirit.

54. As M. Welker ("The Spirit in Philosophical, Theological, and Interdisciplinary Perspectives," p. 225 herein) argues, differently from philosophical traditions, the biblical teaching (e.g., John 16:13) conceives of the Spirit not as "a self-referential personality" but as the one who will bear witness to Christ.

55. Dupuis, *Toward a Christian Theology*, p. 196.

56. For an important article, see H. Wells, "The Holy Spirit and Theology of the Cross: Significance for Dialogue," *Theological Studies* 53 (1992): 476-78.

57. E. Matei, "The Practice of Community in Social Trinitarianism: A Theological Evaluation with Reference to Dimitru Staniloae and Jürgen Moltmann" (Ph.D. thesis, Fuller Theological Seminary, School of Theology, 2004), p. 186.

thing external to the divine life of the Trinity but an identifying element.[58] Yes, the cross is a scandalous event, but it is also an everlasting testimony to the willingness of the triune God not only to share in the suffering of the world but also to let suffering and pain become part of the divine life. The Spirit, at work in the world after the cross, is the Spirit of the crucified and risen Christ. In a very helpful way, Michael Welker emphasizes that the biblical view of the Spirit "is not a self-referential personality but an utterly empathetic personality with a multicontextual presence."[59]

In asking the tough question concerning how Christ's presence and grace reach out to Muslims, Catholics referred to the universal presence and ministry of the Holy Spirit as integrated with — rather than separate from — the cross, based on the groundbreaking statement of Vatican II's *Gaudium et Spes* (# 22):[60]

> All this [the union with the dead and risen Christ] holds true not only for Christians, but for all men of good will in whose hearts grace works in an unseen way. For, since Christ died for all men, and since the ultimate vocation of man is in fact one, and divine, we ought to believe that the Holy Spirit in a manner known only to God offers to every man the possibility of being associated with this paschal mystery.

Does this mean, then, that Islam is a way of salvation? Catholics affirmed that Islam is a way 'towards' God and that, on the level of religion, Muslims are believers who come to God via another way than Christians. Islam is seen as a way to God and as a place of the Spirit. Yet a salvific structure per se of the Islamic faith was not affirmed.[61]

Speaking of the universal presence of the Spirit integrally related to the particularity of Jesus and his cross[62] helps us qualify and critique the

---

58. For Moltmann, this means that the cross is an event between God and God, an inner-divine event (as well as, of course, in relation to the world). One does not need to affirm Moltmann's interpretation, however, to make my point.

59. Welker, "The Spirit in Philosophical, Theological, and Interdisciplinary Perspective," p. 225.

60. See further Jukko, *Trinitarian Theology in Christian-Muslim Encounters*, p. 157.

61. See further Kärkkäinen, *Trinity and Religious Pluralism*, p. 159.

62. Dabney ("The Nature of the Spirit," p. 72) claims that the Gospel of Mark (which serves as the main biblical basis for his pneumatological approach to theology) "places the story of the life, death, and resurrection of Jesus Christ in a Pneumatological context."

mantra according to which the Spirit represents universality whereas the Son stands for particularity. Consider biblical passages such as the Prologue to the Gospel of John, which paints a picture of the Word in no less universal terms.[63] If Christology is depicted in both particular and universal terms, what can be said about the Spirit in this respect? The Spirit not only speaks to universality but also of particularity; any talk about the Spirit in a Trinitarian context is always specific even if universal in its scope. Otherwise, we lose all contours to distinguish, Whose Spirit? Furthermore, as Welker has strongly argued elsewhere, all talk about the Spirit needs to be particular in order to be 'concrete' and specific.[64] One also needs to be careful about using the term 'universality' in this context, not only because it smacks too much of modernity and its preference for the kind of 'generic' pneumatologies so evident in much of Christian theology of religions, but also because at the beginning of Christian theology, any kind of universal claim by a small group of religious enthusiasts seemed to be quite a scandalous (and thus particular!) claim.[65]

Now, to add one more dimension to the Spirit-Christ relation, that of the church, we need to ask: How should we speak of this triad?[66] On the basis of that discussion, we will expand the discussion to concern the kingdom's relation, too.

Spirit, Church, and Kingdom

One of the reasons that I find the proposal of the Catholic Dupuis somewhat truncated (as much as I affirm, for instance, its genuinely Trinitarian pneumatology as indicated in the discussion above) is that he tends to undermine the integral relationship between God and God's kingdom as if the latter made Christian theology more exclusive. He also tends to resist the integral relationship between God and the church in the world.[67] Different from Dupuis and many others (such as Knitter), another Catholic, Gavin D'Costa, insists on the integral relationship between the presence of

---

63. See further Dupuis, *Toward a Christian Theology,* pp. 188-90.

64. M. Welker, *God the Spirit* (Minneapolis: Fortress, 1994).

65. See further, Wells, "The Holy Spirit," pp. 476-78.

66. See the important contribution by M. Volf and M. Lee, "The Spirit and Church," *Conrad Grebel Review* 18, no. 3 (Fall 2000): 20-45.

67. For details, see my *Trinity and Religious Pluralism,* pp. 59-66.

the Spirit and the Father and Son, which then translates into an integral relationship between the triune God and the church.

D'Costa contends that the Holy Spirit's presence within other religions is both intrinsically Trinitarian and ecclesiological. It is Trinitarian in referring the Holy Spirit's activity to the paschal mystery of Christ, and ecclesial in referring the paschal event to the Spirit's constitutive community-creating force under the guidance of the Spirit.[68] The gift of the Spirit is not just for individual believers, but aims at the building up of their fellowship. The Spirit unites believers with Christ and into fellowship with others. The story of Pentecost (Acts 2) expresses the fact that the Spirit does not simply assure each believer individually of his or her fellowship with Jesus Christ, but that he thereby, at the same time, brings about the fellowship of believers.[69] In the New Testament, this is expressed in terms of the church being the people of God, the body of Christ, the temple of the Spirit.

The renewal of communion theology has helped us revive the understanding of the Christian God as relational, as Love.[70] Salvation is not 'individualistic' (even though it is personal). To be saved means to be in communion. In the words of the Orthodox Zizioulas, becoming Christian means a move from 'biological' individuality to 'ecclesial' communion. This reflects the way of being of God: God exists as communion. The church is the image of the triune God and as such is inviting and inclusive. The Holy Spirit is the Spirit of communion (2 Cor. 12:13). Establishing the close connection between the triune God and the church does not, however, lead to a kind of 'ecclesiocentrism' that is blind to either the Spirit's presence everywhere in the world and in creation as the principle of all life or to the Spirit's activity in society and history, peoples, cultures, and religions.

What then is the role of the kingdom of God? The kingdom is of course a much larger entity than the church. The church is the sign of the coming of the kingdom of God, and it is drawn into the eschatological movement through which God fulfills his purposes in the world. Having

68. For details and bibliographical references, see my *Trinity and Religious Pluralism,* pp. 69-72. D'Costa finds the biblical support for this mainly in the Johannine Paraclete passages (John 14–16). In my view, those Johannine passages are only one instance of a larger and more convincing New Testament approach; see ibid., pp. 77-78.

69. Pannenberg, *Systematic Theology,* 3:12, 13.

70. Here the definitive work is J. Zizioulas, *Being as Communion: Studies in Personhood and Communion* (Crestwood, N.Y.: St. Vladimir's Seminary Press, 1985).

created the world, God cannot be God without his kingdom, as Pannenberg has most vocally argued.[71] As noted, the Trinity rules out these kinds of 'kingdom-centered' approaches in which the advancement of the kingdom is set in opposition to or divorced from the Father, Son, and Spirit. The Trinity also rules out that kind of 'pneumato-centered' approaches in which the 'universal' ministry of the Spirit is divorced from christological contours.

The kingdom of God is the kingdom of the Father, and in its coming the Son serves as a humble Son in the power of the Spirit. Again, it is a question how much 'wider' the sphere of the kingdom is than the church. But in what way that relationship may be defined, I believe it is mistaken to separate the two so much that the church becomes an obstacle to the coming of the kingdom rather than a God-willed agent that participates in it.

This prompts the question concerning Islam's relation to the church and the kingdom. The French dialogue contended that Muslims can be regarded as co-members in the kingdom of God. This insight brings the task of spiritual discernment to the surface. The mission of the church and the work of the Holy Spirit are given new dimensions when the children of the kingdom are to be recognized in the world. If so, the dialogue continued, both Christians and Muslims should participate in the building of the kingdom until it comes in the eschaton. Yet an important distinction was made: Muslims are not building the church, which is the task for Christians, but the kingdom, which is a wider concept. Here there is a close relationship between the kingdom and the Spirit; the building of the kingdom is seen as a sign of the work of the Spirit who acts and makes the messianic kingdom come.[72]

Going back to the notion of the triune God as communion and the Spirit as the principle of relationality, let us reflect on the implications for the encounter with the Other.[73]

---

71. Pannenberg, *Systematic Theology*, 1:311-13 especially. This is not limiting God's freedom since it is in his sovereign freedom that God created the world.

72. Jukko, *Trinitarian Theology in Muslim-Christian Encounters*, pp. 193-97.

73. "God's radical relativity *ad extra* is a mirror image of the same radicalism *ad intra*: that is to say, the whole universe, as image or 'vestige' of the Trinity, is endowed with the character of radical relativity. . . . Things are but reciprocal constitutive relationships." R. Panikkar and R. R. Barr, *The Silence of God: An Answer of the Buddha* (Maryknoll, N.Y.: Orbis, 1989), p. 142.

"The Holy Spirit's Invitation to Relational Engagement"[74]

The triune God as a perichoretic communion is a helpful way to think the dynamic and tension between one and many. The Trinity as communion gives room for both genuine diversity (otherwise we could not talk about the Trinity) and unity (otherwise we could not talk about one God). Trinity "unites transcendence and immanence, creation and redemption in such a way that from the Christian standpoint dialogue [with Muslims in this case] becomes possible and meaningful," so the Catholics engaged in the dialogue with Muslims affirmed.[75] Communion serves as the paradigm for relating to the Other among human beings, too. It is not about denying differences nor eliminating distinctiveness as various sorts of 'rough parity'–type pluralisms typically do; rather, communion is about encountering the Other in a mutually learning, yet challenging atmosphere.

The Christian, coming from a particular perspective, is both encouraged and entitled to witness to the triune God of the Bible and his will to salvation, yet at the same time he or she is prepared to learn from the Other. This helps the Christian to get to know the Other and may also lead to the deepening of one's own faith. "The other is always interesting in their difference and may be the possible face of God, or the face of violence, greed, and death. Furthermore, the other may teach Christians to know and worship their own trinitarian God more truthfully and richly." Thus, D'Costa believes that Trinitarian theology provides the "context for a critical, reverent, and open engagement with otherness, without any predictable outcome."[76]

I further agree with D'Costa that other religions are not salvific as such in my Christian perspective, but other religions are important for the Christian church in that they help the church to penetrate more deeply into the divine mystery. This is the essence of what D'Costa calls the Spirit's call to "relational engagement." The acknowledgment of the gifts of God in other religions by virtue of the presence of the Spirit — as well as the critical discernment of these gifts by the power of the same Spirit — means a real Trinitarian basis to Christianity's openness toward other religions. It also ties the church to dialogue with the Other: wherever the presence of the Spirit — and thus the presence of God — is to be found, it bears some relation to the

---

74. Section title in D'Costa, *Meeting of Religions*, p. 109.
75. Jukko, *Trinitarian Theology in Muslim-Christian Encounters*, p. 221.
76. D'Costa, *Meeting of Religions*, p. 9.

church. Thus, the discernment of the activity of the Holy Spirit within other religions must also bring the church more truthfully into the presence of the triune God. Again, to cite D'Costa, "if the Spirit is at work in the religions, then the gifts of the Spirit need to be discovered, fostered, and received into the church. If the church fails to be receptive, it may be unwittingly practicing cultural and religious idolatry."[77] The church better be ready for surprises since there is no knowing a priori what beauty, truth, holiness, and other "gifts" may be waiting for it.[78] Catholics affirmed that it is the Holy Spirit who urges Christians to dialogue and who makes Christians discover aspects of their own faith that they have not known or recognized in Christ. Even more, "the Christian-Muslim encounter can help, among Christians, to receive the revelation of God in Jesus Christ."[79]

Both Welker and Polkinghorne[80] speak of the "context-sensitivity" and "encounter-sensitivity" of the Holy Spirit. This means that the Holy Spirit is not "a power which acts and operates in each and every context in 'the same way'" and that "[a]ll associations of uniformity and homogeneity" must be balanced by statements that speak of diversity. The Spirit's presence and ministry are both multicontextual and polyphonic. Not only that, but "[t]he context-sensitivity and encounter-sensitivity of the Spirit is also correlated with His vulnerability."[81] Spirit-inspired and Spirit-guided dialogue with followers of other faiths is always particular and specific. The challenges to and riches of the Muslim faith are not necessarily the same as those encountered in other faiths.

Concluding Reflections and Tasks for the Future

The church is a community in search of truth. Interfaith dialogue reflects — as the Catholic-Muslim dialogue affirmed — the dialogical nature of God, who in the Son enters the world he has created and through the active

77. Ibid., p. 115.

78. Ibid., p. 133.

79. Jukko, *Trinitarian Theology in Muslim-Christian Encounters*, p. 161, quotation on p. 219.

80. Welker gives a reference to Polkinghorne, *Faith in the Living God: A Dialogue* (London: SPCK/Philadelphia: Fortress, 2001), pp. 71ff.

81. Welker, "Spirit in Philosophical, Theological, and Interdisciplinary Perspectives," p. 227.

presence of the Holy Spirit seeks every person created in God's image.[82] In its service the church is drawn into the movement of the coming of the kingdom, humbly and boldly giving its testimony to Christ's Lordship and God's grace available to all.[83] As a truth-seeking community, the church is also called to receive new insights in its dialogue with religions.

The present essay has ventured to offer a few tentative guidelines as to how to speak of the presence and ministry of the Holy Spirit among religions. Nothing more than a beginning of a prolegomenon to a pneumatological theology of religions in a Trinitarian framework can be offered in the confines of a short essay. Many critical tasks arise out of this reflection such as the following:

First, how do we establish the principle of continuity in pneumatology so that salvation communicated by the Spirit is not foreign to the created order? Here the work of Dabney with its idea of the theology of the third article — pneumatology — seems promising.

Second, related to this is the question of the role of the Spirit in relation to the general religious nature of humanity.[84] Amos Yong's desire to develop a distinctively Pentecostal pneumatological theology of creation and anthropology raises hopes.[85] Dabney's work also bears on this question in that for him anthropology serves as the springboard for doing theology in the postmodern context.

Third, the need to establish criteria for spiritual discernment is a continuing task for the theology of religions. The task of spiritual discernment, however, is wider and more comprehensive than often perceived. In addition to developing criteria for discerning evil/demonic spirits, discernment also has much to do with the capacity and resources to identify the work of God's/divine Spirit vis-à-vis other spirits.[86]

82. See further my *Trinity and Religious Pluralism*, pp. 160-61.
83. See further Jukko, *Trinitarian Theology in Muslim-Christian Encounters*, pp. 213-14.
84. Here we could learn a lot from the theological anthropologies of both Pannenberg and Rahner.
85. A. Yong, "*Ruach,* the Primordial Chaos, and the Breath of Life: Emergence Theory and the Creation Narratives in Pneumatological Perspective," pp. 183-204 herein.
86. The scientist Donald G. York's attempt to develop the biblical idea of Wisdom as the work of the Spirit of God especially in relation to decision making may offer some seed thought to this task. See Donald G. York and Anna York, "The Spirit in Evidence: Stories of How Decisions Are Made," herein, pp. 215-20 especially.

Fourth, it would be highly interesting to ask, what is the significance of the 'syncretistic' nature of the Christian faith to our topic?[87] How is this related to the Spirit's call for engagement?

Fifth, it would be also important to continue reflection on the epistemological contours of a pneumatological theology of religions.[88] Of course, this essay in itself is already a step in that direction. What I have in mind, in addition, is the recent debate on this side of the Atlantic concerning the topic of 'foundationalism' in a postmodern context. This prompts the question of whether building a theology of religions with a Trinitarian "foundation" implies a foundationalist epistemology. I don't think so, but in this essay I cannot deal with the issue.[89]

Yet the most important task is to continue a careful and painstaking dialogue with a particular religion. Prolegomena by definition are abstract and general; dialogue is particular and specific.[90] Regarding the Muslim-Christian dialogue I tend to agree with the ironic conclusion of the French dialogue:[91]

> In sum, it can be said — paradoxical as it may sound — that even though the proper theological foundation for the interfaith dialogue with Muslims is the Christian doctrine of the Trinity, . . . the doctrine itself cannot be used in actual encounters with Muslims, since the Islamic faith denies it at the outset. . . . How this translates to the Trinitarian conviction, shared by all Christians . . . is one among the crucial

87. Pannenberg, among others, has argued that one of the distinctive features of the Christian faith is its capacity to incorporate elements from various religions more successfully than other faiths.

88. Yong's proposal is that of a "foundational pneumatology" (see ch. 3 in *Beyond the Impasse*).

89. I have touched on this in my *Trinity and Religious Pluralism*, p. 168n. 5.

90. Some of my doctoral students at Fuller Theological Seminary are currently working on utilizing a Trinitarian framework in interfaith dialogue, for example, Lewis Winkler, whose Ph.D. thesis has to do with a dialogue between Pannenberg's Trinitarian doctrine and Islamic monotheism as the latter is expressed in some leading contemporary Islamic theologies. Another doctoral student of mine, Linh Doan of Vietnam, has looked at the more recent theology of the Thich Nhat Hanh (referred to in the beginning of the essay) and its claim for bridges between the Buddhist notion of mindfulness and the Christian view of the Holy Spirit.

91. As summarized and developed by myself in my *Trinity and Religious Pluralism*, p. 162 (with sources to original documentation in Jukko's book).

theological questions to be pondered. Trinity pushes Christians to dialogue with other religions, especially with monotheistic "cousins," yet at the same time it also sets rules for Christian talk about God.

In terms of an epilogue, let me add a final word of warning and qualification to my "Trinitarian rules." While I believe it is urgent theologically to reflect on the Spirit's life in the world and among religions within a rigorous Trinitarian framework, we also have to remind ourselves of the fact that 'knowing' the ways of the Spirit is only possible by doxology. Indeed, Trinitarian doctrine is essentially doxological in its origins and character.[92] To use the poetic expression of yet another Catholic pneumatologist, Hans Urs von Balthasar, the Spirit is "the Unknown beyond the Word." Therefore, von Balthasar reminds us that even without in any way wanting to divorce itself from the Trinitarian contours, faith is also a "venture of transcending the Word into the Spirit." This means that

> The Word no longer leads us by the hand, equipping us with recipes and traveling plans that one need only consult: rather, we are exposed in the dimension of creative invention, sharing in the breath of the Creator Spirit and even . . . breathing him out ourselves together with God. It is only in faith that we can let go of the handrail of the Word, so that we can walk without vertigo in the sphere of freedom; only in believing hope dare we join Peter in leaving the ship to venture out into the billowing infinity of the divine Spirit.[93]

92. See further, McDonnell, "Pneumatology," pp. 197-98.
93. H. U. Von Balthasar, "The Unknown Lying Beyond the Word," in *Exploration in Theology*, vol. 3: *Creator Spirit*, trans. B. McNeill C.R.V. (San Francisco: Ignatius, 1993), pp. 110-11. For applications to dialogue, see Robert Imbelli, "The Unknown Beyond the Word: The Pneumatological Foundations of Dialogue," *Communio* 24 (Summer 1997): 326-35.

The Nature of the Spirit:
Creation as a Premonition of God

D. LYLE DABNEY

Citing Jesus' response to Nicodemus in the third chapter of the Gospel according to John, Michael Welker began his letter of invitation to the participants in the symposium with which these papers originated with the words: "The Spirit, like the wind, blows where it will" (3:8a). I imagine that as each of us read this phrase we immediately recall the rest of that saying: "and you hear the sound of it, but you do not know where it comes from or where it goes. So it is with everyone who is born of the Spirit" (3:8b). It is precisely to the rest of that verse that I would now draw our attention. For these words bring to a point the whole of the preceding conversation between Jesus and this "teacher of Israel," and they are at the same time the point of departure for all that comes after.[1] They also introduce the issue I would like to examine in the following. Nicodemus in this story wants to know 'How?' Interpreting Jesus as another in the long line of men and women sent by God in Israel's history, he has acknowledged that Jesus is "a teacher who has come from God, for no one can do these signs . . . apart from [God's] presence" (3:2). Unexpectedly, Jesus has responded by saying that "no one can see the kingdom of God without being born from above" (3:3). And now this one who "came to Jesus by night" (3:2) literally finds himself in the dark. "How can anyone be born after having grown old?" he asks, "Can one enter a second time into the mother's womb and be born?"

1. For the structure and development of this discourse, see R. E. Brown, *The Gospel according to John, I-XII,* 2nd ed. (Garden City, N.Y.: Doubleday, 1979), pp. 136-37.

(3:4) Thus Jesus speaks of the Spirit of God who comes and goes like the wind and brings about a new creation at will. Those who are born of the Spirit, he teaches, are moved by the Spirit of God in a manner that familiar or ordinary patterns of explanation simply do not clarify — "you hear the sound of it, but you do not know where it comes from or where it goes," for a "divine possibility" (to borrow a term from Rudolf Bultmann) is at work in their lives that is not the sum of the causal forces that human beings usually employ to elucidate the phenomena of our existence.[2] Where Nicodemus sees only an inexplicable mystery, Jesus points to the Spirit as the possibility of God moving through God's creation and new creation of the world: the very possibility of God at work in all those who are brought to the realization of the coming of the kingdom; indeed, the very divine possibility seen in and at work through Jesus Christ himself. Nicodemus wanted to know 'How?' and he missed entirely therefore the 'Who?' — of Jesus the Christ, not another in a long line but the unique recipient and bearer and bestower of God's Spirit (see 1:29-34), and of the Holy Spirit, not simply a divine presence with a man of God but the one who blows through the life, death, and resurrection of Jesus the Christ in this narrative as the possibility of God in and for God's world.

The following chapter wants to draw attention to the Spirit as the possibility of God, and the way this pneumatological perspective allows us to picture God's relation to God's creation and new creation of the world. Just as western debates over soteriology have returned again and again to Paul's Epistle to the Romans in the New Testament, so in Christian theology from Augustine to Aquinas to Luther to Barth, discussions of the doctrine of creation and the relation of God to the world have seemed inevitably to turn to an exposition of the opening chapter in the book of Genesis in the Old Testament.[3] Although by no means exhaustive of the biblical witness to creation,[4] this text more than any other has become the *locus classicus* for the doctrine. The beginning of the book of Genesis, therefore,

2. R. Bultmann, *The Gospel of John: A Commentary,* trans. G. R. Beasley-Murray et al. (Philadelphia: Westminster, 1971; German original, 1966), p. 142.

3. For a recent example, see M. Welker, *Creation and Reality* (Minneapolis: Fortress, 1999).

4. See B. W. Anderson, *Creation in the Old Testament* (Philadelphia: Fortress, 1984). For an example of just how wide-ranging a doctrine of creation can be that draws on the breadth of the witness of scripture, cf. J. Moltmann, *God in Creation: An Ecological Doctrine of Creation* (London: SCM, 1985).

will be the focus for that which follows; and unlike Nicodemus, I will start with the question of 'Who?' First, we will begin with an introduction to the passage itself: its context in the book of Genesis and the structure and general characteristics of the text. Second, with frequent reference to Genesis, we will examine the role played by the Spirit of God in the "creation of the heavens and the earth" and, more specifically, the way that shapes how Christian theology should speak of God as the Creator of the world and the world as God's creation. Here two implications of the 'nature of the Spirit' will be drawn for our interpretation of the 'nature of the world': on the one hand, that creation begins not with the Word but with the Spirit, and on the other, that creation begins therefore not with creaturely necessity but with divine possibility.

If we would understand this opening passage in the Bible depicting the creation of "the heavens and the earth," we must see this text in its context in the book of Genesis.[5] This first book of the Torah and thus of the Bible is called in Hebrew 'in the beginning,' and in the Greek Septuagint 'origin.' In translation it was the Greek title, mediated through the Latin Bible, that our own language took over in naming the book. Genesis is comprised of fifty chapters, and is about 'beginnings,' or 'origins.' It is, in fact, about two distinct origins: on the one hand, that of Israel (roughly chapters 12–50) and, on the other, that of all the universe (roughly chapter 1; the remainder of the book, roughly chapters 2–11, found between the creation account and the calling of Abraham, plays a preparatory role to the Abraham stories in the narrative). While distinct, these two origins or beginnings are depicted as being closely interrelated. To grasp the message of the opening chapter of Genesis, therefore, one must understand that the story of the origin of the universe recounted there is told from the perspective of the story of the origin of Israel found in the later chapters.

The story of Israel begins with the claim that God called Abraham, from whom all Israel descends, and promised him blessing both for himself and his descendants, and, furthermore, that through Abraham God would bless "all the families [or, nations] of the earth" (12:1-3). From the perspective of the worship of the One who has chosen the line of Abraham

---

5. For a very good critical and narrative orientation to Genesis and the Pentateuch, cf. R. S. Hendel, "Genesis, Book of," *Anchor Bible Dictionary*, 2:933-41; J. J. Scullion, "Genesis, The Narrative of," *Anchor Bible Dictionary*, 2:941-62; and R. E. Friedman, "Torah (Pentateuch)," *Anchor Bible Dictionary*, 6:605-22.

to serve as a channel of divine blessing for all creation, Israel took up se-
lected parts of the stories about the origin of the world as recounted in the
traditions of the peoples living around them in the ancient Near East and
transformed them to serve their witness to the One who had laid claim to
their collective life.[6] The opening chapters of Genesis in general, and specifically the first chapter, are, therefore, not to be (mis)taken as a kind of
speculation on 'the way things came to be' — much less as an ancient
equivalent of a 'modern' or 'scientific' account of the origin of the universe
— but rather recognized as a confession of faith concerning the relationship existing between the "God of Abraham, Isaac, and Jacob" (Exod. 3:6)
and all the world — as well as how that relationship with God determines
the nature of the world. Indeed, the first chapter of Genesis is best understood as a "doxological interpretation of the first commandment,"[7] which
instructed Israel to worship no other gods (Exod. 20:3-4), and thus as reflecting that passage which would become a daily prayer during the long
exile of the Jews, "Hear, O Israel: The LORD is our God, the LORD is one"
(Deut. 6:4). Its subject matter is, in the first instance, *God* — and secondly,
the manner in which *all creation,* including Israel, stands in relationship to
God.

The creation narrative in Genesis, therefore, is not primarily about
'*how* the world came to be,' but rather about '*who* is the world's Creator
and what does that mean for the creation.' By speaking of creation in this
way, Genesis demonstrates the connection between the story of Israel and
that of all the world: the God of all creation is the One who has called and
thereby created Israel so that God's good purposes of blessing all creation
might be achieved. Thus the story of 'God and Israel' (chs. 12–50) is to be
understood within the larger story of 'God and all the world' (chs. 1–11).
Conversely, the story of 'God and all the world' (1–11), and more specifically, the story of 'God's creation of the heavens and the earth' (roughly, ch.
1), is to be understood in relation to the story of 'God and Israel' (12–50),
for it is the latter that provides the controlling perspective for the former.

The precise parameters of the story of 'God's creation of the heavens

6. See M. Bauks, *Die Welt am Anfang: Vom Verhältnis von Vorwelt und Weltentstehung
in Gen 1 und in der altorientalischen Literatur* (Neukirchen-Vluyn: Neukirchener Verlag,
1997); B. S. Childs, *Myth and Reality in the Old Testament* (London: SCM, 1962).
7. G. Gloege, "Schöpfung IV B. Dogmatisch," in K. Galling (ed.) *Die Religion in
Geschichte und Gegenwart: Handwörterbuch für Theologie und Religionswissenschaft*
(Tübingen: Mohr Siebeck, 3rd ed. 1961), 5:1485.

and the earth,' identified above as 'roughly, chapter 1,' can be identified by
attending to the structure of Genesis. The book has a clearly demarcated
form. It is structured as an extended genealogy, with its major divisions
marked by the repeated appearance of the genealogical phrase "these are
the generations of . . ." (2:4; 5:1; 6:9; 10:1; 11:10; 11:27; 25:12; 25:19; 36:1; 37:2),
which in translation means something like 'this is the story of . . .' or even
'this is what became of. . . .' Thus the first of these genealogies, "The Generations of" (or, "The Story of . . .") the Heavens and the Earth (2:4–4:26), is
followed by that of Adam (5:1–6:8), Noah (6:9–9:29), the Sons of Noah
(10:1–11:9), Shem (11:10-26), Terah (11:27–25:11), Ishmael (25:12-18), Isaac
(25:19–35:29), Esau (36:1–37:1), and Jacob (37:2–50:26). The book advances
its story line, therefore, through a series of discrete if interrelated 'genealogical' subnarratives.

What this immediately makes clear is that 1:1–2:3 stands outside the
formal structure of Genesis. The story of "God's creation of the heavens
and the earth" is therefore not 1:1-31, but rather 1:1–2:3. And this passage is
to be understood not as a link in the 'generations' that make up the story,
but as that which goes before and stands outside the rest of the tale. For
1:1–2:3 functions as the preface or prologue to the book of Genesis, indeed,
to the Torah as a whole.[8] And not just in Genesis or in the Torah, but in
truth in the whole of the biblical witness, that of the Old Testament and of
the New Testament as well. It is in this horizon that we are to read all the
subsequent stories of divine command and human disobedience, of divine
judgment and human estrangement, of divine promise and human hope,
and of human repentance and divine forgiveness: all unfold in the midst of
the tale of creation from chaos to consummation on the day of God's Sabbath rest for all things.[9]

8. See S. D. McBride, Jr., "Divine Protocol: Genesis 1:1–2:3 as Prologue to the Pentateuch," in idem and W. P. Brown (eds.), *God Who Creates: Essays in Honor of W. Sibley
Towner* (Grand Rapids: Eerdmans, 2000), pp. 3-41.

9. Here perhaps it is helpful to note that chapter 2, 2:4-25, is often described as a 'second creation story' and is then contrasted with the 'first' found in 1:1–2:3. But while it is certainly true that 2:4-25 depicts God creating the man and placing him in the garden, and
while it may be true that the account now found in chapter 2 originated and circulated at
some point in Israel's history as an independent creation story, nevertheless, in terms of its
role in the narrative of Genesis, this description seriously misrepresents the passage. It is not
the case that Israel had two 'creation stories' and, unable or unwilling to decide between
them, simply included both. Rather, *chapter 1* serves in Genesis, indeed, in the whole of the
Pentateuch, as *the* account of the creation of the world. *Chapter 2*, as part of the first major

That prologue, 1:1–2:3, is itself clearly structured. Genesis 1:1 serves as a kind of general statement summarizing the content of the whole passage, a statement then echoed in 2:1. The passage as a whole is structured by the literary device of depicting God's creation as occurring on seven consecutive days, corresponding to the seven days of Israel's week; a period of time culminating with the Sabbath, which itself corresponds to the seventh day upon which Israel was commanded by God to observe a day of rest as a sign of the covenant between themselves and their Redeemer. Genesis 1:1–2:3 tells the story of the creation of the world, therefore, in the categories of Israel's own story of redemption (cf. Deut. 5:12-15). Thus these seven 'days' clearly function as a literary device used to interpret creation in terms of a process culminating in the Sabbath day of covenanted rest. As such, the prologue establishes the 'horizon' upon which all that follows is to be seen, for it depicts the overarching context for the successive accounts of the 'generations' which follow. It speaks, therefore, not of the first in a chain of events but rather of the all-encompassing event within which all else is to be understood: an unfolding event culminating in all creation coming to God's Sabbath rest. As such, as S. Dean McBride comments, "the chronicle not only documents what happened at creation 'in the beginning'; it also epitomizes divine procedure and purpose, setting an agenda that previews the creator's continuing relationship to an ordered but still malleable cosmos."[10] Thus the theme of the prologue — as for Genesis as a whole — is God's promise. Just as the story of the origin of the world and its condition (chs. 1–11) is told in Genesis from the perspective of and in terms reminiscent of the origin of Israel (chs. 12–50), so the story of 'God's creation of the heavens and the earth' (1:1–2:3) is portrayed as fraught with divine promise in correspondence to the promises of God to Israel which are con-

---

genealogical subnarrative, "The Story of [or, 'What Became of'] the Heavens and the Earth," 2:4–4:26, plays a completely different role in that narrative. It is closely connected, even subordinated, to the account of disobedience and exile from the garden in chapters 3 and 4. It does not provide some 'alternative' account of 'how the world came to be,' as if that was what chapter 1 was all about, but rather functions as the indispensable 'preface' in 2:4–4:26 which establishes the categories used to describe the breadth and depth of the ramifications of human failure. Within the context of Genesis, therefore, chapter 2 has no independent role and is not a 'second creation story' to be played off against the 'first,' i.e., 1:1–2:3. It is, rather, that which makes possible the depiction in chapters 3 and 4 of the corruption of all that God has created.

10. McBride, "Divine Protocol," p. 7.

stitutive of the stories of the patriarchs: Abraham, Isaac, and Jacob (see 12:1-3), the promise that God will bless 'every nation on the face of the earth.'

In summary, then, we can say that the story of God's "creation of the heavens and the earth," 1:1–2:3, declares that the One whom Israel worships and serves is the Creator and Sustainer of all the universe (1:1; 2:1); and is Lord therefore over all, indeed, precisely over all those objects venerated as 'gods' in the myths of the peoples around Israel in the ancient Near East: the primeval waters of chaos (1:2; see Isa. 45:19), the sun, moon, and stars (1:14ff.; see Deut. 4:19; Zeph. 1:5), and the 'great sea monsters' of the primeval sea (1:21; see Pss. 74:12-13; 104:25ff.; Isa. 51:9ff.). God's creation is depicted as taking place through a process of seven days, culminating in the day of promise, the day of Sabbath rest. While both the 'waters' (1:20) and the 'earth' (1:24) are made a part of God's creative activity, the creatures of the 'sixth day', human beings, play a special role in creation, as is indicated by the manner in which their creation is introduced, the description of them as being made "in the image and likeness of God," and their being given "dominion" over creation (1:26-31). The point is thus made that this world is neither purposeless nor inimical to human existence, for it is ruled not by a pantheon of viciously warring gods — as in many of the mythic tales of the ancient Near East — but by the One who is alone God, the LORD worshiped by Israel as Redeemer and Creator. Moreover, that rule is by no means to be thought to be despotic and exploitive — again, as was the case in many of the tales of the ancient Near East — but rather gracious and inclusive of the human in the unfolding of the story of the creation and the Creator. Thus Israel's confession of faith in *God the Creator* is at the same time a confession of the essential goodness of *God's creation* as a whole and of human life in particular. For it is a world made by the One who intends to bring it to its proper end: the "rest" of the Sabbath day.

Now, having offered an initial introduction to a reading of the story of God's "creation of the heavens and the earth" in Genesis 1:1–2:3, let us turn our attention to the role played by the Spirit of God in this narrative in order to begin to bring some clarity to what the doctrine of creation might look like when interpreted from a pneumatological standpoint. Just what does the 'nature of the Spirit' in this narrative mean for the way we understand the 'nature of the world'? I will argue in the following that such a theology: (1) begins with the Spirit in its account of the world as creation and,

and thus (2) interprets the world as defined not by necessity but by possibility, that is, as fraught with the very possibility of God's Spirit.

The first point to be made is that a doctrine of creation viewed from the standpoint we are pursuing here starts with God's Spirit — and that in contrast to other forms of theology which would insist upon beginning with God's Word. This shift in perspective is immediately apparent in our reading of Genesis, where the Spirit's presence precedes and is presupposed by the speaking of the Word. Thus we read in the story of God's "creation of the heavens and the earth" (1:2), "Now the earth was a formless void and darkness covered the face of the deep, while a wind from God swept over the face of the waters," before we hear, "Then God said, 'Let there be light'; and there was light," in 1:3. It is in the context of the blowing of God's wind or breath that God's Word is spoken, and this "wind from God" is to be understood as nothing other than the Spirit of God.[11] If, therefore, we pose the question as to what we must say first in the doctrine of creation, if we speak of God, then before we can simply assert, *Deus dixit*, "God said" (Gen. 1:3), we must *first* say that the "divine wind or breath" or the "Spirit of God" was sweeping over the chaotic abyss (Gen. 1:2). For the Word presupposes the Spirit in creation; indeed, the Word is spoken in the Spirit.

Now here I must emphasize that this is by no means to be taken as an attempt to subordinate Christology to Pneumatology, nor Word to Spirit. Rather, it is an attempt to take seriously the biblical witness to the story of the Word made flesh itself, the Gospel narratives of the life, death, and resurrection of Jesus Christ. For just as the presence of the Spirit precedes the speaking of the Word in Genesis 1, so we find in the testimony of the New Testament to Jesus Christ, that it is first said to the woman, "the Holy Spirit will come upon you, and the power of the Most High will overshadow you" (Luke 1:35; cf. Matt. 1:18), before the birth of the Son of God is proclaimed, or, as the Gospel according to John presents it: "the Word became flesh" (John 1:14). Just as in creation, so in re-creation the Spirit is once again portrayed as that which is presupposed by the Word. The point is not to play off Word and Spirit, but rather to show how they relate to one another, what we must say first if we say what is central. For just as the human word is born on the breath of the mouth and moves through wavelike

11. For the debates concerning this interpretation, cf. S. Tengstrom, *TWAT* 7 (1990): 385-418, 402ff.

motion of the air and thus is perceived by another, so it is that from the very first the Word of the One who is Wholly Other has presupposed God's breath or Spirit: "By the word of the LORD the heavens were made, and all their host by the breath of his mouth" (Ps. 33:6). Therefore, stressing the Spirit first in a theology of the third article does not displace, replace, or in any way make Christ last. Rather, it makes Christ central.[12] One cannot ultimately speak of Christ until one has spoken of that chrism with the Spirit that makes Jesus of Nazareth God's Christ. One cannot adequately speak of Word until one has first spoken of Spirit.

Rather, starting with the Spirit of God in the story of God's creation, we are able to identify what comes first in the relation of God and world and thereby begin to speak of that ubiquitous and mysterious presence of God in the world, a presence whereby God is creation's 'Other,' and that which enables creation to be truly 'other' — both to God and to one another. Contrary to what one might initially assume, the concept of 'otherness' presupposes and demands not only a difference between two persons or things, but also their relatedness. To say that x is other than y, for example, is not simply to make a statement about x alone. For implicit in those words is the notion of comparison and relation of x to y. The sentence, "x is other than y," means, therefore, x is different *as compared to, in relation to, y*. Thus, while the statement certainly *denies* identity between x and y, it also implicitly *affirms* relationship between the two. Only that which is both different and related is 'other.' That with which we are identical is not 'other'; it is simply a repetition of ourselves. That to which we have no relation, on the other hand, is likewise no 'other'; it is, as far as we are concerned, simply 'not.' The otherness of God and our otherness to God and to one another are to be understood in precisely this manner. How is it that a world can exist that is related to God and yet is not God? How can creatures exist who are other than and yet related to one another? How is it that the Creator can relate to the creature as the Wholly Other, the One who is truly and utterly other than ourselves? How is it that the Word of God can be the Word of the Wholly Other and not just our own word 'spoken in a loud voice?' The answer is to be found in the Spirit of God, the presence of God in the world, in that we are established and maintained in

---

12. On mutuality between Spirit and Word rather than a subordination of Spirit to Word, cf. Y. Congar, *The Word and the Spirit*, trans. D. Smith (London: Geoffrey Chapman, 1986).

relationship with the One who is truly Other, the Wholly Other, with whom we are not identical and yet with whom we are always related.

And in that difference in relationship we are at the same time related to one another and to the entirety of God's creation.

Thus the story of God's "creation of the heavens and the earth," Genesis 1:1–2:3, can depict the creation of the world in a way that avoids both the notion that creation is somehow an extension, that is, an 'emanation' or 'procession,' of divine being and the notion that the world is somehow not intrinsically related to God, that is, that the presence of the world somehow implies the absence of God. Creation, according to this story, is neither identical with nor autonomous from its Creator. So, if God is depicted in 1:1 as the transcendent Creator of all things, the One who is other *than,* indeed, who is the uncreated 'Other' *to* all that which is created, then it by no means intimates that God is *absent from* creation. That point is immediately underlined in 1:2 where the primordial state of the world is portrayed, a formless emptiness whose watery abyss is enveloped in darkness. Yet even there in the chaotic darkness — that which in the ancient Near East stood over and against the world and over and against divine order — the "wind" or "breath" or "Spirit" or God is present as the possibility and promise of creation: the possibility that the emptiness might yet be filled, the darkness might yet be made light, and the chaotic waters might yet be subdued and brought to order. For the sweeping of the wind or breath or Spirit of God across the waters means that chaos's lack of capacity for God does not preclude God's possibility for the world.

In the presence of that Spirit there then follows the account of the six days of creation. Each day is described in a highly stylized manner, making use of a set of common elements which are repeated and added to in a constantly shifting pattern through the sequence of days. Thus, while each day begins with God speaking a word of command and ends with the numbering of the day, other elements which appear include statements that what God commanded occurred, that God acted to separate or gather, that God saw that it was good, that God acted to make, that the earth or the waters brought forth what God had commanded, and that God named what he had made. In this way creation is depicted as a complex activity of *ordering* (separating, gathering, setting in place), *making* (light, the dome of the sky, lights, vegetation, creatures of the sea and sky, land animals, and human beings), *naming* (day and night, sky, earth, and seas), *including* (the earth, the waters, and human beings each participate in the process of creation), and *blessing* (of the animals, of humanity, of the Sabbath day) by means of which God fills the empty darkness and makes it light. And into all of this there is woven the presupposition of the presence of the Spirit in which God speaks, by which God orders and makes and includes and blesses. From the darkness of chaos to the light of the cosmic Sabbath, the Spirit is the presence of God in the world. Because the Spirit is the presence of God in the world, the world is not God, but the world is never without God.

By virtue of the Spirit as the life-giving presence of God in the world, we might say then that, from the very first, we are 'Otherwise engaged in the Spirit' and are thus ever and again encompassed in events of emergent commonality. Not as a manifestation of a creaturely *capax Dei*, but rather as the expression of a divine *capax creaturae*, the creature is never without the Creator. For the Spirit of God is that which relates us to God and to one another ever and again at each moment of our existence. Indeed, according to the biblical testimony, from the very inception of our lives we live 'out of' the presence of God's spiritual breath, borne away from ourselves on the winds of the Spirit to the 'other' of our neighbor and to the 'Wholly Other' of our Creator. At no point in our existence are we abandoned or left alone, but rather at every moment we are 'Otherwise engaged' by the God whose Spirit is the source and the maintenance of our very being. We live therefore, literally, 'eccentric' lives; lives, that is, having their center not in themselves, but in an o/Other. For from the very beginning there is a relationship between Creator and creature from God's side, a relationship in the Spirit as the breath of God that gives breath to all creation, which is the possibility of God for the world and the possibility of the world for God, a relationship that even permits the speaking of a/the w/Word to an o/Other and the hearing of the w/Word of the o/Other.

For breathing not only effects life and movement in the creature, but it also relates all living things to the otherness of a reality outside of themselves, to that which is other than themselves, in the most concrete way possible. Moreover, air is not simply the condition of our creaturely existence, it is the all-encompassing element in which we, as in God, "live and move and have our being" (Acts 17:28). It is by virtue of the Spirit, therefore, that even and again *the common* emerges at all levels of our creaturely existence. Thus, just as the 'east wind' drives the various waters westward or bends the many different plants of the field in a *common* direction, thereby effecting in the many a *common* result without in any way relativizing their individual differences, so the divine wind of God's Spirit can move upon the waters of chaos at the first or among a people at a certain time and place and bend their lives to a *common* purpose and a distinctive social existence. The Spirit of God is thus not to be identified with individualized human spirit aspiring to the Divine, but neither is it the subjectivity of an individualized God making an object of the human. Rather, in contrast to 'subjective' or 'objective,' the Spirit of God is better conceived as 'transjective,' that is to say, that by which we as individuals are transcended, engaged, oriented beyond ourselves, and related to God and neighbor from the very beginning.

The common emerges among us above all in and through our language; and it is precisely through our speech that we most truly become transjective beings ourselves. According to the witness of Genesis, creation occurs through the speaking of the Word in the Spirit. The creature of the sixth day, that pluriform creature which is male and female and designated God's image, is thus to be understood as a creature of Spirit and Word. As such, we are not only brought into being by the speaking of God's Word in the Spirit but are from the very beginning linguistic beings who lead linguistic lives, construing the world through the language we speak. Because the Creator is *Deus loquens,* the creature made in the image of the Creator is a 'creaturely creator,' and thus *homo linguisticus.*[13] For we are ourselves a construal of the Word in the Spirit, and our words, coming from the mouth of the *imago Dei,* bespeak the Word of God the Creator. The wind of the Spirit, therefore, the 'breath of God' is that which is constantly bringing us to the realization of the world through w/(W)ord, involving us in and with and beyond one another with God in God's world. We live in a shared world, 'beyond ourselves,' 'beside ourselves,' through the emergence of the common in language, our words borne by a breath not ultimately our own, indeed, our words speaking of that which ultimately is not simply ourselves.

The second point to be made concerning the way this pneumatological perspective leads us to interpret creation has to do with the notion of the Spirit as the possibility of God. Possibility has not enjoyed pride of place in Western theology, but that changes when we turn to the Spirit. As Eberhard Jüngel pointed out in his essay "Die Welt als Möglichkeit und

---

13. See N. Wolterstorff, *Divine Discourse: Philosophical Reflections on the Claim That God Speaks* (Cambridge: Cambridge University Press, 1995), p. ix.

Wirklichkeit,"[14] it was an act the consequences of which for the history of the Western intellectual tradition are almost impossible to overestimate, when Aristotle declared in his *Metaphysics* that the real was necessarily prior to the possible (*Met.* Θ, 1049 b 5; cf. Λ, 1072 a 9). The logical correlate of the claim is, of course, that the real defines the parameters of the possible; and this notion has became constitutive for Western thought as a whole. It has shaped the development of our conceptions of substance, of being, of time, and of language — and has gone beyond shaping our thinking to impacting our doing (our technology!) as well — from the classical age to our own. The success of the claim, the compelling power and pervasive character of this notion can be seen in the tremendous influence not just in philosophy but in theology as well. That influence is clearly on display, for instance, in medieval Scholasticism and the enduring influence it has exercised. Aquinas, of course, referred to Aristotle as 'the Philosopher' in the same way that he made reference to Paul as 'the Apostle.' And his account of creation reveals the presupposition of the priority of the real over the possible and the defining of the possible in terms of the reality of being in a hierarchy from the necessary to the contingent. But a pneumatological theology does not begin with a metaphysical claim for the ontologically real, for it forswears the claim that being is given to be read off the world or inferred from existence. It starts rather with the Spirit of God who in the death and resurrection of Jesus Christ is identified as the possibility of God that through the Word brings the real into emergent being. It is the Spirit who raises Jesus Christ from the dead who blows across the waters at the beginning and, at the speaking of the Word, brings forth creation from chaos. As George Montague wrote: "Because God's Spirit is hovering over it, the chaos becomes promise."[15]

This is, in fact, precisely the way the story of God's "creation of the heavens and the earth" in Genesis 1:1–2:3 tells its tale: from beginning to end it is the story of God bringing forth creation in the possibility of the Spirit through the speaking of the Word. And this possibility is not just that God might be for the world, but also that the world might be for God. In the preliminary creative activities of the first two days of the 'week of

---

14. E. Jüngel, "Die Welt als Möglichkeit und Wirklichkeit," *Unterwegs zur Sache: Theologische Bemerkungen*, 2. Aufl. (München: Chr. Kaiser Verlag, 1988), pp. 206-33.

15. G. T. Montague, *The Holy Spirit: Growth of a Biblical Tradition* (New York: Paulist, 1976), p. 67.

days' ending with the Sabbath depicted there, God is portrayed in a manner that could be characterized as a 'subject' acting upon an 'object.' But from the third day on, once the light had been created (day one) and the waters separated (day two) and dry land made to appear (day three), the manner of God's creative activity often takes on a very different character indeed. For on the third day, in the midst of God's creative week, God's creating begins to take the creation itself into the process of further creation, and the process of *creatio continua* becomes at the same time a process of *creatio ex creatione*. Thus we read on day three: "Then God said, '*Let the earth put forth* vegetation: plants yielding seed, and fruit trees of every kind on earth that bear fruit with the seed in it'" (1:11), and on day five God commands, "*Let the waters bring forth* swarms of living creatures, and let birds fly above the earth across the dome of the sky" (1:20), and again, "*Let the earth bring forth* living creatures of every kind: cattle and creeping things and wild animals of the earth of every kind, and everything that creeps upon the ground of every kind" (1:24-25). And thus the earth and the waters and the sky itself are included in the ongoing 'transjective' creation of the world in which structures of commonality not only emerge and engender further commonalities, but are woven into the very warp and the woof of the world in such a manner that they are intrinsic to the nature of creation itself.

Yet it is not before the sixth day that this aspect of creation comes to its climax. For there we read that not only does God include the creation in further acts of creation, thus engendering communities of commonality, but that God takes up the human in a special relationship with the Creator so that 'he,' that is, 'Adam' (1:27a) — 'the' human who in fact is the pluralistic community of male and female (1:27c) — might be nothing less than the image of God on earth (1:27b), a 'creaturely creator.' "Because [Adam] has been created in the image of God," writes Sergei Bulgakov, "he is called to create."[16] That image is to be understood not as ontological but as 'missional,' as participating in the creative activity of God in the world through word and deed: specifically as 'filling' and 'subduing' and exercising 'dominion' over creation (1:28) and thus preparing creation for the seventh day of Sabbath rest (2:2). The "creation of the heavens and the earth," therefore, is not simply about God acting in a vacuum or upon an object; it

---

16. S. Bulgakov, "Religion and Art," in E. L. Mascall (ed.), *The Church of God: An Anglo-Russian Symposium* (London: SPCK, 1934), p. 175.

is about a process in which creation itself is taken up in acts of further creation. God's creative Word is not simply spoken to creation but rather is spoken through creation in the Spirit. For in the Spirit and through the Word God brings us into being as God's own image in the world, a being which is itself a bearer of God's Word in the Spirit, a being whose words are made part and parcel of God's bringing into being God's world as God's other. As creatures of Word and Spirit, therefore, we are made to take part in God's speaking of the Word of creation in the Spirit.

But in none of these acts of further creation are we to suppose that there is some innate *capax* of nature in that which is taken up in creating that would allow it to bring about the 'new' or the 'further' out of itself. Reading this narrative, who would guess at the beginning of day three when dry land appeared (1:9) that the land itself would bring forth life, both vegetable (1:11-12) and animal (1:24-25)? For this is a process in which God's possibility, the possibility of the Spirit, unexpectedly emerges in ever new acts of creation, acts in which God's *capax creaturae* take the creature into the very processes of creation itself. It was centuries after the priestly traditions found in Genesis 1 depicted 'God's creation of the heavens and the earth' as beginning with chaos, that first the Jewish and then the Christian traditions argued that God's creation is *ex nihilo*. I think one can certainly argue that the Old Testament notion of the waters of chaos 'in the beginning' is the functional equivalent of 'nothing', but the point must still be made that there is a difference between the claim that the world is *creatio ex nihilo* and the realization that the process that marks that creation is not only *creatio continua,* but also *creatio ex creatione,* and that — from beginning to end — in the possibility of the Spirit of God the Creator.[17]

When we — unlike Nicodemus — begin with the question 'Who?' rather than 'How?' we find that our understanding of the presence and activity of God in the world profoundly changes. In regard to the doctrine of creation, we learn that this is neither an event of divine emanation and causation nor of human realization of sin nor of divine determination; it is, rather, an event in which God takes up the creature into the divine possibility of speaking the Creator's Word of creation in anticipation of the promise of the seventh day of Sabbath rest. Creation is thus an act of dis-

---

17. See J. McIntyre, *The Shape of Pneumatology: Studies in the Doctrine of the Holy Spirit* (Edinburgh: T&T Clark, 1997), pp. 37ff. Cf. J. M. Houston, *I Believe in the Creator* (Grand Rapids: Eerdmans, 1980), pp. 272-73.

covery, brought forth in divine condescension and grace. And its promise — the theme of Genesis 1:1–2:3 — is rooted not in the capacity of the creature but in the possibility of God, the Holy Spirit, who yet blows through the chaos on the way to the new creation of all things.

Workings of the Spirit:
Simplicity or Complexity?

KATHRYN TANNER

This chapter explores a bifurcation or polarization in the understanding of the workings of the Spirit in Christian thought and practice. On the one view (which I believe to be the dominant one in modern times), the Spirit is thought to work immediately — both instantaneously and directly, without any obvious mediating forms — in exceptional events, rather than in the ordinary run of human affairs, upon the interior depths of individual persons, apart from the operation of their own faculties, in ways that ensure moral probity and infallible certainty of religious insight. On the other side, the Spirit is thought to work gradually, and without final resolution, in and through the usual fully human and fully fallible, often messy and conflict-ridden public processes of give-and-take in ordinary life. On this second view, the Spirit does not begin to work where ordinary sorts of human operation come to an end. To the contrary, the workings of the Spirit emerge from out of the whole of those ordinary operations, in and over their gradual and apparently meandering course, to surprising, indeed unpredictable, effect. On the one hand, then, immediacy, interiority, privacy, singularity, and the bypassing of the fallibility and sinful corruption of the human both in the Spirit's operations and effects; on the other hand, historical process, mediation, publicity, surprise within the course of the commonplace, and the ability of the Spirit to make do with the fallibility, corruption, and confusions of human life for its own purposes. This second understanding of the workings of the Spirit holds great potential, I suggest, for the contemporary science-and-religion dialogue. It resonates with both the method and conclusions of contemporary scientific investigation into the complexity of natural processes.

A Specifically Modern Controversy?

While presaged by earlier controversies (which share with the case at hand, as I will suggest in a moment, questions about religious authority), this specific bifurcated understanding of the workings of the Spirit is peculiar to modern times. It erupts in the sixteenth and seventeenth centuries — in Britain in particular — around the disputed question of 'enthusiasm.' Radical sects and individuals in Britain, associated with the zeal of Puritanism, millenarianism, and new prophecy — Fifth Monarchy Men, Levelers, Diggers, Quakers, and Ranters, to name just a few — claimed direct inspiration and special revelations in their opposition to established church and social orders, culminating in the upheaval of the English Civil War in the mid-seventeenth century. But this controversy over the workings of the Spirit had a wider geographical range and reflects very general religious trends typical of the period.[1]

In the first place, this bifurcation in thought about the Spirit has everything to do with a number of other bifurcations that are characteristic of modern religious thought and life generally. For example, the split here between interior and exterior, personal and public, seems to mirror the way that faith tends to bifurcate into the faith by which one believes and the faith one believes in, faith as either personal trust or assent to the propositions making up the confession of faith, a bifurcation underlying the division between Protestant pietists and scholastics since the seventeenth century. Like what happens at both poles of the modern understanding of faith, especially the first view of the workings of the Spirit narrows down the standard account, splinters off certain aspects of an earlier, widely shared view about the Spirit, and gives them undue emphasis. Of course the Spirit can work without mediation, and in a completely antagonistic relation to the operations of our usual faculties, but now this occasional course becomes the Spirit's typical one. The second view of the Spirit, on

---

1. See M. Heyd, "The Reaction to Enthusiasm in the Seventeenth Century: Towards an Integrative Approach," *Journal of Modern History* 53, no. 2 (June 1981): 264 (for the controversy's specifically modern character) and 275-76 (for its international range).

my reading of it, is not so much the opposite extreme, an equally one-sided, narrowed view, as the attempt to bring back the fuller picture in an updated way.

Perhaps more obviously proving my point here, the split in views of the Spirit also has everything to do with the bifurcation between faith and reason that breaks out in modern times. Christian factions do not simply line up here on one side or the other of the split — irrational faith or faithless reason — as equally one-sided devolutions from a previous, more harmonious integration of religious and rational forms of assent and commitment. The question for Christian controversy primarily concerns whether the split between the two is to be affirmed or not. When reason challenges the faith, should the claims of reason be repulsed as an inappropriate incursion on faith's rightful domain, or should efforts be made to reconcile the two on a new basis?

In the case of the Spirit, the challenge from rational reflection seems to be based on the recognition of the fully human character of religious processes, a recognition hard to square with the usual claims to religious authority — claims to be speaking, for example, a divine word or truth. Those who speak in God's name, who predicate their own authority on God's, are merely human beings, with their own narrow interests, erroneous views, partial perspectives, and moral failings. Appeals to the Spirit that interpret its workings as an unmediated divine influence on human life, bypassing human faculties and human historical processes, would be a way of repulsing this challenge by fundamentally accepting the terms of it. Fully human historical processes and religious ways of sanctioning claims are incompatible with one another; appeals to the Spirit — unlike appeals to the more apparently humanly mediated forms of scripture or church traditions — can simply erase the influence of those historical processes and with them any challenge to religious authority. God simply spoke to me directly, overthrowing in an instant everything that I would otherwise have believed. The following summary judgment of W. C. Braithwaite captures nicely the religious dynamic here on the part of so-called enthusiasts such as the early Quakers: a refusal to acknowledge human processes seemed the only recourse if the unquestionable character of religious authority was to be assured. "They believed that inspiration gave infallibility, a belief that men have often held with respect to the writers of scripture, and they had to learn, with the help of some painful lessons, what we are learning today about the writers of scripture, that the inspired servant of God remains a man, liable to much of human error and weakness."[2]

This unquestionable authority, which the understanding of the Spirit's immediate workings in this way shored up, could then be extended to other more compromised, because more obviously humanly mediated, sources of religious authority. Especially in more mainstream Protestant circles it becomes common to argue that the traditional authority of church teaching and practice stems from the authority of scripture, and that the authority of scripture depends, in turn, upon the fact that the authors of it were inspired by the Spirit in the aforementioned way. Out of the blue, singled out without rhyme or reason, apart from anything they were in and of themselves, the biblical writers were taken up by the Spirit as its passive mouthpieces. In a way that contravened the whole character of their human circumstances, when they appeared to speak themselves, the Spirit was speaking in their place.

The second view of the workings of the Spirit would contest the initial opposition between religious sources of authority and fully human processes, and offer a picture of the Spirit's workings that reconciles the two. In so doing, one might argue, it contests modern trends in the understanding of the way God works while accepting, to a greater extent than the other view of the Spirit does, a modern realism about human nature.

Rather than taking the place of human reason (for example), divine inspiration works through its exercise: "Reason is always the means of apprehension, and 'that is not revealed, which is not made intelligible.'"[3] Yet no illusions are held about inspiration's instrument: "for fallible to fail, is no more than for frail to be broken; and for mortal to die."[4] Every human being and all human beings together, without exception, are fallible, prone to corruption from partial interests and narrow-mindedness, and therefore in need of correction from others, their taken-for-granted views properly subject to change over the course of time, and properly laid open to challenge from competing views of their contemporaries. God need not,

2. W. C. Braithwaite, *The Beginnings of Quakerism* (1923), p. 109, cited in Geoffrey Nuttall, *The Holy Spirit in Puritan Faith and Experience* (Chicago and London: University of Chicago Press, 1992 [1947]), p. 54.

3. H. R. McAdoo, *The Spirit of Anglicanism* (London: Adam and Charles Black, 1965), p. 89, citing the Cambridge Platonist Benjamin Whichcote, *Whichcote's Aphorisms* (1753), p. 1168.

4. McAdoo, *The Spirit of Anglicanism*, citing Whichcote's *Select Sermons* (1698), p. 323.

however, work independently of these facts of the matter, from outside them, but in them: "Doth the Spirit work on a man as on a beast or a stone? and cause you to speak as a clock that striketh it knoweth not what; or play on man's soul, as upon an instrument of music that hath neither knowledge of the melody, nor any pleasure in it? No, the Spirit of God supposeth nature, and worketh on man as man; by exciting your own understanding and will to do their parts."[5] "The Spirit of God moveth according to our principles, it openeth our understandings to see that it is best to trust in God; it moveth so sweetly, as if it were an inbred principle, and all with our own spirits."[6]

Bucking Enlightenment trends in the understanding of divine agency, God's working is not identified here with exceptional, occasional interventions that interrupt the ordinary operations of natural processes. One deceives oneself "to suspect the special presence of God in anything vehement or unusual."[7] It is wrong to think that "faith and sanctity are not to be had by study and reason, but by supernatural inspiration. . . . Faith and sanctity are not miracles, but brought to pass by education, discipline, correction, and other natural ways."[8] God is as much at work in the ordinary run of things as in unusual happenings, because the usual run of things is not being understood from the first in naturalistic terms, as if what happened there took place on its own, apart from God's agency. "They are not to be blamed as neglecting or undervaluing the idea of grace . . . who remind men that they should use reason and the principles of creation, and those who 'take offence to hear reason spoken of' are mistaken, for these things have a more than human foundation."[9]

If human life is what it is (for all the corrupting influence of sin) because of God's working and not in independent self-sufficiency from God, there is no reason to think that God is working more the less we are. And that means we cannot rule out a divine sanction for beliefs we come up

---

5. R. Baxter, *Practical Works*, vol. 4 (Orme ed., 1830), p. 226, cited in Nuttall, *Holy Spirit*, p. 169.

6. R. Sibbes, *Works*, 1:197, cited in Nuttall, *Holy Spirit*, p. 36.

7. H. More, *Enthusiasmus Triumphatus* (1712), pp. 11-12, cited in Truman Guy Steffan, "The Social Argument Against Enthusiasm (1650-1660)," *Studies in English* (University of Texas Publication, 1941): 52.

8. T. Hobbes, *Leviathan* (1651), p. 172, cited in Steffan, "Social Argument," p. 58.

9. McAdoo, *Spirit of Anglicanism*, p. 87, citing Whichcote, *Several Discourses* (1701), no. XXIII.

with on 'our own' — say, on the basis of the ordinary operations of our reason in conversation with others who disagree with us. The very fact that we come up with them in that way does not exclude their having divine sanction; God might very well be behind them for all that. So, for example, if God's laws for human life are given indirectly through human processes of judgment over time, it might very well be that the "voice of men" is "the sentence of God himself."[10]

God is likely to be behind the beliefs we hold, however, only in their very status as temporary, changing, site-specific, fallible truths. If God usually works with, rather than overriding, the ordinary character of human life, we have every reason to think that God sanctions thereby the limited, fallible, correctable truths typical of it. It is as changing and defensible truths, then, that human claims would gain divine sanction. Rather than split off divine sanction from the mutable with human origins, we can admit that what God wants for human life can be altered, corrected, and improved over time to suit changing circumstances. For example, it is the subject matter and not the source of a law that establishes whether it holds in the same form for all time; a law for mutable people is therefore itself properly alterable whether God or mere human decision is behind it.[11]

Divine sanction would in this way not bring with it an insistence on indefeasible certainty or uncontestable veracity. Something about the human is changed through the workings of the Spirit, but it is not the fully finite character of our acts. Surely divine influence here is for the purpose of remedying the sinfulness of human operations. But removal of sin means not the discarding of the finite human character of our operations, but their elevation, strengthening, purification, and improvement. Something is different about spirit-filled human processes, but it no longer makes sense to think of this difference in terms of something more than and added to the human. Instead, the difference is something in these human processes themselves, part and parcel of them. Human processes, for example, with a new direction, rather than the chaotic formlessness of many uncoordinated voices or the shapeless convergence of multiple causal trajectories. As Michael Welker affirms in his contribution to this volume: "the multicontextual and polyphonic presence of the Spirit does by no

---

10. R. Hooker, *Of the Laws of Ecclesiastical Polity* (1593), bk. 1.8.3.
11. See Hooker, *Laws*, 1.15.3.

means create chaos and lead to the loss of clear orientation."[12] Something definite emerges from our acts in history, as we work together and against one another, something that is not fully imaginable, controllable, or fore-seeable by us — certainly not predictable from any one of our personal perspectives as individuals. Different too is the shape of human processes, their new communal organization. "[A] complex and lively community [is] constituted by the Holy Spirit."[13] Instead of short-circuiting the messy course of human history in a rush for certainty or narrowly channeling history's pluriform course with a demand for control, one can continue in such human processes patiently and without anxiety, in the confidence that, even in our ignorance of it, God's Spirit is making its way in and through them.

Let's review the argument between the first and second ways of ap-pealing to the Spirit in terms of the modern problematic I have just been discussing, in the hopes of clarifying things a bit further. Most generally, it is the mediation of the workings of God in human life that leaves religious claims to divine validation open to question and in that way threatens to overturn the whole apple cart in which unquestioned assurance and ap-peals to divine sanction typically go together: both critics and defenders of the faith who appeal to the unmediated working of the Spirit accept the idea that the primary point of the appeal to divine validation is to main-tain an unquestionable authority for religious claims. Understanding the same challenge more narrowly: it is the existence of any inferential process at all when making appeals to divine validation of religious claims that opens them to question, that allows for the entrance of the question, But how can you be sure? Perhaps it is only a mere human being speaking, from a limited and interested point of view, and not God?

Appeals to the direct, immediate working of the Spirit on individual persons are from this point of view an attempt to regain an unquestionable self-evidence for the divine sanction of religious claims, using the resources available for this purpose in the empirical philosophies and scientific meth-ods of the day. This is not mere hearsay; I am not forced to put my trust in the word of others (the writers of scripture or church teachers) about what

12. Cf. M. Welker, "The Spirit in Philosophical, Theological, and Interdisciplinary Perspectives," pp. 221-32 herein.

13. Cf. Welker, "The Spirit in Philosophical, Theological, and Interdisciplinary Per-spectives."

God has done, a trust that might conceivably be misplaced. Nor am I left to draw the conclusion of divine direction of human life from indirect evidence (say, from the effects of the Spirit's workings on human life). Instead, God came to me directly, and I had the immediate experience of God working on me to change my views and my life. I have no more reason to question this than I have to question that the light shines when I see it; the experience itself is self-validating in an uncontestable way.

> How do you know the word to be the word? It carrieth proof and evidence in itself. It is an evidence that the fire is hot to him that feeleth it, and that the sun shineth to him that looks on it; how much more doth the word. . . . I am sure I felt it, it warmed my heart, and converted me. There is no other principle to prove the word, but experience from the working of it.[14]

> For as in natural things, you know, that by the same light whereby I see the Sun, by the same light I know that I see him: So there is in the very manifestation of God to the soule, it carries a witnesse in it self, it is so cleare, that when I have it, though I never had it before, and I cannot demonstratively speak a word what it is, yet I know as it is Gods sight, so I know as I see him.[15]

> Let the Sun arise in the firmament, and there is no need of Witnesses to prove and confirme unto a seeing man that it is day. . . . Let the least child bring a candle into a roome that before was darke, and it would be madnesse to go about to prove with substantiall Witnesses, men of Gravity and Authority, that Light is brought in. Doth it not evince its selfe, with an Assurance above all that can be obtained by any Testimony whatever?[16]

If you weren't there to experience these things — and by definition you weren't since these were experiences that singled me out personally, expe-

14. Sibbes, *Works* (ed. A. B. Gorsart, 1862), 4:334-35, 363; 2:495, cited in Nuttall, *Holy Spirit*, p. 39.

15. W. Craddock, *Gospel-Holinesse* (1651), "To the Reader," and p. 32, cited in Nuttall, *Holy Spirit*, p. 40.

16. J. Owen, *Of the Divine Originall, Authority, self-evidencing Light, and Power of the Scriptures* (1659), pp. 72-73, cited in Nuttall, *Holy Spirit*, p. 41.

riences shielded from public view in the depths of my interior life — you have no grounds to challenge them — no more than a blind man has the right to question what a sighted person sees.

> I can no more convey a sense of this difference (between Reason and Spirit) into any soule, that hath not seen these two Lights shining in it self: than I can convey the difference between Salt and Sugar; to him who hath never tasted sweet or sharp. These things are discerned only by the exercise of senses.[17]

Upholders of the second view of the Spirit — even when they share this same empiricist bent — typically attack the self-evidence of the Spirit's influence on individual persons and work to reinstate fallible human judgments, often from public evidence, into every appeal to divine sanction. Even in the case of a private revelation of the Spirit to me personally, beyond anything found in scripture or church teachings and therefore beyond the range of those usual public tests, I am drawing the conclusion that the Spirit is at work on me from the evidence of my own private experience — for example, from the overwhelming way I become convinced of something, out of the blue, on the occasion of reading a Bible verse, in the prayerful search for divine direction, subsequently confirmed for me by my ability to lead a markedly different way of life. The inferential process of human judgment here properly admits of question — perhaps even more than in other forms of religious authorization since I am thrown on my own resources in forming these judgments without the help and correction of others in making them. "It is true, reason is fallible; or . . . subject to abuse and deception; . . . but if reason . . . be fallible, so are the pretences of revelation subject to abuse; and what are we now the nearer?"[18] My vanity, my pride — even my simple credulity — might easily be at work here leading me astray, making me think I have been touched by the Spirit when I have not.

Although "revelations and inspirations seem to fall upon us from heaven, they did ascend from the earth, from our selves, from our own melancholy, and pride, or too much homeliness and familiarity in our ac-

---

17. P. Sterry, *The Spirits Conviction of Sinne* (1645), p. 24, cited in Nuttall, *Holy Spirit*, p. 139.

18. J. Taylor, *Works* (ed. R. Heber, 1828), 11:462, cited in McAdoo, *Spirit of Anglicanism*, pp. 64-65.

cesses and conversation with God, or a facility in believing, or in often dreaming the same thing."[19] Appeals to the direct working of the Spirit on individual persons are therefore no more able to avoid critical questioning than any other sort of appeal to divine sanction — say, appeals to divine sanction in virtue of conformity with scripture or church teaching. "[T]his guide of his *light within* [must be brought] to the trial. God when he makes the prophet does not unmake the man. He leaves all his faculties in the natural state, to enable hum to judge of his inspirations, whether they be of divine original or no."[20] The second account of the Spirit's working would simply accept (with critics of the faith) the unavoidable fallibility of religious ways of authorizing human claims, but understand this (against both the critics and the faithful appealing to an unmediated personal working of the Spirit on them) as part and parcel of the very old view of what appeals to the Spirit bring with them — the need for a complex process of testing and discernment in community.

> [I]f this internal light . . . be conformable to the principles of reason, or to the word of God . . . we may safely receive it for true . . . if it receive no testimony nor evidence from either of these rules, we cannot take it for revelation . . . till we have some other mark that it is revelation, besides our believing that it is so. Thus we see the holy men of old, who had revelations from God, had something else besides that internal light of assurance in their own minds to testify to them that it was from God. They were not left to their own persuasions alone . . . but had outward signs to convince them of the Author of those revelations. And when they were to convince others, they had a power given them to justify the truth of their commission.[21]

Appeals to the Spirit as an Attack on Religious Authorities

But the story that I've told so far is inadequate — even at the level of gross generality at which it remains. Appeals to the Spirit in modern times, as in

---

19. J. Donne, *Fifty Sermons* (1649), p. 201, cited in Steffan, "Social Argument," p. 47.

20. J. Locke, *An Essay Concerning Human Understanding* (ed. Alexander Campbell Fraser, 1959), bk. 4, ch. 19.14.

21. Locke, *Essay*, 4.19.15.

earlier ones, are generally not for the purpose of supplementing and shoring up contested forms of religious authority, but ways of furthering that attack. The direct inspiration of the Spirit becomes, then, an alternative source of religious authority with which to contest the usual ones — appeals to the authority of scripture or church teaching or the God-given light of reason as that might find expression in the long-standing opinion of educated clerical elites. Perhaps most moderately expressed in the words of the early Puritan Richard Sibbes:

> There is a great difference between us and our adversaries . . . They say we must believe . . . because of the church. I say no. The church, we believe, hath a kind of working here, but that is in the last place. For God himself in his word, is chief. The inward arguments from the word itself, and from the Spirit are the next. The church is the remotest witness, the remotest help of all.[22]

Or more radically by John Owen:

> There is no need of Tradition . . . no need of the Authority of any Churches. . . . A Church may beare up the light, it is not the light. It beares witnesse to it, but kindles not one divine beame to further its discovery.[23]

And more radically still by Peter Sterry:

> The Papists . . . perswade us to receive the testimony, not of the Spirit but of the Church, for a Touchstone of Truth. . . . Thus the Church's authority, not the Demonstration of the Holy Ghost, shall be the light of Faith to Truth. . . . But wee need no visible Judge on earth, to determine our consciences; what is Scripture; what is the essence of Scripture. We have an invisible Judge and Witnesse in our own breasts.[24]

Appeals to the direct personal inspiration of the Spirit are not, then, so much answering challenges posed to the usual sources of religious au-

22. Sibbes, *Works*, 3:374, cited in Nuttall, *Holy Spirit*, p. 43.
23. Owen, *Divine Originall*, pp. 44, 76, cited in Nuttall, *Holy Spirit*, pp. 43-44.
24. Sterry, *Spirits Conviction*, p. 28, cited in Nuttall, *Holy Spirit*, p. 44.

thority (as I've been suggesting so far) as putting themselves in league with such challenges. They are generally part of a minority Christian attack on those established religious views and practices that use scripture or tradition as a defense against criticism. Appeals to the direct working of the Spirit are proffered as a means of prophetic dissent against otherwise entrenched scripture-based religious views or traditional church teachings. They also work as a defense against the persecution of dissenting religious opinion when such persecution is authorized and fomented by the idea that the majority view has the divine sanction of either scripture or church teaching behind it.

This remains, nonetheless, a distinctively modern dynamic. It does not easily fit, in the first place, with the analysis of charismatic-versus-institutional authority so often employed, usefully I believe, in discussions of earlier periods in the church. In the early church, the authority of those holding institutional office might be contested by individuals claiming special gifts from the Spirit of wisdom or moral and religious virtuosity.[25] But these are qualities that, for all their personal character, are publicly evident and communally recognized. Their acquisition, moreover, is generally recognized to require slow and patient processes of training — for example, ascetic disciplines. Nothing rides, in short, on their interiority or lack of mediation by ordinary human processes.

What the insistence on the latter does is make the attack on other forms of religious authority much more thoroughgoing — more extensive and fundamental — than anything previously seen. The attack on public mediations of the Spirit is no longer equivalent to a simple attack on institutional forms of authority, on the authority one has in virtue of the office or role one has in the church. Nor does it only bring with it the ability to bypass the usual readings of scripture or sacramental forms when communicating with the Spirit, and thereby move beyond them to more profound truths about God and more rigorous requirements of human life. It is also an attack on the authority of all communally or socially validated forms of intellectual, religious, or moral achievement that take their rise from long, slow processes of training or learning. It is in short a way of issuing a religious challenge to all the usual sources of religious authority on the part of persons without any obvious, communally recognized gifts of the Spirit —

---

25. For these conflicts between different sources of authority in the early church, see, e.g., R. Williams, *Arius* (Grand Rapids: Eerdmans, 2002).

those without learning, and without any socially recognized graces of a religious or moral sort. Appealing to the direct influence of the Spirit upon them, they need not wait for the development and recognition of such gifts through the usual channels controlled by church authorities. And the hidden interiority of the Spirit's working effectively deflects attention from their actual publicly recognized personal characters; it is a working that makes up for their lack of authority according to commonly accepted standards on all other social, educational, moral, and religious fronts.

The range of persons with the capacity to claim religious authority is not only expanded here beyond the range of what was hitherto possible — beyond, for example, typical fights previously between, on the one hand, those claiming authority in virtue of their moral standing or their leadership of, in effect, a school of Christian wise men, and, on the other hand, those claiming the authority of office, however weak their preaching or lax their moral lives. This expansion of who can claim authority presupposes a more thoroughgoing attack on the usual sources of religious authority themselves across the board. Appeals to the Spirit are not a way of taking sides in a controversy between one commonly accepted way of justifying religious authority versus another commonly accepted one, in which the primary question is how to rank them in relation to one another. Instead, an appeal to the direct workings of the Spirit amounts to a fundamental questioning of all of them.

The extensiveness of this attack on the usual sources of religious authority — whether person specific or institutional — has everything to do with the fundamental level at which sources of religious authority were challenged in modern times.[26] A general skepticism about the usual sources of religious authorization was fomented from within the Christian fold by Reformation controversies that pitted scripture (and private conscience in the reading of it) against established church traditions, in ways that apparently precluded argumentative settlement. The controversies took place here at too fundamental a level to be effectively resolved. The most basic or bedrock criteria of religious truth, merely presumed hitherto, became subject to questioning by one's co-religionists in ways that only encouraged a skeptical regress of mutual recrimination: How do you know church teaching is reliable? Church teaching purports to conform to

---

26. See R. Popkin, *The History of Scepticism from Erasmus to Spinoza* (Berkeley, Calif.: University of California Press, 1979), ch. 1.

scripture, but perhaps it does so only according to a corrupt tradition of interpretation that makes a habit out of misreading it. The clear teaching of scripture might trump church traditions but what, besides the normative principles for reading it supplied by the church, is to prevent wildly disparate and arbitrary interpretations of Scripture according to the unconstrained opinions of individual fancy? Without argumentative avenues of resolution, these intractable disputes over religious authority break out into a century of violence — religious persecution of dissenting views and religious warfare — that only further discredits and undermines all the usual sources of religious authorization. Unchecked religious fervor or zeal for competing religious viewpoints that divine sanction forbids any of the warring parties from questioning promotes the use of force on all sides and becomes, thereby, a simple recipe for ongoing bloodshed.

Appeals to the immediate working of the Spirit, occurring as they so often do (e.g., in the course of the English Civil War) among unlettered and socially disreputable lay religious dissenters, might be understood, in keeping with these worries about the violence-prone character of the usual sources of divine sanction, to be an attempt to break open the ossified rigidity of religious claims made on the usual grounds.[27] New voices need to be included; religious views, held onto ever so tightly by way of appeals to an unbending scriptural witness or unwavering church tradition, need to be open for the unpredictable revisions of a Spirit on the move again in the present day, in expected persons and places. The stultifying fixity of a written word or infallible teaching office would in this way be contested so as to invalidate the use of force against dissenting religious minorities.

Understanding the appeal to an immediate working of the Spirit in individual lives in this way — as a counter to authoritarian justifications of religious persecution — it could be that the second view of the Spirit is merely designed to blunt, even crush, its prophetic spirit. The second view of how the Spirit works is not directed with the same force as the first against the usual sources of religious authority; it seems to dull the very attack on those sources that the first appeal to the Spirit makes possible, by now extending the workings of Spirit to the usual sources themselves. The

27. See, e.g., M. Walzer, *The Revolution of the Saints* (Cambridge, Mass.: Harvard University Press, 1965); and C. Hill, *The World Turned Upside Down* (London: Penguin, 1975).

Spirit is not simply at work directly in individual persons to say a new thing, but at work in the institutional forms of the established churches, in the reason of an educated clergy entitled by their training to draw conclusions about how scripture is to be read, in all sorts of patient processes that require skills formed over time by some people more than others, in fundamentally unequal fashion.

No doubt the second understanding of the workings of the Spirit can have a conservative effect.[28] It can be used to restrict the workings of the Spirit to the regular, predictable channels of church tradition and church life — for example, to sacraments routinely administered by an ordained clergy. Anything out of the ordinary — anything novel or 'singular,' in the language of the day — becomes in this way suspect, simply because it fails to conform to the common and the run of the mill. The unusual is taken for a sign, not of the Spirit, but of the demonic. Advocates of the first view of the Spirit would then be holding out for a free Spirit against its domesticated captivity in rigidly controlled institutional forms. What they properly object to, in the way the second account of the Spirit reconciles the Spirit with institutional forms, is this:

> the infinitely abounding spirit of God, which blows when and where it listeth, and ministers in Christians according to the gift, and prophesies according to the will of the Almighty God . . . is subject to the Laws and ordinances of men . . . to outward ceremonies, as Ordination, etc. God must not speak till man give him leave; not teach nor Preach, but whom man allows, and approves, and ordains.[29]

This second account of the workings of the Spirit can also, however, be an effort to do better what the first view is trying to do: attack dogmatism and fanaticism in claims for divine sanction. The conservative potential of the second understanding of the Spirit is often altered, indeed, in the confrontation with so-called enthusiasm, so as to incorporate its concerns and give them their due. Rather than attack the usual sources with unmitigated ferocity from the outside (as the account of the immediate workings of the Spirit suggests), the appeal to the Spirit on the second view would be a way of loosening up the usual sources of religious authority by increasing

---

28. See Steffan, "Social Argument," pp. 53-60, for examples.
29. J. Saltmarsh, *Sparkles of Glory* (1647), p. v, cited in Nuttall, *Holy Spirit*, p. 84.

their flexibility, tolerance for diversity of opinion, and openness to change. By talking about the Spirit at work in them, one would be trying to increase the complexity of the usual sources to bring about their greater inclusiveness and internal diversity. More open-ended processes of religious formation would ensue, with stability no longer secured, in a top down fashion, through enforced redundancy and mechanical repetition of a linear sort.

So as to reconcile it with the anti-authoritarianism of the first, the second way of appealing to the Spirit opens the usual sources of authority up for criticism on grounds that, while requiring practice, are commonly exercised in some form or other by everyone. For example, consenting to the teachings of established church authorities is a particular case of putting one's trust in what other people say. Rather than rejecting that sort of authority altogether and relying on your own personal experience — what the Spirit has witnessed to you personally — one can subject those authorities to critical standards for trust employed in everyday life: Are they in a better position than you to know? Do they have reason to lie to you? Are their faculties impaired or their views compromised by moral corruption and narrow self-interest? Or when considering the Bible as an authoritative report about the life that Jesus led, one may use the usual standards for witnesses in common trials. "In the testimony of others, is to be considered: 1. The number. 2. The integrity. 3. The skill of the witnesses. 4. The design of the author, where it is a testimony out of a book cited. 5. The consistency of the parts, and circumstances of the relation. 6. Contrary testimonies."[30]

The Spirit at work everywhere here — in the teachings of the church, in one's personal religious experience, and in the complex processes of bringing them together for purposes of mutual adjudication — would in this way only open up the life of the church to greater flexibility and greater appreciation for the surprise of the new. Taking the other route — reserving appeal to the Spirit, as the first view does, to cases where the Spirit comes directly to individual persons — tends, to the contrary as we have seen, only to solidify the association of the highest forms of religious authority with simple self-evidence of an uncontestable sort. The Spirit trumps all those other purported authorities because I cannot doubt it; my experience of the Spirit speaks for itself in an indubitable fashion. Far from countering fanatical zeal and a dogmatism of religious viewpoint that ex-

30. Locke, *Essay,* 4.15.4.

cludes all possibility of criticism from the outside, appeal to the direct workings of the Spirit in one's personal experience would in this way simply reinstate fanaticism and dogmatism on new grounds. Uncritical fervor for what the Spirit has revealed to you personally would enter the fray, along with all the other competing claimants to similarly absolute forms of divine sanction, bringing along with it its very own justifications for violence. Enthusiasm would only aid and abet that "zeal for opinions that hath fill'd our hemisphear with smoke and darkness . . . by dear experience we know the fury of those flames it hath kindled" — a reference to religious warfare in England, and elsewhere no doubt, in the sixteenth and seventeenth centuries.[31]

Chastened by this criticism of its own violent and dogmatic potential, insistence on the immediate workings of the Spirit in the interior of individual lives can itself easily be modified to stress the need for external tests and complex public forms of accountability. Both sides in the modern controversy over the workings of the Spirit would in this way be transformed in a kind of dialectical relation of opposition to one another.[32] External critique becomes the impetus for internal reforms among advocates of the immediate workings of the Spirit. Scripture is one such public test of long standing:

> The breath of the Spirit in us is suitable to the Spirit's breathing in the Scriptures; the same Spirit doth not breathe contrary notions. But there be, you will say, strong Illusions. True. Bring them therefore to some rules of discerning. Bring all your joy, and peace, and confidence to the word. They go together. As a pair of indentures, one answers another.[33]

Rational assessment is another:

> [I]f we give to reason, memory, study, books, methods, forms, etc., but their proper place in subordination to Christ and to his Spirit, they are

---

31. J. Glanville, *The Vanity of Dogmatizing* (1661), p. 209, cited in Steffan, "Social Argument," p. 41.

32. See Heyd, "Reaction to Enthusiasm," pp. 262, 273, 276, 280; and J. R. Jacob and M. C. Jacob, "The Anglican Origins of Modern Science: The Metaphysical Foundations of the Whig Constitution," *Isis* 71, no. 257 (June 1980): 254, 255, 258, 267.

33. Sibbes, *Works*, 5:427, 441, cited in Nuttall, *Holy Spirit*, p. 43.

so far from being quenchers of the Spirit, that they are necessary in their places, and such means as we must use, if ever we will expect the Spirit's help. . . . He that hath both the Spirit of sanctification, and acquired gifts of knowledge together, is the complete Christian, and likely to know much more, than he that hath either of these alone.[34]

The so-called "primitivism and pragmatism" of the Pentecostal movement — supernatural workings of the Spirit amidst great organizational savvy and rather tight institutional controls on their expression — is one contemporary example of such a drift in the direction of the second view.[35] The more this sort of thing happens the more the first view of the workings of the Spirit becomes indistinguishable, indeed, in all but emphasis, from the second.

Import for the Religion-Science Dialogue

The first view of the immediate workings of the Spirit is clearly influenced, as I mentioned earlier in passing, by the empirical philosophies and scientific methods that took their rise in the modern period. This is an "experimental" approach in its reliance on personal experience and its suspicion of traditional and textual authorities. But certainly with the end of the English Civil War and the restoration of the establishment church along with many of the old structures of national governance, scientific opinion in Britain, as represented by the Royal Society, clearly aligned itself against any associations with "enthusiasm."[36] "Scientific progress would come through painstaking inquiry, the collection of evidence, and the testing of hypotheses. Knowledge then was not . . . the result of . . . God's direct revelation to the saints. God instead revealed Himself indirectly, [by means that] required close study in order to bear fruit."[37] "Patient, industrious

---

34. Baxter, *Works*, 5:567 and 20:179, cited in Nuttall, *Holy Spirit*, p. 84.

35. See G. Wacker, *Heaven Below: Early Pentecostals and American Culture* (Cambridge, Mass.: Harvard University Press, 2001). See also in this volume: Wacker, "Early Pentecostals and the Study of Popular Religious Movements," and M. Poloma, "The Future of American Pentecostal Identity."

36. This is the major thesis of Jacob and Jacob, "Anglican Origins." See also Heyd, "Reaction to Enthusiasm," pp. 272-73, 277.

37. Jacob and Jacob, "Anglican Origins," p. 256.

scrutiny" was necessary to uncover the workings of God in the order of nature; there would be no "easy shortcuts" to the truth, as enthusiasts hoped for via direct revelation, on either religious or scientific matters.[38]

Indirect revelation in the workings of the world, in keeping with the second understanding of the Spirit, requires methods of inquiry typical, then, of modern science. But this resonance between science and the second view of the Spirit is only heightened by the sort of conclusions about the world that present-day science draws. This is a world of "intrinsic unpredictability," whose characteristically "open grain" nevertheless has the "self-organizing power to generate spontaneously large-scale patterns of remarkably ordered behavior," in and through its very "contingent happenstance."[39] This is a world in which the Spirit might work "modestly," in continuous fashion throughout the totality of natural processes.[40] Contrary to the often socially and politically conservative character of the Royal Society after the 1650s, this is also a world open, as the second view of the Spirit insists, to an unpredictable future, beyond any ultimate human control and beyond any self-serving human interest in fixed orders or rigid institutional mechanisms for enforcing the status quo.[41]

38. Jacob and Jacob, "Anglican Origins," p. 256; Heyd, "Reaction to Enthusiasm," p. 277. R. Boyle is a fine example of this opinion. See J. R. Jacob, *Robert Boyle and the English Revolution* (New York: Burt Franklin, 1977), pp. 98-112.

39. See J. Polkinghorne, "The Hidden Spirit and the Cosmos," pp. 169-82 herein.

40. See Welker, "Spirit in Philosophical, Theological, and Interdisciplinary Perspectives." This is a central claim of Polkinghorne, "Hidden Spirit."

41. Jacob and Jacob, "Anglican Origins," especially pp. 253, 265-67.

II. The Spirit in Pentecostal Theology

The Kingdom and the Power:
Spirit Baptism in Pentecostal
and Ecumenical Perspective

FRANK D. MACCHIA

Pentecostalism began at the turn of the twentieth century as a child of the American Holiness movement. The Holiness movement took from John Wesley his quest for "perfection" (unwavering loyalty of the will to the love of Christ) but, under the influence of American revivalism, came to view this as a crisis experience called the "baptism in the Holy Spirit." Christians were called through Spirit baptism to full sanctification by surrendering all to Christ. Pentecostalism arose later out of the Holiness movement basically from an alternative interpretation of Spirit baptism. Influenced profoundly by the narrative of Luke's Acts, Pentecostals came to view Spirit baptism as an empowerment for witness as evidenced by heightened participation in extraordinary gifts of the Spirit, especially speaking in tongues (Acts 1:8; 2:4). The sanctification experience was then popularly viewed by the Pentecostals as *preparatory* to the empowering experience of Spirit baptism. Those who joined Pentecostalism from outside of the strict boundaries of the Holiness movement also accepted Spirit baptism as an empowerment for witness but did so without recognizing the need for a dramatic sanctification experience as an intermediate step (sanctification being viewed by these "baptistic" Pentecostals as the "finished work" of Christ accessible in the Christian's gradual growth in grace). This debate within early Pentecostalism over the nature of sanctification was eventually overshadowed by the fact that Spirit baptism as an empowerment for gifted witness became the hallmark of the movement. Driven by this experience of Spirit baptism, Pentecostalism spread rapidly to become arguably the largest family of Protestant churches in the world.

When one thinks of Pentecostal theology, therefore, what usually comes to mind is the doctrine of the baptism in the Holy Spirit as an experience of empowerment for Christian service evidenced by speaking in tongues and distinct from both Christian conversion and water baptism (or the sacraments of Christian initiation). Of course, not all Pentecostals historically and globally understand Spirit baptism in this way. For example, Oneness Pentecostals (who hold to a uniquely christocentric and modalistic understanding of the Trinity) view Spirit baptism as the gift of the Spirit given in integral connection with a Christian initiation that involves repentance, faith, and water baptism in Jesus' Name. With this diversity admitted, I do think that enough Pentecostals globally hold to the belief that Spirit baptism is a charismatic empowerment for service distinct from conversion or Christian initiation to qualify this belief as distinctively Pentecostal.

This essay arises out of the conviction that the Pentecostal experience holds significant potential for expanding standard understandings of Spirit baptism so as to involve an experience of prophetic calling and empowerment. Yet, I am convinced that this Pentecostal contribution to an ecumenical pneumatology will inspire Pentecostals to expand their own understanding of Spirit baptism. My goal, therefore, is to suggest that the Pentecostal doctrine of Spirit baptism can be renewed so as to contribute to an ecumenical pneumatology in a way that will allow other voices to challenge and expand their own theological distinctive. First, we need to discuss the place of the doctrine in Pentecostal theology so as to create a meaningful setting for the renewal of the doctrine in the future of Pentecostal theological discourse.

The Place of Spirit Baptism in Pentecostal Theology

With some qualification, I think it is fair to say that the doctrine of the baptism in the Holy Spirit has been globally the "crown jewel" of Pentecostal theology. I agree with Simon Chan that Pentecostals are not in agreement over all of their distinctives but that "what comes through over and over again in their discussions and writings is a certain kind of spiritual experience of an intense, direct, and overwhelming nature centering on the person of Christ which they schematize as 'baptism in the Holy Spirit.'"[1]

Spirit baptism, however, has recently declined in significance among Pentecostal theologians. Part of the reason for this is that historical research has tended to shift the axis of Pentecostal distinctives away from Spirit baptism to other theological interests. Walter Hollenweger's research revealed a vast doctrinal diversity among Pentecostals worldwide and even within the U.S. both now and from the beginning of the movement. His classic, *The Pentecostals,* fell like a bombshell in the late sixties and early seventies upon geographically sheltered Pentecostal groups surprised by the doctrinal diversity of the movement globally.[2]

Hollenweger not only diversified the doctrinal distinctives of Pentecostal theology, but he also shifted what was most distinctive about Pentecostal theology from doctrinal points to how theology itself was conceived. He wrote, "A description of these theologies cannot begin with their concepts. I have rather to choose another way and describe how they are conceived, carried and might finally be born."[3] Hollenweger focused not on doctrinal issues but on the oral and narrative nature of theological conception and discourse among Pentecostals. This shift in focus made Spirit baptism seem like an accident of history, a holdover from the Holiness movement that is not at all significant to what is most distinctive about Pentecostal theology. The narrow and ecumenically irrelevant understanding of Pentecostalism as a revivalistic "tongues movement" was replaced in Hollenweger's work with a Pentecostalism that seemed ecumenically relevant, at the forefront of a way of doing theology that is not burdened with post-Enlightenment standards of rational discourse.

While recognizing the value of Hollenweger's approach to Pentecostal theology, one must also note that doctrinal issues cannot be so easily detached from the symbolic framework that shapes how a movement experiences God and thinks theologically. Furthermore, Spirit baptism is not only a doctrine but a metaphor that can function imaginatively in ways

1. S. Chan, *Pentecostal Theology and the Christian Spiritual Tradition* (Sheffield: Sheffield Academic Press, 2003), p. 7.

2. W. J. Hollenweger's stated purpose was "to discover with Pentecostals the rich variety of the Pentecostal movement." "Preface to the First and Second Editions," *The Pentecostals* (2nd ed.; Peabody, Mass.: Hendrickson, 1988), p. xxi.

3. W. J. Hollenweger, "Theology of the New World," *The Expository Times* 87 (May 1976): 228.

other than doctrinal conceptualization. Of course, we cannot deny that there was doctrinal diversity early on and historically among Pentecostals globally. But this diversity does not mean that there was not some kind of coherent, distinctive theological vision among Pentecostals. Donald Dayton and D. William Faupel[4] accepted the fact that Pentecostals were diverse doctrinally and, therefore, not just about Spirit baptism and tongues, but they also showed that there was a kind of theologically coherent understanding of God's redemptive work through Christ and the Holy Spirit in early Pentecostal theology that tended to stay with the majority of those active in the movement. Dayton showed that early Pentecostal theology advocated a fourfold devotion to Jesus as Savior, Spirit Baptizer, Healer, and Coming King. D. William Faupel highlighted the final element of this fourfold gospel as that which was decisive, namely, the eschatological. Pentecostalism was mainly about the latter "rain" of the Spirit to restore the gifts and power of Pentecost to the church in order to empower global mission before Christ's soon return. Pentecostals viewed the church as a "missionary fellowship," which (in the words of Grant Wacker) was "riding the crest of the wave of history" toward the end of the latter days of the Spirit.

It may be argued that what is really being displaced in the research above is not so much Spirit baptism biblically presented in its broad eschatological, redemptive, and charismatic dimensions, but rather the narrow definition of Spirit baptism that most Pentecostals used to define their high-voltage experience with God, especially as evidenced by speaking in tongues. Not since Harold Hunter's and Howard Ervin's theologies of Spirit baptism published nearly two decades ago[5] has there been a similar work written by a Pentecostal theologian. Steven J. Land's seminal effort at writing a Pentecostal theology, *Pentecostal Spirituality,* devotes no more than a few pages to the doctrine. He explicitly takes issue with Dale Bruner's description of Pentecostal theology as *"pneumatobaptistocentric"* (Spirit baptism centered). Land regards Bruner's description as "missing

4. D. W. Dayton, *Theological Roots of Pentecostalism* (Grand Rapids: Zondervan, 1988); D. William Faupel, *The Everlasting Gospel: The Significance of Eschatology in the Development of Pentecostal Thought* (Sheffield: Sheffield Academic Press, 1996).

5. H. D. Hunter, *Spirit Baptism: A Pentecostal Alternative* (Lanham, Md.: University Press of America, 1983); H. M. Ervin, *Conversion-Initiation and the Baptism in the Holy Spirit: A Critique of James D. G. Dunn, Baptism in the Holy Spirit* (Peabody, Mass.: Hendrickson, 1984).

the point altogether" concerning what is really distinctive about Pentecostal theology, which is in Land's view the sanctification of the affections as part of an eschatological passion for the kingdom of God yet to come.[6] Russell P. Spittler even wrote that the most popular understanding of Spirit baptism as "subsequent" to regeneration or Christian initiation is a "non-issue," since Pentecostals were more concerned with spiritual renewal than with creating a new *ordo salutis*.[7] In the context of historical theology, a recent book written on Spirit baptism by Pentecostal theologian Koo Dong Yun presents the popular classical Pentecostal treatment of this doctrine as little more than a historical curiosity.[8] Even the significant efforts by New Testament scholars Robert Menzies[9] and Roger Stronstad[10] to focus on the unique charismatic pneumatology of Luke in order to open up fresh possibilities for viewing Spirit baptism as prophetic or charismatic inspiration has received no significant response from the most prolific among contemporary Pentecostal theologians, who have focused on broad pneumatological themes toward the construction of an ecumenical pneumatology.

I affirm this ecumenical interest, and I have contributed to it. I have come recently, however, to wonder whether or not the displacement of Spirit baptism, the "crown jewel" of Christian experience, is a good idea. Spirit baptism is the metaphor used by John the Baptist to characterize and inaugurate the person and work of Jesus in the Gospels. We can also note that the metaphor is taken up in Acts to denote what happens at Pentecost as well. Paul makes at least one explicit reference to it in his letters (1 Cor. 12:13) and maybe implicit references as well (e.g., Eph. 4:10). Though the metaphor is somewhat ambiguous, is uniquely connected to John the Baptist's characterization of Jesus' ministry, and may have waned somewhat in use over the early decades of Christian proclamation, it has a

6. J. Land, *Pentecostal Spirituality: A Passion for the Kingdom* (Sheffield: Sheffield Academic Press, 1993), pp. 62-63.

7. R. P. Spittler, "Suggested Areas for Further Research in Pentecostal Studies," *Pneuma* 5:2 (Fall 1983): 51.

8. K. Dong Yun, *Baptism in the Holy Spirit: An Ecumenical Theology of Spirit Baptism* (Lanham, Md.: University Press of America, 2003), pp. 23-44.

9. R. Menzies, *Empowered for Witness: The Spirit in Luke-Acts* (Sheffield: Sheffield Academic Press, 1991).

10. R. Stronstad, *Charismatic Theology of St. Luke* (Peabody, Mass.: Hendrickson, 1984).

powerful place in the canon and Christian memory and deserves a greater role in Christian theology than it has gotten in the past.

Pentecostalism is a movement that has helped to bring this metaphor back to the center of our understanding of God's redemptive work in history. Especially in the light of the well-known *Geistvergessenheit* in the West, Spirit baptism can emerge as a powerful metaphor of the pneumatological substance of God's redemptive work through Christ (as Dabney has pointed out[11]). Should we give up this possibility? Why not expand the Pentecostal understanding of Spirit baptism so that it can function as an aid to the formation of a uniquely Pentecostal contribution to an ecumenical pneumatology? The Catholic Charismatic Peter Hocken suggested at a Society for Pentecostal Studies meeting in 1992 that it is possible to take the Pentecostal vision of the latter rain of the Spirit to expand the doctrine of Spirit baptism among Pentecostals pneumatologically and eschatologically.[12] I think it is also possible to mine the accent of our Wesleyan heritage on sanctification. In the remainder of this paper, I will begin a conversation toward the formation of such a project. First, we can discuss briefly major approaches to the doctrine of Spirit baptism. It is important to describe the dialogue partners who will be blessed by *and bless* the Pentecostals in the process of ecumenical exchange.

Spirit Baptism and Regeneration

Spirit baptism among many Reformed and/or Evangelical Christians has been defined as regeneration or new birth through a faith response to the proclamation of the gospel. Typically noted here is the contrast implied by John the Baptist between water and Spirit baptism when speaking of the ministry of Jesus ("I baptize in water *but* he . . ."). Spirit baptism is thus "repentance unto life" (Acts 11:18) or a figurative "baptism" into Christ by faith (1 Cor. 12:13) and not something formalized in a water rite or isolated as a separate stage of spiritual renewal or power.

Karl Barth held this view, noting that Spirit baptism is a liberation

---

11. L. Dabney, "Baptism in the Holy Spirit: Towards a Pneumatological Soteriology," *Society for Pentecostal Studies,* March 8-10, 2001, Oral Roberts University, Tulsa, Oklahoma.

12. P. Hocken, "Baptism in the Holy Spirit as Prophetic Statement," *Society for Pentecostal Studies,* Nov. 12-14, 1992, Assemblies of God Theological Seminary, Springfield, Missouri.

involving a radical change in a person, a passage from death to life.[13] As a Reformed theologian (and under the influence of his son Markus's book on baptism), Barth defended the freedom and sovereignty of the Spirit in Spirit baptism. Spirit baptism is not formalized in water baptism nor mediated by the church. The church "is neither author, dispenser, nor mediator of grace and its revelation."[14] The church can at best "participate as assistant and minister" in the "self-attestation or self-impartation of Jesus Christ himself" in the gospel. But Spirit baptism given in one's acceptance of the gospel by faith does call for water baptism as the church's fitting response to God's gracious self-giving.[15]

According to another classic treatment of Spirit baptism from this perspective by James Dunn, Spirit baptism is the bestowal of the Spirit that functions as God's decisive act of establishing Christian identity.[16] The Holy Spirit is the "nerve center" of the Christian life that marks one essentially as a Christian. The Spirit is given in connection with repentance and faith in the gospel, while water baptism bears an indirect relationship to Spirit baptism in the sense that water baptism functions as the fulfillment of one's act of repentance and faith.[17] Though critical of Pentecostal theology, Dunn gives some credence to Pentecostal theology by regarding Spirit baptism as having experiential and charismatic implications for the Christian life (at least eventually) and criticizes the mainline churches for reducing the experience of the Spirit to sacramental forms or psychological categories.[18] There are Pentecostal scholars, such as Gordon Fee and Russell Spittler, who have embraced Dunn's view of Spirit baptism and would, like Dunn, find value in the charismatic experience of the Spirit cherished by the Pentecostal heritage.

13. K. Barth, *Church Dogmatics*, IV/4, ed. G. W. Bromiley and T. F. Torrance (Edinburgh: T&T Clark, 1969), p. 18.

14. Barth, *Church Dogmatics*, IV/4, p. 32.

15. Barth, *Church Dogmatics*, IV/4.

16. J. D. G. Dunn, *The Baptism in the Holy Spirit: A Re-examination of the New Testament Teaching on the Gift of the Spirit in Relation to Pentecostalism Today* (London: SCM, 1970).

17. Dunn, *The Baptism in the Holy Spirit*, p. 97.

18. Dunn, *The Baptism in the Holy Spirit*, pp. 225-26, 229.

FRANK D. MACCHIA

Spirit Baptism and the Sacraments of Initiation

Those from sacramental traditions, such as Kilian McDonnell and George Montague, have sought to understand Spirit baptism as universally experienced among Christians through water baptism or the sacramental rites of initiation (baptism/confirmation and eucharist).[19] Jesus' reception of the Spirit at his baptism thus becomes paradigmatic of the connection between water baptism and the reception of the Spirit among Christians (Acts 2:38; 19:5-6; and 1 Cor. 12:13, which is understood literally as water baptism).[20] There is but "one baptism" in water and Spirit (Eph. 4:5). We are buried with Christ "through baptism," implying an intimate relationship between water baptism and our identification with Christ (Rom. 6:4). But, like Dunn, McDonnell and Montague grant validity to the Pentecostal movement by regarding Spirit baptism as linked in the New Testament and the writings of the church fathers to charismatic experience. In the view of McDonnell and Montague, sacramental grace given in Christian initiation will eventually (either at the moment of initiation or later) burst forth in experiences of charismatic power. Though Pentecostals in their view have a faulty *theology* of Spirit baptism by detaching it wrongly from sacramental initiation, Pentecostals do validly call the church to the *experience* of Spirit baptism in life.[21] This view became popular among charismatics in the mainstream churches.

There are Pentecostals, such as Simon Chan, who have been attracted to this doctrine of Spirit baptism as given sacramentally but released in life experience later.[22] Other Pentecostals fear that Spirit baptism as a release or breakthrough of the Spirit in life precludes the need to seek a definite reception of the Spirit for empowered witness. Catholic theologian Francis Sullivan supports this concern and has quoted persuasively from Thomas Aquinas in favor of a new endowment of the Spirit that is subsequent to sacramental initiation and is not to be viewed as merely the outworking of

19. K. McDonnell and G. T. Montague, *Christian Initiation and Baptism in the Holy Spirit: Evidence from the First Eight Centuries* (Collegeville, Minn.: Liturgical Press, 1991).

20. Viewing Jesus' baptism as paradigmatic of Christian baptism sacramentally understood has had an influence on certain Reformed and Free Church theologians as well. See G. Wainwright, *Christian Initiation* (Richmond, 1969), pp. 50ff.

21. Wainwright, *Christian Initiation*, pp. 376ff.

22. S. Chan, "Evidential Glossolalia and the Doctrine of Subsequence," *Asian Journal of Pentecostal Studies* 2:2 (1999): 195-211.

sacramental grace. Pentecostals and charismatics who desire to view Spirit baptism as a genuinely new beginning in the Christian life would find Sullivan's arguments attractive. However, unlike the Pentecostal view of Spirit baptism as a one-time event after conversion to Christ, Sullivan views every breakthrough or filling of the Spirit as a fresh Spirit baptism.[23] This whole discussion raises the question of how one understands continuity in the Christian life in relation to new beginnings.

Spirit Baptism, Vocation, and Charisms

Pentecostals regard the baptism in the Holy Spirit as an experience of empowerment for witness. The experience is in my view akin to a "prophetic call," which allows believers to participate in various gifts connected with prophetic discernment, such as visions, dreams, various "word gifts," and other gifts of the Spirit highlighted in the New Testament. Acts 1:8 identifies the baptism in the Holy Spirit as a gift of power for witness. Pentecost is thus a charismatic moment in the life of the church already formed as the Easter community under Christ. For Pentecostals, a case in point in support of this understanding of Pentecost is Acts 8, in which the Samaritans "accepted the Word of God" (v. 14) and were "baptized into the name of the Lord Jesus" (v. 16) without having received the Spirit. Robert Menzies argues that the possibility of accepting the gospel and being baptized into Jesus' name without receiving the Spirit would have been unimaginable to Paul (Rom. 8:9).[24] This fact implies for Menzies a fundamental difference between Lukan and Pauline pneumatologies. For Menzies, as well as Roger Stronstad, Luke is indebted to a typically Jewish pneumatology that understands the reception of the Spirit as an empowerment or "charismatic" enrichment (referring to gifts of the Spirit or *charismata*). Paul, however, goes deeper to connect the work of the Spirit to one's initiation to Christ by faith, making the gift of the Spirit fundamental to one's Christian identity. Menzies thus accuses those who see Spirit baptism in Acts as soteriological of reading a Pauline pneumatology into Luke. Menzies then

23. F. A. Sullivan, *Charisms and Charismatic Renewal: A Biblical and Theological Study* (Ann Arbor: Servant, 1982).

24. R. Menzies, "Luke and the Spirit: A Reply to James Dunn," *Journal of Pentecostal Theology* 4 (1994): 127.

uses this charismatic understanding of Spirit baptism in Luke to justify the Pentecostal doctrine of a "Spirit baptism" as a charismatic experience subsequent to conversion.[25]

Of course, Menzies is aware of the fact that his position does little more than open up the *possibility* of viewing Spirit baptism as a post-conversion charismatic empowerment. Even if one accepts his understanding of Luke's use of the verb to "baptize" in the Spirit as charismatic, one could still integrate Luke's pneumatology with Paul's in a way that avoids separating the charismatic and soteriological elements of Spirit baptism. In fact, fracturing the charismatic from the soteriological work of the Spirit has created problems for Pentecostal theology. The result of this fracture is an otherworldly spirituality detached from the concrete guidance available from God's self-disclosure in Christ. In such a theological vacuum, the attempt to relate spirituality to secular life can easily latch on to pragmatic strategies for success for guidance. The consequence is the dark side of Grant Wacker's insightful treatment of the Pentecostal ethos as a synthesis of otherworldly spirituality and a this-worldly pragmatism.[26] As we will see, Pentecostal language was fortunately not consistent in its support of this separation of Spirit baptism from the sanctifying grace inaugurated by Christ.

On a positive note, the Pentecostals viewed this Spirit baptism as distinct from initial Christian conversion or the sacraments of initiation in order to present it to the church as an ongoing challenge to its life in the world. They were revivalists, as much concerned with reviving the saints as with converting the sinners. The nineteenth-century Pietist and social activist Christoph Blumhardt once wrote that one must convert twice, first from the world to God but then, again, from God back to the world.[27] He wrote this in rejection of a piety that is oriented toward God only. He favored instead a divine love that is directed to both God and (from God) the world. The Pentecostal doctrine of the baptism in the Holy Spirit at its best can be seen as advocating a kind of "second conversion," an awakening to one's vocation in the world and giftings to serve as a witness to

25. Cf. Menzies, *Empowered for Witness.*

26. G. Wacker, *Heaven Below: Early Pentecostals and American Culture* (Cambridge, Mass.: Harvard University Press, 2003).

27. Quoted by J. Harder in the introduction to C. Blumhardt, *Ansprachen, Predigten, Andachten, und Schriften,* ed. J. Harder, vol. 1 (Neukirchen-Vluyn: Neukirchener Verlag, 1978), p. 12.

Christ. As Roger Stronstad noted, Pentecostals advocate a "prophethood of believers," since everyone is a bearer of the Spirit to dream dreams, have visions, and speak under the inspiration of the Spirit in praise to God and in witness to Christ.[28]

With regard to sanctification, the formal way that most early Pentecostals devoted to the Holiness movement related Spirit baptism to sanctification was to sharply distinguish between them as stages of initiation to the life of the Spirit, even appropriating them to persons of the Trinity. The Pentecostals following this approach shifted pneumatology from sanctification to Spirit baptism as a charismatic experience. Sanctification was then placed under the work of Christ, whether formally viewed as distinct from regeneration or not. In a brief essay entitled "The Spirit Follows the Blood," one Pentecostal author even denied that the Spirit sanctifies, "for he is not our Savior." It is the blood of Christ that cleanses from sin and purifies in preparation for the gift of power by the Spirit.[29] Indeed, how Christ can be said to do anything in the life of the believer without the agency of the Spirit is baffling. Furthermore, it did not occur to the early Pentecostals who followed this train of thought that this rigid relegation of sanctification to Christ alone contradicts 1 Peter 1:2 as well as the biblical portrayal of the inseparable workings of Word and Spirit and the overlapping nature of soteriological categories in the New Testament. Fortunately, the overriding tendency in Pentecostal theology, as Donald W. Dayton has shown, was to focus on Christ as the one who both saves and Spirit baptizes through the agency of the Spirit. But this christological focal point still did not prevent many Pentecostals from fracturing Christ's saving work from his role as Spirit Baptizer.

This formal distinction, however, is not the whole story. Seymour implied a more integral connection between sanctification and Spirit baptism by stating that Spirit baptism is the gift of power "upon the sanctified, cleansed life."[30] Implied here is that Spirit baptism empowers, renews, or releases the sanctified life toward outward expression and visible signs of renewal. I have also found numerous references in early Pentecostal literature to Spirit baptism as a baptism in the love of God, usually in reference

28. Roger Stronstad, *The Prophethood of Believers* (Sheffield: Sheffield Academic Press, 1999).

29. "The Spirit Follows the Blood," *The Apostolic Faith,* April 1907, p. 3 (author unknown).

30. W. J. Seymour, "The Way into the Holiness," *The Apostolic Faith,* October 1906, p. 4.

to Romans 5:5, which refers to the love of God "shed abroad" in our hearts, a "Pentecostal" image that did not escape the attention of a number of early Pentecostal pioneers.

The Pentecostal image of a divine outpouring is connected here to Wesley's understanding of sanctification as a transformation of the person by the love of God. William Seymour wrote in 1908 in answer to a question about what the evidence of Spirit baptism is: "Divine love, which is charity. Charity is the Spirit of Jesus."[31] Seymour's *Apostolic Faith* paper would say more than once concerning the baptism in the Holy Spirit: "this baptism fills us with divine love."[32] This paper also gives a testimony from a "Nazarene brother" who called his Spirit baptism a "baptism of love."[33] These were not the only voices among the early Pentecostals to write about Spirit baptism as a filling with divine love. Assemblies of God pioneer E. N. Bell, for example, referred to Romans 5:5 to describe Spirit baptism as a baptism in the love of God " — not a scanty sprinkling but a regular 'outpour.'"[34] In an implicit allusion to Romans 5:5, a brother Will Trotter wrote an article entitled "A Revival of Love Needed," in which he wrote, "I tell you that this entire 'tongues movement,' independent of works of grace positions held, needs . . . to get down and get the thing that loves in their hearts, that divine flame shed abroad by the Holy Ghost." He concludes, "Get the flame, the pentecostal flame, if you like the term better — but get it."[35] As yet another example of an identification of Spirit baptism with an "infusion" of divine love, one could find Oneness Pentecostal pioneer Frank Ewart describing Spirit baptism this way: "Calvary unlocked the flow of God's love, which is God's very nature, into the hearts of his creatures."[36] Stanley Frodsham made both tongues and love consequences of

31. "Questions Answered," *Apostolic Faith* 1:9 (June-September 1907): 2.1. I am grateful to C. M. Robeck Jr. for directing me to this quote: "William J. Seymour and the 'Bible Evidence,'" in G. B. McGee (ed.), *Initial Evidence: Historical and Biblical Perspectives on the Pentecostal Doctrine of Spirit Baptism* (Peabody, Mass.: Hendrickson, 1991), p. 81.

32. "The Old Time Pentecost," *The Apostolic Faith*, September 1906, p. 1; note also "Tongues as a Sign," September 1906, p. 2 (authors unknown).

33. "The Old Time Pentecost," *The Apostolic Faith*, September 1906, p. 1 (author unknown).

34. E. N. Bell, "Belivers in Sanctification," *The Christian Evangel*, September 19, 1914, p. 3.

35. W. Trotter, "A Revival of Love Needed," *The Weekly Evangel*, April 3, 1915, p. 1.

36. F. Ewart, "The Revelation of Jesus Christ," in D. W. Dayton (ed.), *Seven Jesus Only Tracts* (New York: Garland, 1985), p. 5.

Pentecost: "Therein we see in their brightest luster the union of gifts and graces in believers."[37]

Without question, Spirit baptism has often been interpreted throughout Pentecostalism with a heavy emphasis on the Spirit as the *power* of God for enhancing worship and service and overcoming the obstacles to the life of faith, especially with the aid of powerful manifestations and gifts of the Spirit. This is true of Pentecostal and charismatic churches in Asia, Africa, the U.S., Europe, and Latin America. "Power encounter" is the byword for global Pentecostal mission.[38] Theologically, this emphasis on spiritual power is tied to the military metaphor for the Christian life favored by Pentecostals. As E. Kingsley Larbi notes with regard to African Pentecostalism, Pentecostalism does not recognize any "demilitarized zone" but rather accents the battle for the victory of the kingdom of God over the forces of sin and darkness.[39] I do not wish to denigrate this Pentecostal focus on power. The love of God is not sentimental. It is also not reducible to an ethical principle, as valuable as that is. God's love is powerfully redemptive and liberating. It is also not confined to the inner transformation of the individual but propels people outward to bear witness to Christ. In my view, the vocational and charismatic elements highlighted by Pentecostals hold potential for expanding our understanding of sanctification so that it involves a "prophetic call."

Part of the reason why Pentecostals resisted a formal connection between sanctification and Spirit baptism was the connection forged early on between Spirit baptism and speaking in tongues. At times, it seemed in the early literature that the merely "sanctified" are not yet Spirit baptized simply because they do not speak in tongues. Yet, when describing why tongues uniquely symbolizes Spirit baptism, Pentecostals turned usually to a notion of what may be termed the sanctification of human speech. The unruly tongue is said to be tamed and transformed into a source of telling truth, praising God, or bearing witness to Christ. Seymour saw tongues as a sign that God is causing the people of God to cross boundaries: "God

---

37. S. H. Frodsham, "Back to Pentecost: The Effects of the Pentecostal Baptism," *The Pentecostal Evangel,* October 30, 1920, p. 2.

38. A representative development of this theme in Pentecostal literature is A. Chia, "A Biblical Theology of Power Manifestation: A Singaporean Quest," *Asian Journal of Pentecostal Studies* 2:1 (1999): 19-33.

39. E. K. Larbi, *Pentecostalism: The Eddies of Ghanaian Christianity* (Dansoman, Accra, Ghana: Centre for Pentecostal and Charismatic Studies, 2001), p. 423.

makes no difference in nationality; Ethiopians, Chinese, Indians, Mexicans, and other nationalities worship together."[40]

Such a connection between Spirit baptism and tongues speech (and other forms of inspired speech) can be theologically significant. Catholic theologian Simon Tugwell, for example, sees scriptural support for the notion that inspired speech is "in some way symptomatic of the whole working of the Holy Spirit in our lives, a typical fruit of the incarnation."[41] Furthermore, Seymour and others referred on occasion to the divine healing of the body, another favored spiritual gift among Pentecostals, as the "sanctification of the body."[42] This language further supports the idea that Pentecostals described Spirit baptism on occasion as an enhancement of sanctification rather than as an additional work beyond it.

It is my view that early Pentecostals separated sanctification from Spirit baptism only by defining sanctification narrowly and negatively as a cleansing or a separation from sin. Sanctification, however, is also positively a consecration unto God in preparation for a holy task, as it was for the Old Testament prophets and Jesus of Nazareth. As an aspect of the life of discipleship to which we are consecrated and called, sanctification involves a transformation by the Spirit of God into the very image of Christ "from glory to glory" (2 Cor. 3:18). It is interesting that the distinction between sanctification and Spirit baptism can be sustained only through a reductionistic understanding of sanctification as an inward cleansing and of Spirit baptism as an outward empowerment for a holy task. In a sense, sanctification was fractured for many early Pentecostals along the line of its negative and positive (as well as inward and outward) effects. This point raises the legitimate question as to the degree to which the separation of sanctification from Spirit baptism was more semantic than substantial. Pentecostal pastor and theologian David Lim thus calls Spirit baptism for Pentecostals "vocational sanctification."[43] In this light, I will include both Holiness and Pentecostal movements as advocating a vocational and at least implicitly charismatic understanding of Spirit baptism.

---

40. W. J. Seymour, "The Same Old Way," *Apostolic Faith,* September 1906, p. 3.

41. S. Tugwell, "The Speech-Giving Spirit," in S. Tugwell et al. (eds.), *New Heaven? New Earth?* (Springfield, Ill.: Templegate, 1976), p. 128.

42. E.g., W. J. Seymour, "The Precious Atonement," *Apostolic Faith,* September 1906, p. 2.

43. In personal conversation with the author.

Final Biblical Reflections:
Towards an Ecumenical Pneumatology

Spirit baptism has historically been defined largely in service to one's ecclesiology. "Word" ecclesiologies that highlight the church as those who are faithful to the word of the gospel would tend to see Spirit baptism as regeneration by faith in Christ through the proclamation of the gospel. Sacramental ecclesiologies that view the church as a sacrament which mediates grace to the world would identify Spirit baptism with water baptism or the sacraments of initiation. Holiness and Pentecostal groups that see the church as the separated and consecrated people called and empowered for gifted service in the world will see Spirit baptism as that which revives or renews the people of God for its prophetic tasks in the world. These ecclesiologies and understandings of Spirit baptism do overlap each other. For example, a sacramental understanding of Spirit baptism can also emphasize the prophetic call implicit in water baptism and/or confirmation. Interestingly, though ecumenical discussions on ecclesiology have become much more complex, discussions on Spirit baptism have not kept pace. It would be interesting, for example, to relate Spirit baptism to the newer understanding of the church as a *koinonia* or communion in the life of God as Trinity.

As interesting as the connection of ecclesiology and Spirit baptism is, I do not believe an ecumenical pneumatology can begin with the nature of the church. Those who view Spirit baptism as fundamentally an ecclesial dynamic will view John the Baptist's use of the metaphor as solely predictive of what will occur at Pentecost at the birth of the church. I want to suggest something else, namely, an understanding of the Baptist's use of the metaphor in its own right first, before we bring Pentecost and the essence of the church into the picture. This move allows us to define Spirit baptism first as related to the *kingdom of God* before it is applied to the church. John's preaching was, "Repent, for the kingdom of God is near" (Matt. 3:1-2). How Spirit baptism relates to what we regard as most important to the life of the church should be developed after Spirit baptism as the ministry of the Messiah to usher in the kingdom of God is acknowledged.

John the Baptist saw himself as standing on the edge of the end of the world announcing the Messiah's act of "baptizing in the Spirit" (only the verb form is used) as the final act of salvation. John knew that his water baptism did not have the power to bring down the Spirit and to end the age. The prophets of old said in effect, "We circumcise the foreskin, but

God will circumcise the heart." So John uses similar prophetic rhetoric to say in effect, "I can baptize in water unto repentance, but the Messiah will baptize in the Spirit unto judgment and purgation/restoration." John's baptism was preparatory, namely, to gather the repentant together in preparation for the final judgment and restoration. But "apocalyptic transcendence" belongs to the Messiah alone. Only from him will the wind of the Spirit blow away the chaff and store the wheat into barns. That the Messiah will be anointed of the Spirit is foretold. As James Dunn in his insightful essay for this volume has noted, insight into the Messiah's role to dispense and baptize in the Spirit is unique to John the Baptist.

Consistent with our eschatological theme, the opening of the heavens at Jesus' baptism is a typical sign depicting an apocalyptic revelation.[44] The descending of the dove is reminiscent perhaps of the Spirit brooding upon the waters of creation and the sign of new creation in the story of Noah.[45] Jesus is being commissioned here to usher in the kingdom of God in power to make all things new: "If I cast out demons by the Spirit of God, the kingdom of God has come upon you" (Matt. 12:28).

It seems clear that Spirit baptism in the Synoptics is granted broad eschatological implications that cannot be exhausted in any version of Christian initiation or of the essence of the church. Interestingly, Donald Hagner insightfully notes that the church connected to the Gospel of Matthew saw parallels between its Christian baptism and Jesus' Jordan experience. But this church also recognized the unique eschatological undertones in the complex of events at the Jordan that await fulfillment at the end of salvation history.[46] I believe that Hagner's insight can be applied quite broadly. The vision of Spirit baptism foretold by John the Baptist and depicted in Jesus' Jordan experience pointed to final judgment and to the final sanctification of the entire creation.

Spirit baptism points to redemption through Christ as substantially pneumatological and eschatological. Pentecost certainly baptizes the disciples in the Spirit, but Luke is quick to note as well the final apocalyptic horizon of this event (Acts 2:17-21). In Spirit baptism, the church is allowed to participate in the final sanctification of creation. Regeneration by faith in

44. J. Nolland, *Luke 1–9:20*, Word Biblical Commentary 35A (Dallas: Word Books, 1989), p. 162.

45. D. A. Hagner, *Matthew 1–13*, Word Biblical Commentary 33A (Dallas: Word Books, 1993), p. 58.

46. Hagner, *Matthew 1–13*, p. 60.

the context of the gospel and the sacraments of initiation do not grant one grace as a "deposit" that can later burst forth in charismatic experience. Rather, the experience of new life in faith, hope, and love in the context of the gospel, the sacraments, and the Holiness/Pentecostal experience of prophetic consecration (with charismatic signs following!) allows one to participate already in a Spirit baptism that is yet to come. The term "participation" *(koinonia)* helps to bring together an emergent eschatology (from below) with a futuristic eschatology (from beyond). The indwelling of the Spirit from within our emerging and diverse experiences of the Spirit continues to help us transcend the past in the present moment through a participation in the powers of the age to come (Heb. 6:5). The Pentecostal belief in the connection between Spirit baptism and sanctification, on the one hand, and between Spirit baptism and the latter rain of the Spirit to end the age, on the other, can nourish an ecumenical doctrine of Spirit baptism in which all of us can have an equal voice.

I believe Michael Welker's excellent essay for this volume, "The Spirit in Philosophical and Theological Perspectives," can aid us in our understanding of the ecclesiological and ecumenical setting of Spirit baptism as an eschatological gift of the Spirit of God. Welker seeks to move beyond the Western philosophical tradition of viewing the Spirit in the context of conscious *self-reference* in order to understand the Spirit as an *empathetic personality* in a *multicontextual presence.* In relation to God the Creator and the Lordship of Jesus, the Spirit draws creation polyphonically into the eternal life of God. Spirit baptism in this understanding of the Spirit would inspire a church that participates in the *koinonia* of God as Trinity and seeks in prophetic empathy with the heart of God and the experiences of others to draw others into this fellowship in a way that cherishes a diversity of contexts and giftings. Simple one-on-one relations and monohierarchical forms of social interactions are implicitly resisted in favor of a participation in the multicontextual and polyphonic work of the Spirit. Pentecostal speaking in tongues as a sign of Spirit baptism symbolizes just such a prophetic empathy (Rom. 8:26) in favor of an experience of the Spirit that sweeps up into itself all languages, contexts, and experiences toward the coming of Christ in great power and glory to fulfill the kingdom of God through new creation (Acts 2). The acceptance of Christ by faith, water baptism, and charismatic, prophetic empowerment in multicontextual experiences will all play a vital role in our experience of this baptism in the Spirit, a metaphor that will continue to shape us as the church in ways unforeseen and unexpected.

Early Pentecostals and the Study of Popular Religious Movements in Modern America

GRANT WACKER

> Breathing strange utterances and mouthing a creed which it would seem no sane mortal could understand, the newest religious sect has started in Los Angeles. . . . [N]ight is made hideous in the neighborhood by the howlings of the worshippers who spend hours swaying forth and back in a nerve-racking attitude of prayer and supplication. They claim to have "the gift of tongues," and to be able to comprehend the babel.

With these memorable — and often quoted — lines, a *Los Angeles Times* reporter tried to describe a local revival meeting he witnessed in the spring of 1906. Though hardly impartial, he seemed somehow to sense the event's singular power. If so, he was right. In the next five years thousands of quite ordinary men and women — white, black, Latino, and Native American — would jam the fire-gutted church on Azusa Street in order to relive the miracles of the Day of Pentecost. They saw visions. They healed the lame. They spoke languages they had never studied. And despite modest means, they raised astonishing amounts of money to send missionaries to the corners of the earth to herald the good news of

---

I wish to thank John C. Greene, Gary B. McGee, Brendan Pietsch, Kristin Sutton, Matthew Sutton, Wayne E. Warner, and the University of Chicago American Religious History Workshop for helping with the conceptualization or research of this essay.

Christ's imminent return. Whether the Azusa Street revival represented *the* spark or one of many sparks that started the worldwide Pentecostal movement remains an open — and hotly debated — question. Whatever the answer, it is clear that in the span of a single century the Pentecostal insurgence has turned into one of the largest and most influential religious stirrings of modern times.[1]

This essay holds three goals. The first is to provide a sketch of Pentecostalism's place on the American and, to a lesser extent, the world religious landscape. The second is to offer a hypothesis for why the movement has flourished. The third is to suggest that understanding Pentecostalism's success may help us understand the success (or failure) of other religious movements in modern America.

Pentecostals in Context

Our narrative begins in the United States in the twilight of the nineteenth century. The main players were two related but distinct Protestant groups: mainstream Evangelicals and radical Evangelicals. We might think of the former as Pentecostals' grandparents and the latter as their parents. Like their grandparents, Pentecostals emphasized conversion, personal sanctification, missionary outreach, and freedom from worldly habits. And like their parents, Pentecostals stressed divine healing, the Lord's imminent return, the Holy Spirit's gifts, and miraculous signs and wonders. But Pentecostals — who often called themselves Holy Ghost believers or, simply, saints — also distinguished themselves from both mainstream and radical Evangelicals. They insisted that the order of salvation entailed, beyond conversion and sanctification, a *third* definable experience called Holy Spirit baptism. The dynamite in the crevice was Pentecostals' uncompromising conviction that all who truly had been baptized by the Holy Spirit — all, in other words, who had experienced that third landmark in the order of salvation — would speak in unknown tongues as a palpable sign of its authenticity. When the king was home, they liked to say, the royal flag

---

1. "Weird Babel of Tongues," *Los Angeles Times*, April 18, 1906, p. 1. The article was unsigned; I assume the author was male. For a concise yet factually rich telling of the Azusa story, see Cecil M. Robeck, "Azusa Street Revival," in Stanley M. Burgess (ed.), *New International Dictionary of Pentecostal and Charismatic Movements* (Grand Rapids: Zondervan, 2002), pp. 344-50.

always flew from the tallest spire of the castle for all to see or, more precisely, for all to hear.[2]

It is hard to tell exactly when that confection of doctrines and practices began to crystallize into institutional shapes. Some say the movement started in the mountains of North Carolina in the late 1890s, some trace it to divine healing meetings in eastern Kansas just after the turn of the century, and others attribute it to the interracial Azusa Street revival. Recently several historians have argued that those American events represented a dramatic intensification of a renewal impulse that had been growing in the British Isles and in South India for four decades.[3] All of those positions are defensible. Whatever the real story, it is clear that in the first decade of the twentieth century hundreds of revival centers felt the breath of fresh life. Independent chapels carrying names like Full Gospel Tabernacle and Apostolic Faith Mission started to spring up in all parts of the United States and in other countries. Though a hefty minority of converts perennially resisted any kind of formal organization, by World War I the majority had gathered themselves into a half dozen organized bodies. The best known included the mostly white Assemblies of God and the mostly black Church of God in Christ.

After World War I, the Pentecostal movement grew extremely diverse. Shabby storefront missions, gleaming mega-churches, unlettered country preachers, sonorous radio voices, and, eventually, flamboyant television personalities all represented the sprawling revival. More important, in the 1960s an emphasis on the Holy Spirit's miraculous gifts broke out in many of the established Protestant denominations and in the Roman Catholic Church. These newer enthusiasts commonly called themselves Charismatics rather than Pentecostals, but the message of divine empowerment proved similar.

After World War I, the Pentecostal movement also grew extremely large. By the year 2000 various studies suggested that the U.S. alone housed

2. Grant Wacker, *Heaven Below: Early Pentecostals and American Culture* (Cambridge, Mass.: Harvard University Press, 2001), ch. 1. The present essay draws scattered passages from this work, used with the permission of Harvard University Press.

3. Gary B. McGee, "'Latter Rain' Falling in the East: Early-Twentieth-Century Pentecostalism in India and the Debate over Speaking in Tongues," *Church History: Studies in Christianity and Culture* 68 (September 1999): 648-65; Alan Anderson, *An Introduction to Pentecostalism* (Cambridge: Cambridge University Press, 2004), esp. ch. 9; and a forthcoming major work by Robert S. Fogarty on the trans-Atlantic divine healing movement, 1875-1930.

at least ten million core adherents, accompanied by ten or perhaps twenty million sympathizers. At the same time, according to the *World Christian Encyclopedia,* around the globe 550 million souls considered themselves Pentecostals or Charismatics. The typical adherent was young, female, modestly educated, and lived south of the equator. Taken together, Pentecostals constituted the largest aggregation of Christians outside the Roman Catholic Church. Almost certainly those numbers swelled in the telling, perhaps wildly so, yet other studies consistently showed that within a hundred years of its beginnings, the Pentecostal-Charismatic movement registered an immense following, both at home and abroad.[4]

In the United States, in the past quarter century, Pentecostals have emerged from sectarian shadows into the bright sunlight of modern culture. Too angular to be entirely respectable, yet too numerous to be overlooked, they have established themselves as conspicuous players in American public life. Mainstream media figures have viewed them in diverse ways, ranging from curiosity to alarm, but rarely indifference. Many pundits have found their political attitudes especially worrisome. The reasons are easy to see. Though a solid minority of Pentecostals — chiefly blacks and Latinos — have proved politically moderate or even liberal, clearly a majority have shared the concerns (if not always the agendas) of the Christian Right. Significantly, the Pentecostal subculture has produced some of the most assertively conservative voices of recent times, including former Secretary of the Interior James Watt, Christian Coalition founder Pat Robertson, and former U.S. Attorney General John Ashcroft.[5]

4. Wacker, *Heaven Below,* appendix. In "Missiometrics 2005: A Global Survey of World Mission," *International Bulletin of Missionary Research 29* (January 2005): 29, David B. Barrett and others project 588,502,000 Pentecostal/charismatic/neo-charismatic adherents by mid-2005.

5. "Born Again Christians Were a Significant Factor in President Bush's Re-Election," *Barna Update,* November 9, 2004, found at http://www.barna.org/FlexPage.aspx?Page= BarnaUpdate&BarnaUpdate ID=174, accessed May 19, 2005. Barna documents white born-again Evangelicals' striking inclination to favor Bush over Kerry in the 2004 election (72 percent versus 27 percent). In 2004 both black and Latino born-again Evangelicals preferred Kerry over Bush (85 percent vs. 15 percent and 53 percent vs. 45 percent), but for both groups the percentage voting Republican was larger than in 2000. Barna does not distinguish Pentecostals, but virtually all Pentecostals would categorize themselves as born-again Evangelicals. Ongoing research by University of Akron political scientist John C. Greene shows that in 2004, 79 percent of white Pentecostals voted for Bush. E-mail from Greene to me, May 20, 2005.

Images of Pentecostals as sexual libertines also have shaped popular perceptions. It is an old tradition. John Steinbeck forever typecast Holy Ghost zealots as poor, illiterate, and licentious in his 1939 classic, *The Grapes of Wrath*. "I used ta get the people jumpin' an' talkin' in tongues and glory-shoutin' till they just fell down an' passed out," said the Reverend Casy, a one-time Holy Ghost preacher. "An' then — you know what I'd do? I'd take one of them girls out in the grass, an' I'd lay with her. Done it ever' time."[6] To a great extent such images are specious. They say more about the fantasies of the perceiver than the actual behavior of the perceived. Even so, believers have brought some of the ill repute on themselves. The religious television empires of the Louisiana evangelist Jimmy Swaggart and of the North Carolina evangelist Jim Bakker self-destructed in the late 1980s amidst the ruins of sexual lapses by their leaders. In the fall of 2004, allegations of a homosexual tryst and hefty payoff to keep it quiet entangled the Pentecostal Paul Crouch, president of Trinity Broadcasting Network, the largest Christian network in the world. Though Crouch vigorously denied wrongdoing and later won a favorable arbitration ruling, the story — splashed across the front page of a Sunday edition of the *Los Angeles Times* — remained to color public perceptions.[7]

Finally, there is the problem of ecstatic religious experience. If average Americans know nothing else about Pentecostals, they know one thing for sure: Holy Ghost believers do unconventional things in their worship services. That perception holds a measure of truth. In the fire-baptized holiness services of the late 1890s, one pioneer remembered, the "people screamed until you could hear them for three miles on a clear night, and until the blood vessels stood out like whip cords."[8] A newspaper reporter visiting Maria Woodworth-Etter's divine healing rallies in Oakland in 1889 said that her prayer meetings sounded like the "female ward of an insane asylum." Still another wrote that in her Indiana revivals one could not "imagine the . . . confusion. Dozens lying around pale and unconscious, rigid and lifeless as though in death. Strong men shouting till they were hoarse, then falling down in a swoon. Women falling over benches and

6. John Steinbeck, *The Grapes of Wrath* (1939; New York: Penguin, 1992), p. 22.

7. William Lobdell, *Los Angeles Times*, September 12, 2004, p. 1; Trinity Broadcasting Network, "TBN's Paul Crouch Sr. Vindicated," Religion News Online, October 17, 2004, accessed May 23, 2005.

8. Charles Fox Parham, *Apostolic Faith* [Kansas], April 1925, p. 9.

trampled under foot."[9] To be sure, studies show that Pentecostals have outstripped their mainline counterparts in the routine work of the church — giving, caring, and teaching.[10] Yet ecstatic experience (though usually not this extreme) undeniably has functioned as a cornerstone of Holy Ghost worship from the beginning to the present. Pentecostal periodicals still brim with stories of supernatural healings and interventions in daily life. If one looks in the right places, miracles continue to dance before believers' eyes as frequently and as wondrously as ever.[11]

Given its growth, size, visibility, and controversial character, it is understandable that the Pentecostal revival has attracted the attention of numerous historians. Not at first, to be sure. For many decades, outsiders largely overlooked it. And insiders cared little about recovering their own story. Jesus was coming soon, so what was the point? Within a decade, however, a small number of partisans, hoping to prove their continuity with historic Christianity, sought to chronicle the way things were "in the beginning." By the 1950s, a cottage industry of Pentecostal history writing was taking shape. That period witnessed the start of critical efforts, mostly by third-generation adherents in secular graduate schools, to reclaim their past. The mid-century writers made Herculean efforts to recover the tradition's basic facts — who, what, when, and where. The 1970s, 1980s, and 1990s marked a new stage of historical consciousness. Insiders, former insiders, and now outsiders too tried to cast the narrative in an explicitly interpretive framework. The turning of the twenty-first century saw additional changes. Led by (mostly) young academics, the most recent scholarship has proved sensitive to the identity-forming role of music, the power of ethnicity, the social construction of gender, the markers of regionalism, the instability of language, the implications of interna-

---

9. *San Francisco Examiner,* January 11, 1890, and *Muncie Daily News,* September 21, 1885, quoted in Wayne Warner, *Maria Woodworth-Etter, For Such a Time as This* (Gainesville: Bridge-Logos, 2004), pp. 109, 340.

10. See, e.g., Christian Smith, *American Evangelicalism: Embattled and Thriving* (Chicago: University of Chicago Press, 1998), pp. 32-35, 231. Smith includes Pentecostals among Evangelicals, who consistently outstrip Fundamentalists, Mainliners, Liberals, and Catholics on participation indices.

11. Margaret Poloma, *The Assemblies of God at the Crossroads: Charisma and Institutional Dilemmas* (Knoxville: University of Tennessee Press, 1989), ch. 9, esp. p. 161, and *Main Street Mystics: The Toronto Blessing and Reviving Pentecostalism* (Walnut Creek, Calif.: Rowman and Littlefield, 2003), part 1.

tionalism, and the theological pluralism ineradicably embedded in the primary records.[12]

This historical literature is remarkably rich. It has helped us figure out, with reasonable (albeit provisional) confidence, where Pentecostals fit on the American religious landscape. But — and this is a towering "but" — it still has not adequately explained why the revival flourished. That task now calls for our attention.

12. The historical literature on American Pentecostalism is voluminous, and the debates about it are heated. For an overview of both, see A. Cerillo and G. Wacker, "Bibliography and Historiography of Pentecostalism in the United States," in Stanley M. Burgess (ed.), *New International Dictionary of Pentecostal and Charismatic Movements* (Grand Rapids: Zondervan, 2002), pp. 382-417. See also Grant Wacker, "Are the Golden Oldies Still Worth Playing? Reflections on History Writing among Early Pentecostals," *Pneuma: Journal of the Society for Pentecostal Studies 8* (Fall 1986): 81-100; and Arlene M. Sanchez Walsh, "Whither Pentecostal Scholarship?" *Books and Culture,* May-June 2004, pp. 34-36.

For striking examples of the best new scholarship see (in chronological order): Douglas Jacobsen, *Thinking in the Spirit: Theologies of the Early Pentecostal Movement* (Bloomington: Indiana University Press, 2003); Randall J. Stephens, "'The Fire Spreads': The Origins of the Southern Holiness and Pentecostal Movements" (Ph.D. dissertation, University of Florida, 2003); Edward J. Gitre, "The 1904-05 Welsh Revival: Modernization, Technologies, and Techniques of the Self," *Church History: Studies in Christianity and Culture 73* (December 2004): 792-827; Roger G. Robins, *A. J. Tomlinson: Plainfolk Modernist* (New York: Oxford University Press, 2004); Kathryn E. Lofton, "Making the Modern in Religious America, 1870-1935" (Ph.D. dissertation, University of North Carolina, 2005), chs. 4-5; Matthew Avery Sutton, "Hollywood Religion: Aimee Semple McPherson, Pentecostalism, and Politics" (Ph.D. dissertation, University of California, Santa Barbara, 2005); Daniel Ramirez, "Migrating Faiths: A Social and Cultural History of Popular Religion in the United States–Mexico Borderlands" (Ph.D. dissertation, Duke University, forthcoming fall 2005).

It is worth noting that most historians of Pentecostalism have liked their subject — and subjects. With the signal exception of Robert M. Anderson's brilliant (and brilliantly tendentious) *Vision of the Disinherited: The Making of American Pentecostalism,* published in 1979, almost all of the serious work produced in the last fifty years has come from critically trained insiders, former insiders, or outsiders sympathetic to the tradition. Indeed, my own pilgrimage may be close to typical. I grew up in the heritage but, as an adult, left it for the more sedate meadows of mainstream evangelical Christianity. Even so, the old songs bring early memories flooding back. That ambivalence is, I suspect, one reason the field remains vital.

Reasons for Pentecostals' Success

By any conventional measure of things, Pentecostals have prospered. Their numbers have swollen, their social status has risen, and their cultural influence has expanded. In the beginning, few outsiders expected the upstarts to survive, let alone flourish. But that new mix of old ingredients somehow worked. The question is why.

The reigning answers fall into three categories. They might be summarized as the compensation, mobilization, and satisfaction models of explanation. The first holds that Holy Ghost believers, not able to gain the economic, social, and cultural benefits they desired in ordinary life, compensated themselves with the rewards of otherworldly religion. The second holds that Holy Ghost leaders effectively created the revival by cultivating a religious need and then providing the institutional means for meeting it. The third holds that in the revival, Holy Ghost seekers sought to satisfy ineffable and irreducible religious longings. All of those approaches have much to commend them, but the first two overlook key data, and the third invokes categories not readily open to public analysis. We need to keep looking.[13]

I propose that another model holds untapped explanatory potential. It can be stated in a single sentence. *The genius of the Pentecostal movement lay in its ability to hold two seemingly incompatible impulses in productive tension.* Taking a cue from the artist Georgia O'Keefe — "it is only by selection, by eliminating, by emphasis, that we get at the real meaning of things"[14] — we might think of them simply as principle versus practicality. Three examples, drawn from the formative experiences of the first generation, suffice to make the point. The first illustrates the workings of principle; the second, practicality; the third, the interaction of the two in a single explosive personality.

Stepping back in time, slipping quietly into early Pentecostals' kitchens and parlors, we hear, first of all, a great deal of talk about Holy Spirit

13. Wacker, *Heaven Below*, p. 10; Grant Wacker, "Taking Another Look at the Vision of the Disinherited," *Religious Studies Review* 8 (1982): 15-22; Grant Wacker, "Searching for Eden with a Satellite Dish: Primitivism, Pragmatism, and the Pentecostal Character," in Richard T. Hughes (ed.), *The Primitive Church in the Modern World* (Urbana: University of Illinois Press, 1995), pp. 39-166, especially the data cited in endnotes 9, 79, 80, 81, and 86.

14. Unattributed quotation exhibited on the wall of the Georgia O'Keefe Museum in Santa Fe, New Mexico, March 2005.

baptism. We hear how the Holy Spirit entered their bodies, took control of their tongues, and gave advice on life's most mundane decisions. We also hear about the Bible, its power, its beauty, and the way it served as the final authority on all questions of daily living as well as human salvation. And we hear about signs and wonders — drunkards delivered, eyes restored, unlettered folk speaking foreign languages they had never studied. The more we listen to those discussions, however, the more we realize that most of them were really about something else. And that something else, of course, was God. Occasionally the longing to touch God bordered on mysticism, a craving to be absorbed into the One or even to obliterate one's own identity into the identity of the All. But typically it suggested a yearning simply to know the divine mind and will as directly and as purely as possible, without the distorting refractions of human volition, traditions, or speculations.

An incident in the life of the Church of God's general overseer, A. J. Tomlinson, shows how forcefully the desire for immediate contact with God could shape Pentecostals' outlook. The event took place in the winter of 1913. Striding forward to address his Tennessee mountain faithful, Tomlinson announced that on this particular occasion he would read his remarks out loud, word for word. His hearers must have been stunned. Pentecostal preachers never read their sermons out loud as seminary-trained ministers did. Indeed, they prided themselves on their ability to speak extemporaneously so that the Holy Spirit could rule their tongues. But this day would be different. Tomlinson dared not leave anything out. "This that I am about to produce," he began, "was principly prepared at the midnight hour when alone with God that it might not be a second-handed production but purely first-handed." That single sentence captured the movement's most heartfelt aspiration. The words that the mountain preacher proposed to speak that day would not be "second-handed," not derivative, not passed though the distortions of human imagination or traditions. Rather they would come directly from God Himself, "purely first-handed."[15]

If our explorations into the materials of early Pentecostalism ended there, with the manifestations of the principled impulse to touch the divine directly, our work would be finished. But if we listen closely, we begin

15. A. J. Tomlinson, [Church of God] *General Assembly Minutes 1906-1914* (Cleveland, TN: White Wing Publishing House, 1992), "1913," p. 163.

to hear — off in the distance — other words, other sounds, not antici-pated. We hear about mundane realities like budgets and schedules and financial accountability. We hear about adjusting doctrine to the needs of the moment, the value of a carefully trained leadership, the importance of working hard and getting ahead. We hear respected leaders calling for good common sense in the conduct of the revival. We even hear heated arguments about power of the human kind, who had it and who did not (or should not). For all of their declarations about living solely in the realm of the supernatural, with the Holy Spirit guiding every step of their lives, early Pentecostals nonetheless displayed a remarkably clear-eyed vision of the way things worked here on earth.

No one better represents that practical impulse than the flamboyant Pentecostal evangelist of the 1920s and 1930s, Aimee Semple McPherson. The statistics pile up like snowdrifts. One evangelistic tour stretching from 1919 to 1922 purportedly drew more attenders than any road show or whistle stop circuit in American history, including those by P. T. Barnum, Harry Houdini, or Teddy Roosevelt. Another burst of barnstorming in 1933 and 1934 led Sister personally to address more than two million persons, two percent of the U.S. population. The five thousand seats of her Angelus Temple filled, emptied, and filled again three times every Sunday and often weeknights too, for twenty years running. On average, she hit the front page of the Los Angeles papers three times a week from 1926 through 1933. In 1923 she founded, and four years later incorporated, her own small but sturdy denomination, the International Church of the Foursquare Gospel. Until Oral Roberts strode out of the Oklahoma prairie in the late 1940s, no other enthusiast came close to rivaling Sister's visibility outside Pentecostal circles.[16]

We miss an important part of McPherson's story — and early Pentecostalism's too — if we overlook the large element of rollicking self-promotion in those narratives. In a cemetery scheme that never quite got off the ground, the noted preacher purportedly marketed burial plots to her premillennialist followers under the logo, "Go Up With Aimee!" One account holds that she priced them by their proximity to her own. Another quips that when Sister "carried the ball of the Foursquare Gospel for a

---

16. Edith L. Blumhofer, *Aimee Semple McPherson: Everybody's Sister* (Grand Rapids: Eerdmans, 1993), esp. pp. 2-3, 6, 161, 174; Daniel Mark Epstein, *Sister Aimee: The Life of Aimee Semple McPherson* (New York: Harcourt Brace Jovanovich, 1993), esp. pp. 146, 156, 438; Matthew Sutton, University of California, Santa Barbara, e-mail to me, April 27, 2005.

touchdown, Jesus ran interference." Between McPherson and Jesus it is sometimes hard to tell who won.[17]

Given Sister's gifts, it comes as no surprise that she erected the fifth religious radio station in the United States, KFSG (Kall Four Square Gospel), and made herself the first woman in the Christian radio business anywhere in the world. Nonetheless, the most interesting part of this story largely has escaped notice. When McPherson put up KFSG she soon ran into conflict with Secretary of Commerce Herbert Hoover for refusing to broadcast on a prescribed frequency. "Please order your minions of Satan to leave my station alone," she barked to Hoover. "You cannot expect the almighty to abide by your wavelength nonsense. When I offer my prayers to Him I must fit into His wave reception." That much was standard Pentecostal absolutizing — a tendency to ratchet every issue into one of ultimate morality. Less noticed but equally important, however, was the confrontation's outcome: after an appropriate display of outrage, McPherson backed down in order to achieve her larger goals. She agreed to broadcast on an assigned frequency. In the end she prevailed, too. In 2000 McPherson's denomination sold some of KFSG's rights for $250,000,000, and the station continued to beam the full gospel message until 2003, long after she — and Hoover — had gone to their heavenly rewards.[18]

If Tomlinson's career illustrates the principled side of early Pentecostal culture, and McPherson's the practical side, Levi R. Lupton's career re-

17. ASM quoted in David L. Clark, "Miracles for a Dime: From Chautauqua Tent to Radio Station with Sister Aimee," *California History,* Winter 1978-79, p. 363. Cemetery plot: Carey McWilliams, "Aimee Semple McPherson: 'Sunlight in My Soul,'" in Isabel Leighton (ed.), *The Aspirin Age, 1919-1941* (New York: Simon and Schuster, 1949), p. 75. Touchdown: Marcus Bach, *They Have Found a Faith* (1946), quoted in Vinson Synan, *The Holiness-Pentecostal Movement in the United States* (Grand Rapids: Eerdmans, 1971), p. 198.

18. ASM quoted in Erik Barnouw, *A History of Broadcasting in the United States,* vol. 1: *A Tower in Babel: To 1933* (1966), p. 180, quoted in George H. Douglas, *The Early Days of Radio Broadcasting* (Jefferson, N.C.: McFarland, 1987), p. 94. See also Herbert Hoover, *The Reminiscences of Herbert Clark Hoover,* Columbia University Oral History Project, 1951 (New York: Columbia University Press, 1975), pp. 11-12. Paul Risser, "KFSG Plans for the Future," FNS [Foursquare News Service] Press Release #62, Nov. 3, 2002; Paul Risser, "Radio Station KFSG to Cease Operation," FNS Press Release, Feb. 9, 2003; Jack Hayford, "Update on Our Foundation," December 6, 2004, http://president.foursquare.org/archives/ announcementsreports/ (accessed May 19, 2005). On February 28, 2003, the station expired after seventy-nine years on the air. Jim Hilliker, "History of KFSG," http://members.aol.com/jeff560/kfsg.html (accessed May 19, 2005).

veals both at once. Today only a handful of specialists know about Lupton, but in the early years no one loomed larger. His story merits telling in some detail. It shows that discrete currents, seemingly flowing at cross purposes, could, nonetheless, combine to produce striking results.

The primary materials about Lupton are surprisingly ample and variegated.[19] Though they do not agree on all details, the broad outlines emerge clearly enough. The main source is a book-length biography self-published in 1911 by C. E. McPherson, a sympathetic but sharp-eyed reporter and minister. McPherson evidently knew Lupton and made it a point to interview him and some of his followers. According to McPherson, Lupton was born into a devout Quaker family in Ohio in 1860 and moved in Quaker circles until he passed from the public record fifty years later. Lupton's early friends and schoolteachers remembered him as unremarkable except for a streak of pronounced willfulness.[20] About 1880 he moved to northeastern Michigan, where he and an associate established (or perhaps reestablished) a lumbering town that they christened Lupton.[21] The town prospered economically. In the middle 1880s, after sowing a "bountiful harvest of wild oats,"[22] Lupton married a Quaker woman and soon professed conversion, sanctification, and a call to ministry among the Society of Friends.[23]

19. C. E. McPherson, *Life of Levi R. Lupton: Twentieth Century Apostle of the Gift of Tongues, Divine Healer, Etc.* (Alliance, O[hio]: by author, 1911). I have spot-checked McPherson against other primary sources, and he seems to have quoted them accurately and fairly. See also G. B. McGee and E. J. Gitre, "Levi Rakestraw Lupton," in Burgess, ed., *New International Dictionary,* pp. 846-47; Gary B. McGee, "Levi Lupton and the Ill-Fated Pentecostal Missionary Union in America," paper presented to the Society for Pentecostal Studies, November 14, 1987; Gary B. McGee, "Levi Lupton: A Forgotten Pioneer of Early Pentecostalism," in Paul Elbert (ed.), *Faces of Renewal: Studies in Honor of Stanley Horton* (Peabody, Mass.: Hendrickson, 1988). Professor McGee, of the Assemblies of God Theological Seminary, is, to the best of my knowledge, the only modern historian who has published sustained critical work on Lupton.

20. McPherson, *Life,* pp. 32-33; *Alliance Daily Review* [Alliance, Ohio], December 13, 1910, p. 3. The chronology of events is not always clear.

21. McPherson, *Life,* pp. 37, 43. This account differs somewhat from two others: "Lupton Deposed as Quaker Leader," *Evening Repository* [Canton, Ohio], December 17, 1910, p. 6, and Lupton, Michigan's "official" town history, as stated in www.hometownvalue.com/lupton.htm (accessed April 10, 2005).

22. McPherson, *Life,* p. 39; see also pp. 43-44, which quote the Cleveland *Plain Dealer,* December 17, 1910.

23. Leah Rudy, genealogist, Lisbon, Ohio, "The Lupton Family Group Sheet," Gary McGee personal files; McGee and Gitre, "Lupton," p. 846.

The next twenty-five years saw a succession of rapid and dramatic changes in Lupton's life. Returning to Ohio in 1891, he took up work as a pastor and itinerant preacher with a radical evangelical emphasis on entire sanctification, the Lord's imminent return, and divine healing. In 1901 Lupton founded the First Friends Church in Alliance, where he built a $6,500 meeting house — dedicated free of debt.[24] The following year he established the World Evangelization Company, an organization designed to speed both the evangelization of the world and Christ's return.[25] The association's title spoke volumes about the grandiose sweep of Lupton's vision. Soon Lupton bought — again, without visible resources of his own — an idyllic twelve-acre plot near the town. The land served as a site for camp meeting facilities and a Missionary Training School and Faith Home. In 1903 the relentlessly entrepreneurial Lupton purchased a remodeled showman's railroad car for $4,500, cash on delivery.[26] With evangelistic messages emblazoned on both sides, the *Gospel Car,* as Lupton named it, crisscrossed the northeastern states heralding his peculiar blend of Quaker piety, progressive social ideals, and radical evangelical theology. The following year the rising evangelist established a monthly called, significantly, *New Acts.*[27] The latter reportedly attained an international circulation approaching 10,000.[28] In 1905, under the aegis of the World Evangelization Company, Lupton and three others launched a spectacularly publicized missionary foray into the heart of Nigeria.

The Africa mission proved to be an ominous portent of things to come, for it was ill planned and quickly collapsed. The years 1905 and 1906 brought more hard times. Back home, a tornado destroyed Lupton's prized 1,000 seat tent. His paper folded and his school dismissed classes. Lupton's

24. McPherson, *Life,* pp. 53-54.

25. Thomas D. Hamm, *The Transformation of American Quakerism: Orthodox Friends 1800-1907* (Bloomington: Indiana University Press, 1988), p. 169.

26. McPherson, *Life,* p. 74. For a photo of the apparently opulent vehicle, see Michael G. Owen, "Preparing Students for the First Harvest: Five Early Ohio Bible Schools — Forerunners of Today's Colleges," *Assemblies of God Heritage,* Winter 1989-90, p. 4.

27. The title was significant. Technically it was named after Arthur T. Pierson's 1893 Duff Missionary Lectureship in Scotland, which "described the resurgent missionary movement of the day." But clearly the import was much broader. Besides the restorationist implications of the New Testament Book of Acts, the title also denoted breathless anticipation that the final era of history had arrived. McGee, "Lupton," p. 7.

28. McPherson, *Life,* p. 78.

increasingly strident message and lack of financial accountability incurred the disfavor of Ohio Friends leaders.[29]

Yet Lupton gave resilience new dimensions of meaning. In December 1906, after hearing about the Azusa mission revival in Los Angeles, Lupton traveled to Akron, Ohio, where an itinerant from Azusa was holding meetings. He subsequently received Holy Spirit baptism with the "evidence," as Pentecostals called it, of speaking in tongues. His wife said that a "halo lit upon his brow."[30] In February 1907 the Friends Quarterly Meeting disowned him.[31]

Many — perhaps most — of Lupton's followers seemed not to care. "One of the singular features about this man," McPherson wrote, "was his ability to make all his followers see matters as he saw them."[32] Lupton's interracial camps in the summers of 1907, 1908, and 1909 became stellar events in the Pentecostal firmament. Many of the brightest stars from the United States, Canada, and even Britain made it a point to attend — and to be seen attending. The North Carolina Pentecostal Holiness leader George Floyd Taylor literally spent the family food money in order to get there. At the camp, Taylor carefully noted in his diary, he found a chance to rub shoulders with Pentecostal celebrities like the Californian Frank Bartleman and the British Anglican vicar A. A. Boddy.[33] At the close of the 1907 camp — which attracted seven hundred souls from twenty-one states — Lupton changed the name of his enterprise from the World Evangelization Company to the Apostolic Evangelization Company, evidently aiming to highlight the miraculous power of the New Testament model. He designated himself the director and started calling himself "the Apostle Levi."[34]

Along with this new focus on apostolic signs and wonders, Lupton began to pour most of his resources, now augmented by a flourishing

29. Hamm, *Transformation,* p. 170.

30. Lupton's wife quoted in McGee and Gitre, "Lupton," p. 846.

31. McPherson, *Life,* pp. 112-13; Owen, "Preparing," pp. 3-5; McGee, "Lupton," p. 10; Hamm, *Transformation,* p. 171. McGee and Hamm offer somewhat different interpretations as to why the Friends Meeting disowned Lupton, McGee emphasizing insubordination, Hamm tongues.

32. McPherson, *Life,* p. 242.

33. George Floyd Taylor, "Diary," June 6, 10, and 18, 1908, North Carolina State History Archives, Raleigh, North Carolina.

34. McGee and Gitre, "Lupton," p. 847.

poultry business, into the missionary training school. Initially he, like his better-known contemporary Charles Fox Parham, felt certain that all tongues were actual foreign languages designed to speed the spreading of the gospel to the ends of the earth.[35] Some seventy-five missionaries, including several who eventually acquired mythic status within the movement, either passed through Lupton's school or advertised their services in *New Acts*. In 1909 Lupton put together the Pentecostal Missionary Union in order to systematize the training and financial support of foreign missionaries. Most likely the first Pentecostal organization of national scope, the Pentecostal Missionary Union provoked bitter opposition from those who disliked regularization in any form. Lupton paid no attention.

By 1910 Lupton had moved to the forefront of the burgeoning Pentecostal revival. Blessed with endless stamina, he proved uncannily gifted as a divine healer and articulator of Holy Ghost theology. And the money rolled in. In 1907 the missionary home and land, legally held by the World Evangelization Company, was deeded to Lupton and his wife and a friend. Later it passed to Lupton alone.[36] According to McPherson, Lupton "lived like a prince in his castle," financially accountable to no one.[37]

But trouble was brewing. For two or three years Lupton had disregarded warnings that his relationship with an attractive, 26-year-old female stenographer in his school appeared indiscreet.[38] In December 1910 he publicly confessed that the woman recently had borne a "precious manchild" and that he was the father. "'An enemy hath done this,'" he explained.[39] He expressed deep remorse, even falling into a trance. In classic

---

35. McPherson, *Life*, pp. 69, 143; *Evening Repository* [Canton, Ohio], December 14, 1910, p. 1.

36. *Evening Repository* [Canton, Ohio], December 15, 1910, p. 14; *Alliance Daily Review* [Alliance, Ohio], December 24, 1910, p. 1.

37. McPherson, *Life*, pp. 101-4, quotation on p. 103.

38. McGee, "Lupton," p. 19. In the primary accounts the woman is variously described as a student, teacher, office worker, secretary, and stenographer. In calling her a stenographer, I am following the first headline, "Founder of Missionary Home Confesses to Sin: Tells of Some Criminal Intimacy with His Stenographer," in *Alliance Daily Review*, December 13, 1910, p. 1. The woman's name runs through the primary sources. Since her identity is not material to my argument, and since direct family members are alive, I have omitted it.

39. Levi R. Lupton, in *Alliance Daily Review*, December 13, 1910, p. 1, statement dated December 10, 1910. Apparently Lupton made a more or less private confession to the Missionary Home family in early November, following the child's birth in October. McPherson, *Life*, pp. 183, 186-87.

Pentecostal fashion, Lupton described the scene as a clash between cosmic powers of good and evil: "An awful battle was fought that night with the combined forces of darkness, which almost resulted in the overthrow of my natural life, but at a late hour the victory was won."[40] Lupton's partner invoked the same categories, explaining her behavior as the "outcome of the mysterious manipulations of the powers of darkness."[41]

Things moved from bad to worse. To everyone's dismay, Lupton, his wife, his partner, and their child all continued to live together in the Missionary Home, apparently with his wife's approval.[42] Many made a point publicly to disassociate themselves from the Ohio prophet.[43] *New Acts* ceased publication. Within days the Missionary Training School and Faith Home, the Apostolic Evangelization Company, and the Pentecostal Missionary Union fell apart.[44] Before the year was out, Lupton and his wife headed back to Michigan and his partner and the baby returned to her family in Cleveland.[45]

Almost nothing is known about Lupton's later years. He may have moved to Detroit and taken up a new career selling stoves.[46] Or to Buffalo to sell mining stocks.[47] Or both. The record is too patchy to know for sure. All we know is that in 1929 he died, forgotten.[48]

As noted, Lupton's stormy career illumines larger patterns. The prin-

---

40. Levi R. Lupton, in *Alliance Daily Review* [Alliance, Ohio], December 13, 1910, p. 1, statement dated December 10, 1910.

41. Young woman quoted in McPherson, *Life,* p. 192.

42. McPherson, *Life,* pp. 173, 187-88, 213-15; see also *Evening Repository* [Canton, Ohio], December 14, 1910, p. 14, and December 16, 1910, p. 10; *Alliance Daily Review* [Alliance, Ohio], December 19, 1910, p. 4.

43. See, e.g., *Alliance Daily Review* [Alliance, Ohio], December 20, 1910, p. 5; and J. T. Boddy, *Alliance Daily Review* [Alliance, Ohio], December 23, 1910, p. 5.

44. McGee and Gitre, "Lupton," p. 847. The Chicago-based *Latter Rain Evangel* took over *New Acts*'s subscriptions.

45. *Alliance Daily Review* [Alliance, Ohio], December 21, 1910, p. 3, and December 23, 1910, p. 1.

46. *Alliance Daily Review* [Alliance, Ohio], December 20, 1910, p. 1; December 23, 1910, p. 5; December 24, 1910, p. 1. It is not clear what happened to the women. Four years after the uproar a local newspaper reported a "well confirmed rumor" that Lupton's wife had divorced him and that he had married "his affinity." The Quaker historian Thomas Hamm says that Lupton "abandoned his wife to elope with the secretary at his school." *Alliance Daily Review* [Alliance, Ohio], November 12, 1914, p. 1; Hamm, *Transformation,* p. 171.

47. *Alliance Daily Review* [Alliance, Ohio], November 12, 1914, p. 1.

48. McGee and Gitre, "Lupton," p. 846.

cipled side of his personality and public ministry was the part that insiders undoubtedly found especially compelling. He was gifted with many of those elusive talents that made a person truly and inexplicably charismatic. The steady stream of visitors to the faith home, the continual flow of missionary students, and the considerable funds given to the enterprise make clear that ordinary folk believed in his gifts, almost at any cost. Then too Lupton displayed a remarkable capacity for radical ecstasy. When he received Holy Spirit baptism, he recalled, he lay on the floor for nine hours straight, conscious yet unable to move any part of his body, even his eyelids. In time he received the gift of multiple languages, personal messages for cohorts, and other instructions that the Lord (significantly) would not let him reveal.[49]

At the same time — and this is the key point — Lupton's practical ability to get along in the real world proved just as striking as his otherworldly propensities. Clearly he possessed more than his fair share of street smarts. There is no reason to think that he completed more than a public school education, if that. Yet somewhere along the way he picked up an easy way with words, which he parlayed into windy expositions on all sorts of topics, religious and secular, in his monthly *New Acts*. Lupton's knowledge of Scripture, Christian theology, and world affairs was neither profound nor astute, but he proved exceptionally alert. He simply knew a lot about what was going on, both locally and globally. Further, Lupton's entrepreneurial skills, however unbuttoned they may have seemed from the perspective of a trained accountant, obviously greatly exceeded the abilities of the average person. Omnicompetent, he readily moved from lumbering to real estate to poultry to stove (or mining) sales. Despite a severe illness and miraculous healing experience as a young adult, Lupton evinced exceptional stamina and resistance to disease. Continually on the go, he also displayed remarkable resourcefulness in his missionary travels, reputedly exploring portions of Nigeria never seen by a white person. Finally, he never asked permission. As Lupton's biographer dryly put it, he had "little use for committees that came to criticise his work."[50]

One additional point merits notice. In the end, Lupton's followers proved just as practical — just as canny — as he was. When the hard truth about his moral lapse finally emerged, they faced the reality head-on —

49. Lupton, *New Acts,* February 1907, p. 3.
50. McPherson, *Life,* p. 112.

and made a choice. As far as I can tell, all of them, without exception, abandoned him. By doing so, they seemed to be signaling their determination to uphold conventional standards of sexual morality and, presumably, financial accountability. Institutional memory followed suit. Though early accounts by insiders occasionally mentioned the Alliance camps and the Pentecostal Missionary Union, Lupton's name simply disappeared from the record. The erasure of his identity was so complete that he remained unknown until professional historians rediscovered it in the 1980s.[51]

Tomlinson, McPherson, and Lupton present a complex but coherent group portrait. They show that early Pentecostals' ability to balance the most eye-popping features of the supernatural with the most chest-thumping features of the natural, and to do it without admitting that they were doing it, formed a recognizable (though not unique) profile in early-twentieth-century America. They did it by insisting that God's Holy Spirit, now living inside their very bodies, rendered them spiritually and, to a remarkable extent, physically invincible. Pray as if everything depended on God. Work as if nothing did. Mind the results.

Pentecostals and Other Religious Movements

Finally, I wish to hazard a few thoughts about how early Pentecostals may help us understand the inner structure — the working DNA — of other popular religious movements, especially in modern America. I will focus on three points.

First of all, first-generation Pentecostals call us to remember what we easily forget: that real life is untidy. In their ability to hold seemingly incompatible impulses in productive tension, Holy Ghost folk dramatically exemplified that untidiness. And in their untidiness, they provide us with an almost test-tube perfect illustration of the need for supple historical methods. In the last twenty years, historians, seeking to capture the past's complexity, have elaborated an approach sometimes called the study of "lived religion." As the historian David D. Hall describes it, this approach

51. McGee, "Lupton," *Faces*, pp. 192, 203. In the 1980s, McGee, undertaking the first biographical dictionary article on Lupton, secured Lupton's death date from his granddaughter — a token of the obscurity into which he had fallen. Letter from McGee to me, April 27, 1990.

deems practice — what people actually did, irrespective of what theologians, philosophers, editors, social scientists, and denominational officials think they ought to have done — as the vital, organizing center of religion. Rather than trying to smooth out or explain away the ambiguous, overlapping, or contradictory meanings that ordinary people ascribed to their experience, lived religion seeks to honor those meanings by taking them as its starting point. Beyond that, it esteems change and exchange. Recognizing the "time-bound shape of practice," lived religion assumes the likelihood of development over fixity and of contingency over inevitability. And it challenges unexamined assumptions about the inevitability of opposition between elite and popular, or between imposed and indigenous, or between core and periphery. It looks instead for signs of complicity, collaboration, and cross-fertilization.[52]

Lived religion does more than simply acknowledge the untidiness in religion, however. It also acknowledges that religion — untidy and otherwise — penetrates aspects of life that we conventionally regard as not religious at all, as perfectly mundane. Like traditional social histories of religion, lived religion looks beyond "official" texts (such as sermons, catechisms, and systematic theologies) to "unofficial" ones (such as sacred artifacts, missionary letters, and devotional lyrics). But unlike traditional social histories of religion, lived religion also tries to see how sacred sensibilities seeped into and colored everyday practices, sometimes supporting them, sometimes contesting them. In the words of the historian Julie Byrne — who, significantly, writes about religion and sports — lived religion follows the "fluid piety that always overflows official vessels."[53] It searches for the evidences of faith in the midst of life, and of life in the midst of faith. Early Pentecostals give the practitioners of lived religion a lot to work on.

Second, early Pentecostals' story suggests that their distinctiveness — their angularity — enhanced rather than diminished their growth. It is important to remember that not all religious groups experience meaningful opposition. Some fit right in, all too well. My colleague Stanley Hauerwas likes to quip that long after Christianity is dead and gone, the United

---

52. David D. Hall, ed., *Lived Religion in America: Toward a History of Practice* (Princeton: Princeton University Press, 1997), pp. vii-xiii.

53. Julie Byrne, *O God of the Players: The Story of the Immaculata Mighty Macs* (New York: Columbia University Press, 2003), p. 11.

Methodist Church will still be flourishing. No one ever said that about Pentecostals. From the outset, Pentecostals' spiritual and in many cases biological parents marshaled impressive resources to crush the menace in their midst. Arson and fistfights punctuated the story. Abusive words flew back and forth for decades. In 1907, Jesse Penn-Lewis, the redoubtable matriarch of the British Keswick movement, judged that Pentecostals represented an "onslaught of Satan." In 1913 the beloved Pentecostal songwriter Herbert Buffum returned the favor. Focusing on the American holiness warrior Alma White, Buffum dismissed her "slanderous reports . . . concerning God's elect and select people" as "turkey-buzzard vomit."[54] So it went, year after year, until the polemics finally subsided into sullen silence in the 1930s.

That confrontation is worth studying because it illumines larger patterns of conflict in American religious history. It exemplifies the survival strategies that appear when some but not all of the members of a religious family acquire a new vision of life's possibilities. To outsiders the areas of disagreement between the parent and the child appeared so negligible to be laughable. Yet that was precisely the point. The fight lasted as long as it did and hurt as much as it did because the antagonists poured so much combative energy into such a tiny patch of cultural space. Both sides believed that they were grappling over matters of ultimate significance. It was not a polite discussion about "styles" or "options" but a brawl fought without rules, in the mud, with every rhetorical weapon at their disposal. The protagonists battled for keeps because the issues were for keeps.

Finally, normalcy. If the first lesson that early Pentecostals teach — or at least might teach — about the adherents of other religious movements is their untidiness, and the second is their distinctiveness, the third is their normalcy. First-generation Pentecostals' conceptual world was as exquisitely complex as the conceptual world of a Ralph Waldo Emerson or of an Emily Dickinson. Though the premises and the conclusions of their thinking were, to put it mildly, different from such elites, the intricacy of the consciousness that created them was not. The primary materials make clear that Holy Ghost partisans laughed and hurt like anyone else.

That fact, which runs like a crimson thread through the data, alerts

54. [Jesse] Penn-Lewis, *Life of Faith*, November 15, 1907, p. 1037, and Herbert Buffum, *Gold Tried in the Fire*, April 1913, p. 7 (item unsigned but almost certainly by Buffum, the editor).

us to the likelihood that the converts to other religious movements in modern America also have proved perfectly normal in every respect except one: the peculiarity of their religious allegiance. Sooner or later most have paused to reflect on the meaning of their lives, both alone and together. Most have marked the passage of years with symbols and ceremonies. Most have set apart holy sites for the worship of God. And most have measured their days by ethical standards derived from ancient Scriptures and primal traditions. Through prayer they have tried to make the fragile, flickering candle of life burn a bit brighter and a bit longer. The challenge, then, is to let them speak with all the pathos and beauty, frailty and power, of their original voices.[55]

To say that early Pentecostals merit our attention is not to say that the task is always pleasant. Even by their own standards they often proved petty and mean-spirited. In a way, though, that is precisely the point. As the classicist Peter Brown put it, to the honest historian, the dead "appear exactly as they were — every bit as odd as we are, as problematical, as difficult of access. To explore such people with sympathy, with trained insight, and with a large measure of common cunning, is to learn again to appreciate . . . [that] 'Man is a vast deep.'"[56] Historians should not spare Pentecostals — or the partisans of any religious movement — from criticism when they deserve it, nor exempt them from praise when they deserve that, too. Rather, they should try simply to follow the golden rule: to write about the people of the past as fairly as we hope they would have written about us. In many history books the actors end up as faces with the tears removed. We need to put back the tears.

55. For one of literally countless examples — in this case, a thoughtful, "grassroots" Mormon example — see Jan Shipps and John W. Welch, eds., *The Journals of William E. McLellin, 1831-1836* (Provo, Utah: Brigham Young University Studies, 1994), part II. More broadly, see Jim Sharpe, "History from Below," in Peter Burke (ed.), *New Perspectives on Historical Writing* (University Park: Pennsylvania State University Press, 1991). I owe the larger point of this point to David C. Steinmetz, *Memory and Mission: Theological Reflections on the Christian Past* (Nashville: Abingdon, 1988), especially pp. 31-32.

56. Peter Brown, *Religion and Society in the Age of Saint Augustine* (New York: Harper and Row, 1972), p. 21.

The Future of American Pentecostal Identity: The Assemblies of God at a Crossroad

MARGARET POLOMA

*Charisma, in final analysis, is a gift — a breath that is illusive and frag-
ile. She can launch a new institution and breathe life into existing ones.
The Assemblies of God, birthed by her spirit, has been renewed by her
grace. Whether she will continue to seek and to find a home within the
Assemblies of God remains a critical question that only the future can
answer.*[1]

The Assemblies of God (AG) with some 2.6 million members and over
12,000 congregations in the United States is the second largest Pentecostal
denomination in the United States. Its national membership is second
only to the predominantly black Church of God in Christ (COGIC), but
its global membership of over 50 million exceeds that of any other single
Pentecostal body. The AG, it can be convincingly argued, thus provides a
good vantage for assessing the future of American — particularly white
American — Pentecostal identity.

Over twenty years have passed since I launched the first sociological
study of the Assemblies of God — a research adventure published in 1989
as *The Assemblies of God at the Crossroads*. My conclusion about the fate of
charisma in this rapidly growing Pentecostal denomination was cautious

---

1. M. Poloma, *The Assemblies of God at the Crossroads: Charisma and Institutional Dilemmas* (Knoxville: University of Tennessee Press, 1989), p. 243.

and tentative. Its destiny, despite the gloomy Weberian prognosis on the inevitable routinization of charisma, was then colored by the revitalization of the Assemblies of God (AG) brought about by the rise of the Charismatic movement during the 1960s and 1970s that brought Pentecostal experiences into the mainline Christian churches. The Charismatic movement soon waxed and waned just as did the earlier revival on Azusa Street in Los Angeles (1906-1909) that birthed Pentecostalism during the first decade of the twentieth century. It was not long, however, before another move of the Spirit, the so-called "Third Wave," crossed the American continent during the 1980s — a move that marked the rise of more contemporary and youth-oriented charismatic groups, many of which developed out of the Jesus Movement of the 1970s.[2] As the millennium came to a close, rumors of a fresh renewal in the early 1990s attracted international attention with the outbreak of the so-called Toronto Blessing — a revival that developed in the Third Wave sector but soon spilled over into the Pentecostal and Charismatic streams of the Spirit movement.[3]

With its nightly revival meetings beginning in January 1994 attracting pilgrims from around the world, the Toronto Airport Christian Fellowship with its Third Wave approach to Pentecostalism became the epicenter of fresh revival fire. Its embers torched another revival at an Assembly of God congregation in Pensacola, Florida, on Father's Day, 1995. Brownsville Assembly of God (BAOG), where revival found an inroad into the increasingly routinized and bureaucratized Pentecostal stream of the Spirit-filled movement, promised to revive traditional Pentecostalism much like the Toronto Blessing had refreshed the Third Wave.[4]

2. Although most Pentecostals were wary of both the Charismatic movement and the Third Wave (just as they were of the New Order of the Latter Rain movement of the 1940s), the AG was revitalized by an influx of new converts from more recent revivals. The rapid growth of the AG during the 1970s and 1980s, which reached a plateau by the mid-1980s when the renewal crested, can be linked to revitalization movements that originated outside the AG. See also D. Miller, *Reinventing American Protestantism* (Berkeley: University of California Press, 1997) and D. Di Sabatino, *The Jesus People Movement: An Annotated Bibliography and General Resource* (Westport, CT: Greenwood Press, 1999).

3. Cf. M. Poloma, *Main Street Mystics: The Toronto Blessing and Reviving Pentecostalism* (Walnut Creek, Calif.: Alta Mira Press, 2003).

4. M. Poloma, "The 'Toronto Blessing': Charisma, Institutionalisation and Revival," *Journal for Scientific Study of Religion* 37:2 (1997): 257-71; "Inspecting the Fruit of the 'Toronto Blessing': A Sociological Assessment," *Pneuma: The Journal of the Society for Pentecostal Studies* 20:1 (1998): 43-70; "The Pensacola Revival," in W. Roof (editor in chief), *Contem-*

The "Pensacola Outpouring" at BAOG caused some degree of tension within the Assemblies of God, as it raised questions about denominational identity and blurred the boundaries between classic Pentecostalism and its post-1950s offshoots. But tension has always found a home within the AG; and, as I have discussed at length elsewhere,[5] a degree of tension between charisma and structure has been an important factor in accounting for the vitality enjoyed by the AG. As Lewis Coser convincingly argued over forty years ago, tension and conflict can have positive institutional consequences.[6] Tension with an outgroup (external conflict), for example, can serve to establish a strong group identity, and Pentecostalism's status as a "third force" within Christianity owes much to the hostility Pentecostalism experienced as a newly emerging sect during the first half of the twentieth century. Tension within the group (internal conflict) can also have positive repercussions, especially for loosely knit structures such as the Assemblies of God.

Maintaining a free flow of charisma, however, requires skill not unlike that of a unicycle rider; despite great skill there is always the risk of a fall. This fear of falling into the abyss of "carnal" unregulated religious experience has commonly caused established Pentecostalism to quench the fresh flow of the charismata ("gifts of the Holy Spirit," including glossolalia, healing, miracles, etc.) as it sought to protect its fragile emergent structure and its reputation as an Evangelical denomination. Fresh charismatic outbursts seem to find more fertile ground outside organized denominations in the growing numbers of parachurch networks and independent churches. Sociologist Peter Berger was correct in his passing assessment that "religious experiences are institutionally dangerous." Newly formed networks and emerging congregations appear to have less to risk in embracing fresh experiences than do established sects and denominations.[7]

---

porary American Religion (New York: Macmillan Reference USA, 2000), pp. 82-83; "Pensacola (Brownsville) Revival," in Michael McClymond (ed.), *Encyclopedia of Religious Revivals in America* (Greenwood Publishing Group, 2005; in press).

5. Cf. Poloma, *The Assemblies of God at the Crossroads*.

6. Cf. L. Coser, *Continuities in the Study of Social Conflict* (Glencoe, Ill.: The Free Press, 1967).

7. The birth of the AG itself provides an excellent example of embracing risk and dealing with institutional resistance to seemingly unregulated religious experience. Those who reported being Spirit baptized during the first decade of the twentieth century, complete with paranormal experiences (especially glossolalia, but also healing, prophecy, deliv-

Tolerance for a moderate amount of tension between charisma and institution, however, is seemingly built into the DNA of Pentecostalism, where religious distinctiveness centers on paranormal experiences believed to be generated by Spirit baptism. The inherent tension between what Grant Wacker has called primitivism and pragmatism — the paranormal working of the Holy Spirit and the organizational matrix that promotes the Pentecostal mission — is rooted in its earliest history. As Wacker succinctly summarizes his insightful thesis: "The genius of the Pentecostal movement lay in its ability to hold two seemingly incompatible impulses in productive tension."[8]

I call the two impulses the primitive and the pragmatic. The dynamic tension between the two faces of Pentecostalism — charismatic experiences (the "primitive") and organizational structure (a facet of the "pragmatic") continues to be central for maintaining a distinct Pentecostal identity.

In this article I will use the general framework provided by Thomas O'Dea in his "five dilemmas in the institutionalization of religion,"[9] with a particular focus on what he terms "the dilemma of mixed motivation." As we will see, mixed motivation contrasts with a "singleness of purpose" of pneumatic empowerment reflected in Pentecostal identity. The data to assess American Pentecostal identity comes from my involvement in the larger Organizing Religious Work project conducted by the Hartford Institute in the late 1990s during which I conducted a survey (n=447) of AG pastors and had access to interviews that provide "thick description" to supplement the statistics.[10]

The empirical findings, interpreted within a Weberian theoretical context provided by O'Dea's institutional dilemmas, can be succinctly

---

erance, and miracles), usually (voluntarily or involuntarily) withdrew from what they regarded as "dead denominations." History was to repeat itself throughout the twentieth century with the development of fresh charismatic experiences and the splits and schisms resulting from failed attempts to agree on the essence and meaning of such experiences.

8. G. Wacker, *Heaven Below: Early Pentecostals and American Culture* (Cambridge, Mass.: Harvard University Press, 2001), p. 10.

9. Cf. T. O'Dea and J. O'Dea Aviad, *The Sociology of Religion* (Englewood Cliffs, N.J.: Prentice-Hall, 1983).

10. I would like to acknowledge the assistance and helpful feedback from others involved in the Organizing Religious Work project at the Hartford Institute for Religious research, especially D. Roozen and S. Thumma.

summarized as follows: *the Assemblies of God has a solid core identity around which there are varying levels of ambiguity.* The ambiguity that exists on peripheral issues appears to function as a safety-valve mechanism feeding the ongoing dialectical interrelationship between charisma and institution building.[11] Periodic revivals have the potential to strengthen Pentecostal identity, but the emergent culture and structure of the Assemblies of God often mutes and limits the impact of fresh pneumatic experiences within the denomination. To the extent that revivals have been marginalized by many white American Pentecostals as they seek acceptance from the post-Enlightenment Evangelical and larger secular communities, important distinctives that characterize Pentecostal identity have been jeopardized.

O'Dea's Dilemmas and the Institutionalization of Religion: Ambiguities and Creative Tension

Thomas O'Dea's well-known "five institutional dilemmas" point to the inherent tension found to some degree in all religious organizations. Each dilemma reflects the "basic antimony" or "fundamental tension" that exists between charisma (i.e., the immediacy of direct religious experience) and institutional forces. The ongoing tension between spontaneity and stability that permeates all five dilemmas can be described as "transforming the religious experience to render it continuously available to the mass of men [*sic*] and to provide for it a stable institutional context."[12] Once free-flowing, nonnormative, and seemingly chaotic, charisma must (at least to some extent) be transformed into something that is stable, normal, and ordered. Although an important catalyst in the development of all world religions, charisma is usually quenched in favor of the patterned and predictable institutional features of social life. Each of the dilemmas — mixed motivation, symbol, delimitation, power, and administrative order — can provide a unique vantage point to explore the working of the Assemblies of God, but the dilemma of mixed motivation is perhaps the best

11. Cf. S. Eisenstadt, Introduction to *Max Weber on Charisma and Institution Building* (Chicago: University of Chicago Press, 1969).

12. T. O'Dea, "Sociological Dilemmas in the Institutionalization of Religion," *Journal for the Scientific Study of Religion* 1 (1961): 38.

predictor of the routinization process and the future of American Pentecostal identity.

The Dilemma of Mixed Motivation: Assessing Identity

According to O'Dea's theory, the emergence of a stable structure brings with it the capability of eliciting a wide range of individual motives that follow the ideal-typical state where a charismatic leader is able to generate "single mindedness."[13] It should be noted at the onset that the Pentecostal/Charismatic movement (PCM) has never had a single charismatic leader similar to Methodism's John Wesley, Quakerism's George Fox, Mormonism's Joseph Smith, or Christian Science's Mary Baker Eddy. Since it is a movement that has popularized and democratized charisma, the relationship between a charismatic leader and his disciples described by O'Dea has not been the prime motivating factor. Rather, the "single mindedness" of the movement has been energized by a common experience of the Holy Spirit out of which a diffused leadership and weblike organizations have emerged. In other words, the acceptance and personal experience of pneumatic experiences and self-identification as a people of the Spirit (rather than a single charismatic leader) have been the prime catalyst for the rise and growth of Pentecostalism. Countless churches, networks, and small sects came out of the particular experiences of the Holy Spirit that were reported in the nineteenth century. The experiences became better labeled and identified in the early twentieth century and soon began a global trek from the Azusa Street Revival in Los Angeles (from 1906-1909).[14] Within a few years (in 1914) leaders and pastors of some of these newly emergent Pentecostal groups came together in Hot Springs, Arkansas, a meeting that gave birth to the Assemblies of God, the largest and most influential white Pentecostal denomination in the United States.

Mixed motivation is here assessed through a discussion of religious identity issues and ambiguities in its distinctive worldview. A passage from

13. Cf. T. O'Dea and J. O'Dea Aviad, *The Sociology of Religion.*

14. Wacker (*Heaven Below*, p. 2) identifies Pentecostals as one of a genre of believers that he calls "radical evangelicals," who emphasized a fourfold gospel of "personal salvation, Holy Ghost baptism, divine healing, and the Lord's soon return." The emphasis of the streams differs somewhat, with classic Pentecostals putting their focus on "Holy Ghost baptism."

Zechariah 4:6 that serves as a motto for the AG provides a succinct statement about Pentecostal identity: "'Not by might, nor by power, but by my
Spirit,' says the LORD Almighty." This simple profession reflects what AG
theologian Frank Macchia describes as a "paradigm shift from an exclusive
focus on holiness to an outward thrust that invoked a dynamic filling and
an empowerment for global witness."[15]

As routinization extracts its due, however, this emphasis on "dynamic filling" and "empowerment" increasingly has shifted from personal
experience to doctrinal decree. Testimonies of lived experience that empowered early believers begin to take a back seat to a selective reconstruction of AG history and doctrine that often fails to capture the diversity that
found expression in the larger Pentecostal/Charismatic movements
(PCM). As Robeck[16] has effectively argued in his discussion of Pentecostal
identity, Pentecostalism has demonstrated a host of "indigenous entries"
including "Oneness Pentecostalism," "World Faith Pentecostalism," "Feminist Pentecostalism," and even "Gay Pentecostalism," all of which have
been rejected by the Assemblies of God. The AG has increasingly defined
itself primarily as "Evangelical Pentecostalism," or perhaps more accurately as "Evangelicalism plus tongues." Robeck goes on to state:

> Pentecostals have historically disagreed with one another on what con-
> stitutes a real Pentecostal, and, as a result, on what constitutes genuine
> Pentecostalism. The fact may not be easy for some Pentecostals to ac-
> cept, but it is true nonetheless. Each group seems to want to identify its
> own specific character as providing the best, if not *the only legitimate
> identity* for all real Pentecostals. *Insofar as their distinctives become all
> that define Pentecostalism, the real character, contribution, and impact
> of the whole Movement may be lost.*[17]

What has indeed happened is that the breadth and depth of the PCM
is eclipsed as each segment identifies with a single appendage much like

15. F. Macchia, "The Struggle for Global Witness: Shifting Paradigms in Pentecostal
Theology," in M. Dempster, B. Klaus, and D. Petersen (eds.), *The Globalization of
Pentecostalism* (Carlisle, Calif.: Paternoster Publishing, 1999), p. 16.

16. C. Robeck, "Toward Healing Our Divisions: Reflecting on Pentecostal Diversity
and Common Witness," The 28th Annual Meeting of the Society for Pentecostal Studies,
March 11-13, 1999.

17. C. Robeck, "Toward Healing Our Divisions," p. 5. Italics added for emphasis.

the blind men in their respective attempts to describe the proverbial elephant. The essence of Pentecostalism as a "new paradigm" — with the natural and supernatural engaged in a dialectical dance — is compromised by rationalist accommodative forces that threaten to dilute Pentecostal identity. As Evangelicals came to a recognized place in the American religious pantheon, some Pentecostals preferred to put aside the "new paradigm" to embrace a modernist religious identity that downplays controversial issues that come with "dynamic filling" and "empowerment."

Pentecostalism as a Distinct Worldview

It should be noted that Spirit-filled Christianity, unlike Christian Fundamentalism and Evangelicalism, is not primarily a reaction to modernity. It has proactively developed certain characteristics which taken together make its worldview distinct from other forms of Christianity, both of the liberal and conservative stripes. The Pentecostal worldview is experientially centered, with followers in a dynamic and personal relationship with a Deity who is both immanent and transcendent. According to Johns, "The Spirit-filled believer has a predisposition to see a transcendent God at work in, with, through, above and beyond all events. Therefore, all space is sacred space and all time is sacred time."[18] God is seen as active in all events past, present, and future, which work together in a kind of master plan. It is a worldview that tends to be "transrational," professing that knowledge is "not limited to realms of reason and sensory experience." Consistent with this transrational characteristic, Pentecostal Christians also tend to be anti-creedal, believing that "knowing" comes from a right relationship with God rather than through reason or even through the five senses. Theirs is a God who can and often does defy the laws of nature with the miraculous and unexplainable. Without doubt the Bible holds an important place in their worldview, but for many it is a kind of catalyst and litmus test for the authenticity of personal and corporate experience rather than a manual of rigid doctrine and practices. As Johns succinctly states: "In summary, a Pentecostal paradigm for knowledge and truth springs

---

18. J. Johns, "Yielding to the Spirit: The Dynamics of a Pentecostal Model of Praxis," in M. Dempster, B. Klaus, and D. Petersen (eds.), *The Globalization of Pentecostalism* (Carlisle, Calif.: Paternoster Publishing, 1999), p. 75.

from an experiential knowledge of God which alters the believer's approach to reading and interpreting reality."[19]

This paradigm is shared by both classic Pentecostalism and more recent PCM streams, especially those affected by revival fires. The newer groups, together with some classic Pentecostals, may self-identify as "Charismatic" or as "Spirit-filled" Christians (rather than Pentecostal). Often products of more recent revivals, they are stronger in what Grant Wacker has called *primitivism*[20] (and often weaker on *pragmatism*). The most obvious behavioral distinction between the two major streams of the PCM in North America can be found in the level of intensity in their respective rituals.[21] Differences also exist in spirituality, self-identity, and organizational structures. Those who self-identify as "Charismatic" are more likely to be open to a wider range of paranormal experiences (including prophecy, miracles, healing, and physical manifestations of an altered state of consciousness) as signs of Spirit baptism, while most Pentecostals tend to place a doctrinal emphasis on the gift of tongues (as does the AG). Furthermore, Pentecostal denominations (like the AG) tend to have well-developed bureaucratic structures, while many thriving neo-Pentecostal organizations tend to be nondenominational, with members focusing on relational ties expressed in loosely knit networks.[22]

What can be said about the PCM, regardless of the stream, is that it is more about a distinct spirituality than about religion.[23] Members share a common transcendent worldview rather than particular doctrines, defined ritual practices, or denominational involvement. This worldview is a curious blend of premodern miracles, modern technology, and postmodern mysticism in which the natural blends with the supernatural.

---

19. Johns, "Yielding to the Spirit," p. 79.

20. Cf. Wacker, *Heaven Below*.

21. Cf. D. Albrecht, *Ties in the Spirit: A Ritual Approach to Pentecostal/Charismatic Spirituality* (Sheffield: Sheffield Academic Press, 1999).

22. Scholars have generally not seen revival Pentecostalism in a positive light. The heightened primitivism of neo-Pentecostal spirituality and eschewing of traditional organizational structures has led at least one British sociologist to make the following wager: "I would put my money on the old Pentecostal denominations still to be with us, and thriving at the end of the next century. I'm not prepared to put my shirt on the new churches, and don't relish the long-odds on the Renewal" (A. Walker, "Foreword," in W. K. Kay, *Pentecostals in Britain* [Carlisle, Calif.: Paternoster Publishing, 2000], pp. vii-ix, ix).

23. Cf. Albrecht, *Ties in the Spirit*; S. Land, *Pentecostal Spirituality: A Passion for the Kingdom* (Sheffield: Sheffield Academic Press, 1993).

Signs and wonders analogous to those described in pre-modern biblical accounts are expected as normal occurrences in the lives of believers. Johns asserts that what underlies Pentecostal identity is a Pentecostal epistemology "congruous with the ancient Jewish approach to knowledge" — one that represents an alternative to modern ways of knowing:

> Pentecostals have an alternative epistemology because they have an alternative world-view. At the heart of the Pentecostal world-view is transforming experience with God. God is known through relational encounter which finds its penultimate expression in being filled with the Holy Spirit. This experience becomes the normative epistemological framework and thus shifts the structures by which the individual interprets the world.[24]

The general issue of Pentecostal identity is the core of this analysis — an issue that impacts each of the other dilemmas identified by O'Dea that I have applied to the AG in my earlier work.

A report of the survey findings on the Pentecostal identity of AG pastors will add details to this brief description of Pentecostal identity and the importance of its worldview in maintaining the dialectical tension between charisma and organization that has been at the heart of Pentecostalism's success. Through data provided by the survey questions, identity issues can be empirically explored to reveal core tenets as well as attendant ambiguities. What does it mean to be Pentecostal (specifically AG) in the twenty-first century? Is there congruence between the reported identity self-perceptions of pastors and the congregations they represent? Is there a good fit between these perceptions of identity and the denominational work performed by national and regional administrative offices? These and other related questions are used to tap the core identity and the ambiguities that exist around it, including the importance of being a member of the AG and Pentecostal and social distance between AG and adherents of other religious worldviews.

24. Johns, "Yielding to the Spirit," pp. 74-75.

Pentecostal Core Identity

AG scholar Everett Wilson put the question to pen: "What makes a Pentecostal?"[25] Difficulties of providing a simple description are deeply embedded in Pentecostal history. Wilson concludes that the social identity of Pentecostals is rooted in a worldview based on the "mystical, the 'supernatural' and the allegedly miraculous" that tended to stigmatize and marginalize early Pentecostals. For Wilson, being labeled a Pentecostal was the result of more than a confessional act — it signaled a worldview that separated these believers from other Christians. As Wilson comments:

> Like the proverbial duck, if the person looked like one, walked like one and talked like one — especially if one were supportive of the beliefs and practices that Pentecostals advanced — friends and neighbours could assume that he or she in fact belonged. At least the often-sung refrain, "I'm so glad I can say I am one of them" apparently gained favour not just to establish identity or to convince believers that they were with the right crowd, but because adherents gave assent to the Pentecostal way of looking at reality, something about which they may have felt deeply even when their convictions were not overtly displayed.[26]

Although professing to be a Pentecostal certainly does not tell the whole story of AG identity, it is a good place to begin a discussion of single-mindedness. Are pastors still singing "I am one of them," as the denomination has taken a more accepted place in the religious mosaic? For the vast majority of pastors, the answer appears to be yes — at least as measured by this survey. Self-identity can be gleaned from a question that instructed respondents to "indicate how important it is to identify with each of these groups": Assemblies of God, Pentecostalism, Revival/Renewal, Charismatic Movement/Third Wave, and Evangelicalism. (See the table on p. 158.) Pastors were most likely to report their primary self-identity as being Pentecostal (55 percent claimed it was "extremely impor-

25. E. Wilson, "They Crossed the Red Sea, Didn't They? Critical History and Pentecostal Beginnings," in M. Dempster, B. Klaus, and D. Petersen (eds.), *The Globalization of Pentecostalism* (Carlisle, Calif.: Paternoster Publishing, 1999).

26. Wilson, "They Crossed the Red Sea, Didn't They?" pp. 88-89.

PENTECOSTAL IDENTITY

Pastoral Self-Identity	not important	somewhat important	very important	extremely important
Assemblies of God	2% (10)	14% (59)	36% (155)	49% (211)
Charismatic	32% (134)	40% (164)	20% (82)	8% (34)
Evangelical	6% (27)	25% (107)	36% (155)	33% (139)
Pentecostal	3% (13)	10% (42)	33% (140)	55% (236)
Revival	4% (18)	10% (44)	32% (139)	54% (234)

Congregational Identity	not important	somewhat important	very important	extremely important
Assemblies of God	5% (23)	28% (121)	33% (142)	34% (149)
Charismatic	35% (244)	39% (161)	18% (82)	6% (27)
Evangelical	7% (31)	35% (148)	34% (144)	24% (104)
Pentecostal	4% (16)	19% (81)	35% (150)	42% (184)
Revival	6% (25)	18% (80)	35% (151)	41% (178)

Cooperative Fellowship	none	limited	full
Evangelicals	1% (3)	42% (183)	57% (246)
Charismatic Org.	8% (36)	65% (278)	27% (113)
Other Pentecostals	—	35% (148)	65% (282)
Nondenominational	4% (17)	65% (276)	32% (135)
Non-Christian groups	56% (24)	39% (166)	5% (20)
Mainline Protestant	5% (26)	70% (299)	24% (103)
Mainline Charismatics	8% (33)	66% (279)	26% (110)
Roman Catholic	30% (127)	61% (260)	9% (37)

tant," with another 33 percent saying it was "very important"). Nearly identical figures are reported for a personal identification with being a part of "Renewal/Revival," implying a conscious decision to support a revitalization of Pentecostal identity through fresh religious experiences. Reporting self-identification with the Assemblies of God was only slightly less than being Pentecostal and in Renewal/Revival.[27] Forty-nine percent reported self-identification with the AG as "extremely important," and another 36 percent said it was "very important."[28] The vast majority of the pastors report to having a religious identity that can be described as Pentecostal and being a member of the Assemblies of God. These same pastors also identify very strongly with the need to be involved in revival/renewal, suggesting that Pentecostalism is regarded (at least cognitively) as a dynamic process rather than a staid structure. These labels of self-identity, however, need to be further explored. Probing into the nature of Pentecostal identity will reveal some of the ambiguities that beset the denomination.

Ambiguity around the Core Identity

Despite the strong approval of retaining and reviving Pentecostal identity, an old dilemma lurks beneath the "single mindedness" reflected in the pastors' responses. The AG historically has found itself in the paradoxical position of promoting a distinct Pentecostal perspective while seeking rapport with Fundamentalism and later with a more moderate Evangelicalism, sectors of which have been very critical of the PCM. Within two years after its founding in 1914, the AG's message and mission, as Blumhofer noted, "would be held within the boundaries drawn by traditional evangelical doctrines."[29] Its attempt to become "fundamentalism with a differ-

27. The mean score for Pentecostal identification and for identifying with revival/renewal was 3.4 (on a four-point scale). The mean score for identification with being Assemblies of God was 3.3.

28. Although the solid majority figures are being highlighted, the strength of the minority position should not be overlooked. For 16 percent of the pastors identity with the AG is only "somewhat important" or "not important"; for 14 percent, being in revival is relatively unimportant; and for 13 percent, Pentecostal identity is not particularly relevant.

29. E. Blumhofer, *Restoring the Faith: The Assemblies of God, Pentecostalism, and American Culture* (Urbana and Chicago: University of Illinois Press, 1993), p. 135.

ence" (fundamentalism plus Spirit baptism) was not always well received. Pentecostals, including the AG, became the target of a resolution drawn up by the World's Christian Fundamentals Association in 1928 that went on record as "unreservedly opposed to Modern Pentecostalism." It was not until the development of the more moderate National Association of Evangelicals (NAE) in the early 1940s that the AG found acceptance in this newly formed transdenominational conservative network. However, support for the NAE by AG constituents was far from universal. Edith Blumhofer reports the critical response of one influential AG pastor to AG membership in the NAE:

> This association is not Pentecostal and many of their speakers who are listed for a convention . . . not only do not favor Pentecost, but speak against it. This [cooperating with the NAE] is what I call putting the grave clothes again on Lazarus, while the Scripture says: "Come out from among them, and be ye separate, saith the Lord, and touch not the unclean thing; and I will receive you and will be a Father unto you, and ye shall be my sons and daughters, saith the Lord Almighty."[30]

The old controversy appears to be far from resolved, and it is here that ambiguity surfaces. Clergy remain divided about the threat that Evangelicalism presents to a Pentecostal worldview that provides the AG with its distinct identity. Although a clear majority (60 percent) of pastors agreed or strongly agreed with the statement, "Too many AG churches have stressed a general evangelical identity at the expense of their Pentecostal heritage," a significant minority do not seem to fear any threat from Evangelicalism. At the same time more AG congregations appear to be downplaying their ties to the denomination, often selecting a name for the congregation that gives the impression of its being an independent evangelical church. The rituals in such congregations often follow an evangelical format in which Pentecostal practices are discouraged and squeezed out of public church services.

As can be seen in the table on p. 158, over two-thirds of the pastors responding to the survey self-identified as being Evangelical, a nomenclature that is less important for most respondents than Pentecostal, AG, and Revival/Renewal identities. The Evangelical label is clearly more important,

30. Blumhofer, *Restoring the Faith*, p. 187.

however, than is self-identity with cousins in the Charismatic/Third Wave sector of the PC movement who have been birthed by more recent religious experiences.[31] Despite the Pentecostal-like worldview and experiences of Charismatic/Third Wave churches, only 28 percent of the pastors reported that self-identity with these newer streams of the PCM was "extremely important" or "very important."[32] Thus, while self-identifying as Pentecostal and Evangelical is central to the identity of a clear majority of AG pastors, only a minority self-identify with newer streams of the PCM. It is precisely in these newer streams that revitalization and renewal are often accompanied by a range of "signs and wonders" of early Pentecostalism are more likely to take place.

Further ambiguity may be observed in the response to the question about belief in a dispensationalist interpretation of the Scriptures — a Fundamentalist "fundamental" of longstanding tension within the AG. The dispensationalist perspective, popularized in the notes of the Scofield Bible and permeating sectors of Evangelical Christianity, has been used to disparage Pentecostalism as at best delusional and at worst heretical. As Blumhofer has noted:

> Dispensationalists generally held that miracles had ceased with the Apostles; Pentecostalism thus could not be authentic, for its premise that New Testament gifts would mark the end-times church was false. Rejecting the latter-rain views by which Pentecostals legitimated their

31. Evangelical identity had a mean score of 3 (on a 4-point scale), while Charismatic/Third-Wave identity scores had a mean score of 2 points.

32. In North America the term "Pentecostal" usually refers to persons in denominations born out of or having some connection with the Azusa Street Revival in Los Angeles (1906-1909). "Charismatic" applies to those in mainline and newer (often independent) churches which embraced a Pentecostal worldview in the mid-twentieth century or later. In the U.S. some 23 percent of all evangelical Protestants, 9 percent of mainline Protestants, 13 percent of Roman Catholics, and 36 percent of Black Protestants claim to be "Spirit-filled," another appellation for those persons embracing the PCM (J. C. Green, J. L. Guth, C. E. Smidt, and L. A. Kellstedt, *Religion and the Culture Wars* [Lanham, Md.: Rowman and Littlefield Publishers, 1997], p. 228). Americans who claim to be Spirit-filled tend to self-identify as Pentecostal (4.7 percent) or Charismatic (6.6 percent), but much less frequently as "both Charismatic and Pentecostal" (0.8 percent). It is thus not surprising that these clearly Pentecostal pastors would express some social distance from Charismatics. Despite a worldview and theology that is more similar than dissimilar, most persons involved in the PCM are likely to identify with a particular stream of the movement.

place in church history, dispensationalists effectively eliminated the biblical basis for Pentecostal theology.[33]

Reflecting the fact that many Pentecostals did embrace the Scofield Bible (while rejecting its teachings on spiritual gifts in the contemporary church), 58 percent of the pastors strongly agreed or agreed with the statement, "I believe in a dispensationalist interpretation of Scripture."

Strong identification with Fundamentalists goes back to the earliest days of the AG. As Blumhofer has observed, "The causes espoused by fundamentalists seemed to coincide in meaningful ways with Assemblies of God denominational interests and to offer as well an opportunity for declaring Pentecostal sympathies with doctrinal 'fundamentals.' It was not long before 'right belief replaced right experience,' causing further erosion of AG distinctiveness."[34] The danger that fundamentalism (and its softer evangelical expression) poses for Pentecostal identity has been noted by Cox,[35] Hollenweger,[36] and Spittler,[37] among other scholars. Although the AG can be placed securely within the walls of larger Evangelicalism, there is evidence that such positioning fragments its identity and, as O'Dea's dilemma of mixed motivation suggests, leaves the denomination with possibly dissonant agendas that may not be easy to resolve.

As reflected in figures presented in the table on p. 158, dissonance between what AG ministers say and what they do can be seen in the groups with which they and their congregations are willing to cooperate in promoting issues of common concern. Although over a quarter of the ministers surveyed professed to want strong ties with the Charismatic/Third Wave movement in other sectors of Christianity, a decisive majority would prefer to keep their ties limited to other Pentecostals and Evangelicals. When pastors were asked to indicate the "extent you would like to see the AG cooperate with different religious groups," they were most likely to

33. Blumhofer, *Restoring the Faith*, p. 107.
34. Blumhofer, *Restoring the Faith*, p. 159.
35. Cf. H. Cox, *Fire from Heaven: The Rise of Pentecostal Spirituality and the Reshaping of Religion in the Twenty-first Century* (Reading, Mass.: Addison-Wesley, 1995).
36. Cf. W. Hollenweger, *Pentecostalism: Origins and Developments Worldwide* (Peabody, Mass.: Hendrickson, 1997).
37. Cf. R. Spittler, "Are Pentecostals and Charismatics Fundamentalists? A Review of American Uses of These Categories," in K. Poewe (ed.), *Charismatic Christianity as a Global Culture* (Columbia: University of South Carolina Press, 1994).

choose full cooperation with other Pentecostals. Sixty-five percent (65 percent) of pastors indicated a desire for full support with other Pentecostal churches. Despite paradigmatic differences, over half the pastors (57 percent) advocated full cooperation with Evangelical churches on issues of common concern. Pastors were much less likely to support full cooperation with associations of Charismatics in mainline Protestantism (26 percent) or with independent Charismatic organizations (27 percent).[38]

Summary and Conclusions

Clearly there is widespread acquiescence for a common Pentecostal identity among AG pastors, but the reality of this distinct identity (especially when considered in light of the special preference for Evangelicalism) is less evident. One explanation for the erosion of a distinct Pentecostal identity has been attributed to Pentecostalism's success in spreading a modulated version of their worldview to the larger Christian church. The once popular cessationist teaching that the supernatural gifts were meant only to jumpstart early Christianity (and then ceased) may have lost ground in many Evangelical circles. The old argument against the "signs and wonders" for contemporary Christians appears to be more about semantics and doctrinal statements than common belief. The issue becomes not whether the supra-empirical charismata are possible today but how frequently and intensely they may be expected. While there is undoubtedly some truth to this argument, it does not negate the ambiguity found in American Pentecostal identity that suggests a dilution of its distinct supra-natural worldview.

There does appear to be single-mindedness around key aspects of AG identity that has been found in the survey responses from pastors: the overwhelming majority of them claim that being AG and Pentecostal is "important" or "very important" to them. For many, however, this professed "Pentecostal identity" is increasingly being shaped by pragmatic and organizational forces at the expense of the primitive and experiential di-

38. The mean scores for cooperating with various religious groups "on issues of common concern" (on a three-point scale marking none, limited, and full) are as follows: with Evangelicals=2.6; with Pentecostals=2.6; with Independent/non-denominational churches=2.3; with Charismatic organizations=2.2; with Mainline Protestant churches=2.1; with Roman Catholic Church=1.7; and non-Christian religious groups=1.4.

mensions of early Pentecostalism. This ambiguity is reflected in the preferred collegiality with Evangelicals and the reported desire for social distance from non-Pentecostal charismatic groups (both Protestant and Catholic streams). The latter have often come into Spirit-filled Christianity and a Pentecostal worldview during revivals of the last half of the twentieth century. These revivals, however, have been rejected by many classic Pentecostals. It is the thesis of this article that the rejection of revitalized forms of Spirit-filled Christianity can be correlated to the draw that old Fundamentalism and now Evangelicalism has had for many Pentecostals — and that this preferred company weakens Pentecostal ideology and practice.

Underlying the strong self-identifying ties between Pentecostalism and Evangelicalism remain unresolved differences in worldviews. Evangelicalism is rooted in a rational religious response to the Enlightenment with an emphasis on "right belief." Pentecostalism, on the other hand, has been historically less interested in doctrine than in promoting the primal experiences that nurture its belief system. These primal religious experiences — especially if displayed during a public ritual — are increasingly becoming an embarrassment to many contemporary Pentecostals who would prefer to distance themselves from Pentecostalism's early primitive practices.[39]

Our analysis of the converging of the two seemingly dissonant identities — Pentecostalism and Evangelicalism — suggests that not all is well in white Anglo Pentecostalism. Pentecostal support for Fundamentalist theology and for Evangelical alliances (after the founding of the National Association of Evangelicals in 1943) sowed seeds of ambiguity and tension that are reflected in the survey findings reported here and in other scholarly observations about Pentecostal identity. Nowhere is this clearer than in the tendency of the AG to distance themselves from post-Azusa Street revivals that have birthed new streams of the Spirit movement — catalytic

39. See C. Bridges Johns, "Partners in Scandal: Wesleyan and Pentecostal Scholarship," in T. L. Cross and E. B. Powery (eds.), *The Spirit and the Mind: Essays in Informed Pentecostalism* (Lanham, Md.: University Press of America, 2000), pp. 237-50, for an excellent Pentecostal and postmodern response to M. Noll's *The Scandal of the Evangelical Mind* (Grand Rapids: Eerdmans, 1994) in which Pentecostals are given the dubious honor of creating much of the problem that Noll outlines in Evangelical scholarship. Bridges Johns observes how the Evangelical "mind" has been secularized and urges Pentecostal scholars to "push into the embarrassing rather than pull away in shame."

revivals that have breathed new life into the larger growing global Pente-costal/Charismatic movement. Findings from the AG pastor survey show that while the overwhelming majority of pastors profess to want revival, when it entered the churches in scores of cities and towns across the coun-try in the 1990s, only a minority of AG pastors visited any of these sites or brought revival speakers to their churches.[40]

If Philip Jenkins is correct in his assessment of "the coming of global Christianity," modernist Christianity has had its day on center stage.[41] The form of Christianity that is responsible for much of Christianity's growth south of the equator is an experiential and pneumatic approach that often transcends denominational labels. This ascendancy of a global form of pri-mal Christianity is mirrored in the Assemblies of God in the U.S. where many white Anglo churches are closing while new ethnic churches are thriving. (Significantly for the future of the AG, one fourth of its member-ship is now Hispanic.) The future of American Pentecostalism (as with global Pentecostalism) may not rest with Anglos but rather with the Asians, Africans, and Central and South Americans who are drawn to the pre-modern worldview that frames Pentecostal experiences. The identity espoused by pastors of being "AG, Pentecostal, and Evangelical" appears to be nearly unanimous, but it is one in which there is inherent tension and ambiguity that jeopardizes Pentecostalism's supranatural perspective. A revitalized American Pentecostal identity, however, is potentially in the making in immigrant churches. Among many recent newcomers to Amer-ica's soil can be found "a breathtaking ability to transform weakness into strength"[42] that Jenkins observed in developing nations worldwide.

40. M. Poloma, "The Symbolic Dilemma and the Future of Pentecostalism: Mysti-cism, Ritual and Revival," in E. Patterson and E. Rybarczyk (eds.), *The Future of North Amer-ican Pentecostalism* (Oxford: Oxford University Press, 2005, in press).

41. Cf. P. Jenkins, *The Next Christendom: The Coming of Global Christianity* (Oxford: Oxford University Press, 2002).

42. Jenkins, *The Next Christendom*, p. 220.

III. The Spirit: Connecting Theological,
      Scientific, and Philosophical Insights

The Hidden Spirit and the Cosmos

JOHN POLKINGHORNE

The arid account offered by a metaphysical view based on physical reductionism is one that describes a world void of spirit, either human or divine. Yet, to find room for the theologically indispensable concepts of a spiritual dimension to human nature and of the presence of the divine Spirit active within cosmic history, it is not necessary to go to the other extreme and embrace the metaphysics of platonic dualism. Instead, one can adopt a third metaphysical strategy, based on appealing to those discoveries of twentieth-century science that have revealed the widespread presence of intrinsic unpredictabilities in physical process, and then seeing them as revealing aspects of the nature of the world that are capable of being given metaphysical interpretation as signs of its possessing an openness to the future. One can also look to the increasing insights that physics is beginning to gain into the behavior of complex systems. We shall see that this development strongly encourages the expectation that, as twenty-first-century science progresses, the idea of active information, acting in a top-down fashion to produce ordered patterns of dynamical behavior, will come to stand alongside the bottom-up operation of energy in providing a pair of foundational concepts necessary for an adequate understanding of the causal character of the world.

This extended and more open view of the character of the processes at work in the world offers the prospect of our being able to begin to catch a glimpse of how it might be that our fundamental human experience of acting as intentional agents is compatible with the account of causal structure that science puts forward for consideration by the metaphysicians. A universe of the kind that these ideas suggest is certainly not one in which there is no place for the idea of spirit. On the contrary, there is promise that science will at last find itself in the position to be able to describe a world of which human persons might fittingly conceive themselves to be inhabitants. If that is the case, surely the activity of the Spirit also will be found not to have been banished from the account. The exploration of these possibilities is the subject of this essay; but before embarking on that project, some theological preliminaries are necessary.

Despite the dramatic outpouring of the Spirit at Pentecost, and the exuberance often exhibited in contemporary charismatic experience (such as that discussed in Frank Macchia's analysis of Spirit baptism and in Grant Wacker's historical account of ecstatic religious experience), there is a strong Christian tradition that attributes also a hidden quality to the working of the Paraclete. In Western Christian art, the first two Persons of the Trinity are conventionally represented by the kingly figure of the Father and the crucified figure of the Son, but the Third Person is usually portrayed only by the modest figure of a dove descending. This self-effacing character of the Spirit's presence finds a kind of verbal reinforcement in scripture due to an ambiguity present in both Hebrew and Greek, where the words *ruach* and *pneuma* carry a semantic width that encompasses the range of the English words: "wind," "breath," "spirit." In the Priestly account of creation, are we to translate Genesis 1:2b as saying that "the spirit of God was moving over the face of the waters," or would it be better rendered, "a wind of God swept over the face of the waters"? When Jesus says to Nicodemus, "The wind blows where it chooses and you hear the sound of it, but you do not know where it comes from or where it goes. So it is with everyone who is born of the Spirit" (John 3:8), the Greek of the Gospel contains a kind of theological pun in its double use of *pneuma*.

Taking seriously this veiled presence of the Spirit, expressed in the hidden character of pneumatological action, by no means implies a denial of more manifest activity also. The kind of bivalent working that Kathryn Tanner discusses in her chapter is surely just what one would expect of a divine Person, in contrast to the uniformity of action associated with a mere force such as gravity, unvarying in its characteristics. While the Spirit's activities will sometimes be explicitly exhibited in charismatic gifts and at other times be at work implicitly through hidden means, it is the former that has tended to attract the most attention, while the latter has received less theological discussion. Yet a balanced pneumatology needs to take account of both modes of working.

Writing from within the tradition of Eastern Orthodoxy, Vladimir Lossky made the illuminating suggestion that the covert dimension of pneumatological action reflects a fundamental insight of Trinitarian theology.

> The divine Persons do not themselves assert themselves, but one bears witness to another. It is for this reason that St. John Damascene says that "the Son is the image of the Father and the Spirit the image of the Son." It follows that the third Hypostasis of the Trinity is the only one not having His image in another Person. The Holy Spirit, as Person, remains unmanifested, hidden, concealing Himself in His very appearing.[1]

According to this understanding, the sanctifying work of the Spirit is a continuing activity that awaits its final completion in the creation of the community of the redeemed, a consummation that will be manifested fully only at the *eschaton*. Of the Persons of the Trinity, we can appropriate most specifically to the Spirit the title of *deus absconditus,* the hidden God.

We have acknowledged that a veiling of pneumatological activity is not the only thing to be said about the work of the Paraclete, yet recognition of a degree of reticence in the nature of the Spirit's presence does offer opportunities for the theological understanding of a number of puzzling aspects of the human encounter with divine reality. There is the important and pressing problem posed by the need to understand how the apparently clashing cognitive claims made by the different world faith traditions can be reconciled with the evident presence of authentic spiritual experience within all of them. I have suggested elsewhere that this phenomenon may most helpfully be considered in terms of the salvific working of the hidden Spirit.[2] In my opinion, a Trinitarian Christian can best base a respectful dialogue with those of other faiths on the recognition of the ubiquitous presence of the veiled activity of the anonymous Spirit, rather than by appealing to the more problematic notion of "anonymous Christians."

This essay aims to pursue a different exploitation of the same

---

1. V. Lossky, *The Mystical Theology of the Eastern Church* (Cambridge: James Clarke, 1957), p. 160.

2. J. C. Polkinghorne, *Exploring Reality,* ch. 7, to be published.

pneumatological insight. It seeks to treat in tandem a theological concern with the doctrine of creation and a scientific concern with what we know about the history and process of the universe. It turns out that this leads to the setting out of an explicitly pneumatological perspective on the doctrine of creation, seen in relation to what we know scientifically about the universe, of the kind that Amos Yong calls for in his chapter in this volume. Of course, there will not be iron links of logical entailment connecting the rational perspectives of science and religion, nor will there be a translation scheme by which scientific statements can be transformed into theological statements, or vice versa. Yet there must be a degree of complementary consonance between the two if they really are perspectives onto the one world of actual human encounter with reality.

The expectation of a degree of harmonious congruence between the insights of science and the insights of theology is increased by an understanding that the Spirit is "the Spirit of truth" (John 15:26), and so the Paraclete is expected to be hiddenly at work within all truth-seeking communities, including the community of science. This expectation accords with the affiliation found in the New Testament writings between "Spirit" and "truth," to which Michael Welker draws our attention in his chapter. In scripture, the Spirit is the carrier of the divine gift of wisdom. Concerning that gift, the author of The Wisdom of Solomon wrote that "it is he who gave me unerring knowledge of what exists, to know the structure of the world and the activity of the elements; the beginning and the end of times" (Wis. 7:17-18). The inspiration of the pursuit of science lies within the realm of the Spirit's hidden work. It is a well-documented experience in science that after intense but fruitless engagement with a profound problem, a period of mental rest in which the task is set aside for a while can then be followed by the sudden emergence into consciousness of the sought-for solution, fully formed and articulated. Psychologists will speak of the activity of the unconscious mind, but theologians may well believe that the hidden guidance of the Spirit, received and appropriated in those unconscious depths, has also played a part. Profound thinkers — and creative artists also — often speak of achievements that have about them the character of a gift received.

If it is indeed the case that recognition of the veiled character of the activity of the Spirit is an essential component in pneumatological thinking, one has to ask oneself whether there is any consonant counterpart to be discerned in what science can tell us about the processes of the cosmos. If that account were still to be phrased in terms of the clear and determinate picture of physical process that classical physics had so strongly suggested to Newton's great successor, Pierre Simon Laplace (who considered the notion of a "calculating demon," possessing total knowledge of the present that would then enable him to use Newton's laws completely to predict the future and to retrodict the past), the answer would surely have to be no. The relation of the deity to a clockwork cosmos could surely amount to no more than the spectatorial role of a deistic Clockmaker, watching it all tick away. However, the twentieth century saw the demise of a merely mechanical understanding of physical process. The universe has turned out to be something much more subtle and interesting than a clockwork world. A radical revision of the scientific picture was enforced by the unexpected discovery of widespread *intrinsic* unpredictabilities present in nature. (It is important to recognize that these limitations on the power to predict do not arise from human failure to measure or compute as precisely as we might, but they are originate from inescapable properties of the physical world itself.)

The first of these great revisionary discoveries was made in the 1920s through the insights of quantum physics into the character of subatomic processes. Heisenberg's celebrated uncertainty principle sets limits to the degree of access that is possible to a knowledge of the precise state of physical systems. The reliable ascertainment of the exact values of initial conditions — something that is demanded for Newtonian predictability to be able to function — is in fact forbidden by the intrinsic cloudiness of the quantum world.

A second source of unpredictability came clearly to scientific attention in the early 1960s, although the great French mathematician Henri Poincaré had grasped the essentials of the idea many years earlier. This time the cloudiness of nature was encountered at the level of everyday phenomena, of the kind for whose discussion Newton's ideas had seemed to have proved so effective. Although the equations of Newtonian theory admit of solutions that in principle are precisely determined, in practice it turns out that there are many systems for which these solutions are so exquisitely sensitive to the finest detail of initial circumstance that their exact consequences lie beyond any possibility of absolute calculation. The discovery of this surprising behavior in classical physics has been given the name of "chaos theory."[3] The classic expression of its character is encapsu-

3. See, J. Gleick, *Chaos* (London: Heinemann, 1988).

JOHN POLKINGHORNE

lated in the semi-serious concept of "the butterfly effect." The Earth's
weather systems can be in so sensitive a state that it is not too far-fetched to
say that a butterfly in some faraway jungle, stirring the air with its wings
today, might initiate effects that grew and grew until some weeks later they
precipitated a hurricane a thousand miles distant. Putting the matter more
formally, infinitesimal differences in the initial state of a chaotic system
can exponentiate to produce increasingly radically divergent consequences. The future behavior of these chaotic systems is not, however,
completely random. The adjective "chaotic" has turned out to have been
rather ill-chosen, since order and disorder, the haphazard and the con-
strained, interlace in the subtle patterns of future behavior that are accessible to these systems.

Science's picture of physical process has therefore turned out to be
unexpectedly occluded. In the physical world there are some clocks, but
there are also many clouds.

In fact, the resulting interleaving of order and disorder has been recognized as being the indispensable source of the fruitfulness of the cosmic
process that turned an initial ball of energy into the rich and complex
world of today, the home of saints and scientists. True novelty emerges
only in regimes that we have learnt to characterize as being "at the edge of
chaos." Too far on the orderly side of that border, and things are too rigid
for anything to happen beyond the mere rearrangement of what is already
there. A clockwork world is a boring world. Too far on the disorderly side
of the border, and new entities so readily fall apart that they are unable to
persist. A random world is mere anarchy. Only when regularity and openness operate in a balanced exchange can really new entities emerge and
persist. The fertility of evolutionary process does indeed depend upon an
interaction between "chance" (i.e., contingent particularity) and "necessity" (i.e., lawful regularity).

Our understanding of the workings of the universe is made further
problematic by a current failure to attain a global account that could syn-
thesize the theories that operate in different physical regimes and on different scales. As an example of this lack of understanding of interrelationship, one can point to unsolved problems concerning how quantum
theory and chaos theory might be integrated with each other. The straightforward reconciliation of the two is frustrated by the fact that quantum
theory has an intrinsic scale (set by the magnitude of Planck's fundamental constant), while chaos theory is scale-free, with its fractal nature mak-

ing the character of its behavior "the same all the way down" to the infinitesimal depths. To give another example of our patchy understanding of the nature of the physical process of the world, one can point to the fact that, eighty years after the great initiating discoveries, we still do not understand how measurements on fitful quantum entities yield specific results on each occasion of actual experimental interrogation.[4]

So far we have been describing what contemporary science can tell us about what is known concerning the character of physical process. It offers a picture that is suggestive of an overall view in which regularity and open-endedness interlace, but it is patchy in some of its detail. It is necessary to go on to ask, what implications might these epistemological conclusions have for the actual nature of reality? After all, unpredictability is an epistemological property and there is no necessary entailment from epistemology to ontology. For example, it is a matter for metaphysical discussion and decision whether one should interpret undoubted intrinsic unpredictabilities as signs of actual ontological openness, or merely as signs of an unfortunately necessary ignorance. Those who take a realist philosophical stance, believing that what we know is a reliable guide to what is the case, will incline to taking the former option. This does not mean that they will see unpredictability as representing the presence of an irrational surd in the scientific account, but rather that it indicates the possibility of there being further causal powers at work beyond those described by physics' traditional story of the exchange of energy between constituents.[5] Something of the character of what those additional causal principles might be can be surmised by recognizing an important trend in contemporary scientific thinking that has arisen from the increasing study of the behavior of complex systems, not treated as aggregates of separate parts but considered in the integrity of their wholeness.

One instructive set of examples is provided by physical dissipative systems which are maintained far from thermal equilibrium through the exchange of energy and entropy with their environment.[6] They display astonishing self-organizing propensities, enabling them to generate spontaneously patterns of large-scale orderly behavior. An instance is given by

4. Polkinghorne, *Exploring Reality,* ch. 2, to be published.
5. J. C. Polkinghorne, *Reason and Reality* (London: SPCK/Philadelphia: Trinity Press International, 1991), ch. 3; Polkinghorne, *Belief in God in an Age of Science* (New Haven: Yale University Press, 1998), ch. 3.
6. I. Prigogine and I. Stengers, *Order out of Chaos* (London: Heinemann, 1984).

the phenomenon of Bénard convection. Fluid is contained between two horizontal plates, and heat energy is fed into the system via the lower plate. In certain states of temperature difference between the two plates, the convective motion of the heated fluid is confined within vertical cells of hexagonal cross-section. This represents the generation of strongly correlated motions by trillions upon trillions of molecules.

Another set of examples comes from the study of computer emulations of simple logical networks. An example investigated by Stuart Kauffman is particularly instructive.[7] It is constituted by a Boolean net of connectivity two, but it is easier to envisage what is going on in equivalent hardware terms. Consider a large array of electric light bulbs. Each can be in one of two possible states, "on" or "off." The system evolves in steps and what happens to a particular bulb at the next step is determined, according to some simple rules, by the present states of two other bulbs in the array which are its correlates. The system is started off in a random configuration of illumination, some bulbs on and some bulbs off, and then allowed to develop according to this specification. One might have expected that nothing particularly interesting would happen and that the array would just twinkle away haphazardly for as long it was allowed to do so. In fact, however, it soon generates an astonishing degree of patterned behavior. If there are 10,000 bulbs in the array, they will quickly settle down to circulating through about only 100 patterns of illumination, despite the fact that in principle there are 103,000 such patterns in which the system might have been found.

These examples all display an astonishing self-organizing power to generate spontaneously large-scale dynamical patterns of remarkably ordered behavior. More has turned out truly to be different, the character of the whole exceeding the sum of its parts. At present no general theory is known that would be capable of collating and interpreting the behavior of the many particular instances that have been studied. Yet, in view of the striking phenomena encountered, there can surely be little doubt that such a theory must be awaiting discovery. It is a highly reasonable expectation that when such a theoretical understanding is gained it will place the concept of *information* (meaning the specification of patterned dynamical behavior) alongside energy as a foundational concept for the understanding of complex processes. In the physical cases studied, the systems are all inti-

---

7. S. Kauffman, *At Home in the Universe* (Oxford: Oxford University Press, 1995), ch. 4.

mately linked with their environment (whether through chaotic sensitivity to the slightest external disturbance, or through the input of energy into dissipative systems), so that they cannot properly be considered simply in terms of separate constituents but they require also a complementary holistic treatment. This encourages the expectation that the idea of top-down causality, the influence of the whole upon its parts, will also be a necessary component in the new kind of physical thinking.

This rather long account of the current scientific picture of the process of the physical world (even if it could be sketched here only in outline) has seemed to be a necessary prologue to considering how one might suppose the Spirit to have been at work within the unfolding history of creation. There is well-founded theological expectation that such an account should be possible. When Psalm 33 proclaims that "By the word of the LORD were the heavens made, and all their host by the breath (*ruach*, spirit) of his mouth" (v. 6), the theologian must suppose that more is intended here than simple indulgence in a rhetorical flourish. When the same theologian contemplates science's account of the evolutionary history of the cosmos, considering the tale of the 13.7 billion years that have served to turn an initial ball of energy into the richly diversified and fruitful universe of today, that theologian might surely hope that talk of the universe as a creation can amount to significantly more than just putting a pious gloss on what, in reality, has been no more than simply a sequence of self-contained natural events. If the world is a divine creation, the Creator must surely have played a role in its historically contingent unfolding fruitfulness, as well as being the source of its endowment of potentially fertile regularity. God must be in the "chance" as well as in the "necessity" of evolution.

In fact, the scientific picture of the cosmos as we have explored it does seem to be one that is open to the possibility of theological amplification. In place of the notion of a world of rigid mechanism, we have been given an account of a world of only partial predictability, within whose cloudy processes the causal influences that bring about the future can take a variety of forms. In place of the notion of a world in which all change is driven by the effects of energy alone, we have been offered the prospect of envisaging the operation of principles of self-organizing power that can spontaneously generate unique patterns of future behavior, an idea that opens up the possibility of the causal nexus of the world incorporating a concept of the influence of a kind of "active information," acting holistically in a top-down fashion.[8] Of course, this motivated conjecture of a role for non-energetic causality expressed through pattern-forming propensities falls well short of being an account that would be adequate to the task of describing the ability of a human agent to execute chosen intentions. Yet these are early days, and it seems fair to affirm the hope expressed at the beginning of this chapter, that modern science is at least moving in a direction that could eventually enable it to begin to describe a world of such sufficient flexibility and open richness that we could fittingly imagine ourselves as being among its inhabitants. That achievement would, of course, be a substantial gain for science. (We do not need the help of physics to assure us of our basic human experience of acting as intentional agents.) It also seems fair to say that a world of that kind would also be one within whose open process one could conceive of the Spirit as being continuously at work through the input of pure information into its unfolding history. This would constitute a pneumatological account of continuous creation, divine participation in the evolving fruitfulness of the world, exercised with covert reticence within the open grain of nature. There is no implication here of the theologically problematic idea of the Creator acting against the God-given character of the created world.

If it is indeed the cloudiness of intrinsically unpredictable process that affords the causal space within which pattern-forming influences of these kinds can be active, then the Spirit's interaction with cosmic process could indeed properly be described as the working of the *deus absconditus*. In a world of that veiled sort, it would not be possible to analyze the detail of what was occurring in such a way as to exhibit clearly and explicitly the balance of causal factors at work. It would not be possible to disentangle and itemize what was happening in an event, saying that simple natural forces did this, acts of human or other embodied agents did that, and the Spirit did the third thing. There would be a real pneumatological presence in what was going on in the history of creation, but its operation would be covert rather than overt.

In his insightful book about the Holy Spirit, *The Go-Between God*, John V. Taylor says something close to this when, speaking of the divine relationship to creation, he says, "If we think of a Creator at all, we are to find him always on the inside of creation. And if God is really on the inside, we

8. Polkinghorne, *Belief in God*, p. 63; Polkinghorne, *Faith, Science and Understanding* (London: SPCK/New Haven: Yale University Press, 2000), pp. 96-97 and 123-25.

must find him in the [total] process, not in the gaps."[9] Taylor is protesting against an interventionist picture of divine providence at work in the history of creation, of a kind that would associate the Spirit with acts of naked power exercised through sudden discontinuities. It will be clear that the account we are developing in this essay contrasts strongly with any idea of occasional arbitrary divine disruptions of natural process, for it is based on the picture of the Spirit working within the divinely ordained open grain of nature, rather than against that grain. Of course, the possibility of such openness depends upon the reductionist story, told by the limited kind of science that focuses exclusively on the properties of constituents, not being the total story. The metaphysical strategy of interpreting the intrinsic unpredictabilities found within physical process as being signs of causal openness depends upon recognizing that a purely bits and pieces account has gaps in it, so that by itself it could not be enough. It is important to recognize that these gaps are benign and not vicious, for they correspond to intrinsic features of the way the world is and they are not arbitrary patches of temporary ignorance that could be expected to fade away with the further advance of knowledge. It was the latter that made the old-fashioned idea of a "God of the gaps," confined to working only in patches of current scientific bafflement, such a theologically unacceptable notion. If it is indeed the case that human agency is exercised through some huge generalization of the notion of active information, then we are "people of the gaps" in a perfectly proper and acceptable sense. Equally, the Spirit could be the "Spirit of the gaps" in a similar fashion, an idea that does no violence to the integrity of either science or theology.

Thinking in this manner offers a positive way in which to conceive of divine influence and participation in the development of life. We know, of course, that bio-history has been the arena of evolutionary process. We can join with the distinguished French biochemist and committed atheist, Jacques Monod, in summarizing evolution as arising from the interplay of chance and necessity,[10] in the manner that we have already considered. Yet these are slippery words, and we have to understand them in the right way. We have suggested that necessity stands for the lawful regularity of the world, the specification of the setting which provides the context of fertile potentiality and relatively stable environment within which the shuffling

---

9. J. V. Taylor, *The Go-Between God* (London: SCM, 1972), p. 28.
10. J. Monod, *Chance and Necessity* (London: Collins, 1972).

explorations of evolutionary process alone can bear fruit. The insights of the Anthropic Principle have taught us that the fertility of the natural world depends critically upon the precise form that this necessity takes.[11] This fact is something that Monod's discussion totally failed to take into account. All his emphasis was placed on chance, with necessity simply taken for granted, without discussion. Yet, the given physical fabric of the cosmos had to be "fine-tuned" if there was to be any possibility of carbon-based life developing anywhere at all within it.

We have suggested also that chance does not stand for the operation of a kind of cosmic lottery, but it signifies the particularity of what has actually occurred. By no means everything that could happen has happened, so that there is a considerable degree of historical contingency in the story of the universe and of life. While one may discern that the potentiality for the eventual development of self-conscious beings was, as it were, imprinted on the cosmos immediately following its origin in the Big Bang, because of the precise form taken then and since, by the laws of nature, no one supposes that this development, when it actually came to birth, necessarily involved the emergence of a being with precisely five fingers.

If God is the Creator of the world in a manner that amounts to more than spectatorial deism, then God must have been present and active in this evolving process. Yet that divine presence is not in the form of creation's puppet-master — for the early insight of Charles Kingsley and Frederick Temple that an evolving world is a creation in which creatures are "allowed to make themselves" is surely true — but as an active participant in the great improvisatory act of unfolding cosmic and terrestrial history. It is rather straightforward theologically to understand fruitful potency as being part of the Creator's gift to creation. Within a Trinitarian scheme of thinking, this wonderfully fertile order of the cosmos is naturally appropriated to be the work of the Second Person, the Word "through whom all things were made" (John 1:3) in their remarkable potentiality. But the God who is more than the God of deism must also be present in the chance as well as in the necessity, truly at work within the contingent happenstance of history. The picture we have explored of the Spirit at work "on the inside," operating in a veiled fashion through the input of information into the open grain of natural process, surely meets this theo-

11. J. D. Barrow and F. J. Tipler, *The Anthropic Cosmological Principle* (Oxford: Oxford University Press, 1986); J. Leslie, *Universes* (London: Routledge, 1989).

logical need. By combining these two modes of understanding, the fruitful history of the cosmos, understood as a created world sustained in being by the will of the Father who is the Fount of Being, is also seen to be the story of the work of Word and Spirit, operating, as Irenaeus said long ago, as the "Two Hands of God."[12]

Yet, that kind of language might, at first sight, seem in danger of being impersonally functional, and a further point remains to be made if one is to be able to avoid that theological pitfall. In a remarkable passage in Romans 8:18-27, Paul offers a profound corrective to any such tendency. When he speaks there of the creation being "subjected to futility," from our post-Darwin perspective we think immediately of the blind alleys and extinctions which are inevitable concomitants of evolutionary exploration. We know that change and decay are inescapable features of a world in which the manner in which new forms of life arise necessarily requires the succession of one generation by the next. Paul goes on to describe the Spirit's relation to those caught up in this process, speaking in terms of intercession "with sighs [*stenagmoi* — groanings] too deep for words." This pneumatological involvement with the travail of creation indicates why the Spirit is to be recognized as a divine Person, and not simply as an impersonal divine power at work in the world.

Revaluations of traditional thinking that retain the valid insights of the past but reorganize their detailed expression in the light of contemporary knowledge are characteristic of the kind of development that takes place as different forms of rational inquiry and truthful exploration interact with each other. All our thinking post-Darwin has been profoundly influenced by science's discovery, in its own domain, of the fundamental significance of temporality, so that time is to be understood as the matrix of unfolding fertility and not merely as the index of successive occurrence. The earliest Hebrew thinking about the meaning of the bestowal of spirit seems to have tended to picture it in terms of a static gift of substance, whether in the form of a particular skill (as when Bezalel was empowered for the task of constructing the tabernacle; Exod. 31:2), or in an almost vitalist sense as an indispensable component of a living being (cf. Gen. 2:7; Ps. 104:29-30). Today our manner of thinking is more dynamic and lays a greater emphasis on the unfolding development of structured potentiality. The concept of the Spirit hiddenly at work on the inside of

12. E. Osborn, *Irenaeus of Lyons* (Cambridge: Cambridge University Press), pp. 91-93.

cosmic history, acting through the input of active information into the unfolding story of continuous creation, is a modest attempt to use current scientific insight as a guide to contemporary theological understanding of the fruitfulness of cosmic process and the remarkable story of the development of terrestrial life.

Ruach, the Primordial Chaos, and the Breath of Life: Emergence Theory and the Creation Narratives in Pneumatological Perspective

AMOS YONG

The saying that the Holy Spirit has traditionally been the "shy" or "silent" member of the Trinity and therefore more or less absent or marginalized in the history of Christian thought is also applicable to the theology and science dialogue as that has occurred over the last few generations. More recently, however, we have experienced a kind of renaissance in Christian theological reflection on the Holy Spirit that has invigorated the study of pneumatology proper and provided pneumatological perspectives on other themes of the traditional theological loci. Not surprisingly, then, we have also begun to see proposals exploring the question about what pneumatology can contribute to the theology and science conversation.[1] The hypothesis being tested in this essay is that some of the gains made in recent pneumatological theology can contribute to the theology and science discussion both in terms of helping us think further about the God-world relationship in general and about divine action in particular, and in

---

1. This was first broached with the work of W. Pannenberg, who asked about the possibility of connecting the Christian doctrine of Spirit with field theory (see his essays collected in *Toward a Theology of Nature: Essays on Science and Faith*, ed. Ted Peters [Louisville: Westminster/John Knox Press, 1993], esp. chs. 5-7). Other proposals include: G. L. Murphy, "The Third Article in the Science-Theology Dialogue," *Perspectives on Science and Christian Faith* 45:3 (1993): 162-69; Ernest L. Simmons, "Toward a Kenotic Pneumatology: Quantum Field Theory and the Theology of the Cross," *CTNS Bulletin* 19:2 (1999): 11-16; and, most recently, Denis Edwards, *Breath of Life: A Theology of the Creator Spirit* (Maryknoll, N.Y.: Orbis, 2004).

terms of more clearly delineating a theological methodology that not only tolerates but actually requires engagement with the sciences and with scientific method.

I propose to develop my argument in conversation with Philip Clayton's theory of emergence. Clayton is an ideal dialogue partner because of his attempts over the last few years to wrestle with what he has called the "emergence of spirit."[2]

Section one will provide an overview of Clayton's theory of emergence as developed in his most recent book, *Mind and Emergence*.[3] This will be followed in section two by a rereading of the creation narratives from what I call a canonical-pneumatological perspective. Here, I suggest that resources from recent developments in pneumatological theology can help bridge the gap between the ancient biblical text and modern science. The concluding section will show how the pneumatological perspective presented in part two not only augments Clayton's metaphysical hypothesis from a theological direction, but also provides theological justification for Clayton's concerns about the integrity of science.

Clayton's Theory of Emergence

To be clear, emergence is a philosophical or metaphysical hypothesis rather than a theological doctrine or scientific datum. It is a large-scale theoretical framework derived primarily from our engagement across the spectrum of the natural sciences and answerable chiefly to them. For our purposes, the best way to grasp the scope of Clayton's theory is to identify what he considers to be its eight primary characteristics (pp. 60-62).

First, emergence theory presumes that the world in all its complexity is nevertheless made out of one kind of stuff. Here, Clayton is advocating a kind of *monism* over and against any kind of Cartesian or substance dual-

2. See Clayton, "The Emergence of Spirit," *CTNS Bulletin* 20:4 (Fall 2000): 3-20, and Clayton, "Emerging God," *Christian Century* 121:1 (13 January 2004): 26-30. For Clayton's previous book-length forays into the theology and science conversation, see his *Explanation from Physics to Theology: An Essay in Rationality and Religion* (New Haven: Yale University Press, 1989) and *God and Contemporary Science* (Grand Rapids: Eerdmans, 1997).

3. P. Clayton, *Mind and Emergence: From Quantum to Consciousness* (Oxford: Oxford University Press, 2004). Unless otherwise noted, all references to this book will be given parenthetically by page number in my text.

ism on the one side, and against a crass materialism on the other. Instead, emergentist monism provides a coherent theoretical framework to explain the differentiated but ultimate unity between, for example, consciousness and the material substrate of the world.[4]

Second, emergence theory is able to account for the *hierarchical complexity* of the world. By this, Clayton is calling attention to the "ontological pluralism" (p. 148) of the world manifest, for example, in human creatures who are physical, biological, psychological, and even (Clayton suggests) spiritual realities. Each of these levels or domains emerges from the previous one, but, once emergent, is sufficiently distinct so as to require different kinds of explanation. To proceed along these lines assumes that emergent levels of reality are neither merely aggregates of sublevel entities nor that they can be reduced to those parts.

This leads, third, to the recognition of the *temporal* dimension of emergentist monism. Whether understood through Darwinian theory or otherwise, increasing levels of complexity are structured and have evolved over time. With this, Clayton insists that new elements appear in the world that are dependent upon previous configurations of things (hence monism) but are irreducible not only epistemologically and ontologically but also temporally to their parts. With this latter claim, the processes of emergence are unpredictable. Novelty's evolutionary trail can be recognized in retrospect, but not predetermined in advance.

Fourth, emergence theory is sufficiently comprehensive to recognize that there is *no monolithic law of emergence* that can account for the disparate processes occurring at each level of complexity. This needs a bit of unpacking, so let us briefly digress to distinguish here between what happens at the level of physics and chemistry versus that of biology.

At the level of physics, emergence calls attention to "the development of complex physical and chemical systems which, though verifiable through observation, cannot be derived from fundamental physical principles" (p. 66). Examples Clayton gives, with references to scientific literature, are conductivity, which cannot be reduced to the study of electrons; fluid dynamics, which cannot be deduced from the motion of individual

---

4. Clayton acknowledges here his acceptance of the label "emergentist monism" from fellow science-and-religion scholar, A. Peacocke; see Peacocke, "The Sound of Sheer Silence: How Does God Communicate with Humanity," in R. J. Russell et al. (eds.), *Neuroscience and the Person* (Vatican City: Vatican Observatory Publications, 1999), pp. 214-47.

particles; and ordered patterns such as snowflakes, snow crystals, and other ice phenomena, which cannot be predicted from their chemical structures. At this level, Clayton recognizes that some physicists and chemists would admit only that our current state of knowledge cannot adequately account for these emergent phenomena, but not that we cannot in principle do so given further inquiry. Hence, Clayton is willing to label these examples of *weak emergence* given the possibility that future knowledge will enable an explanation in terms of their constitutive parts.

Stronger forms of emergence, however, can be identified at the biological level. Four kinds of processes govern interactions at this level (pp. 80-84). First, there are differences in scale such that what happens at the level of cells, molecules, and neurons is different from what happens at the level of the central nervous system or the organism as a whole; microstructures and micro-organisms act and react differently than macrostructures and macro-organisms. Second, biochemical processes are sustained in part through feedback loops: cells interact with other cells, plants with their environment, and so on. Beyond the horizontal relationships that constitute feedback loops are more vertically organized relationships that comprise local-global interactions, for example, plants-and-animals-in-their-environment affecting the larger ecosystem, which in turn influences the behavior of the individuals. Finally, there are nested hierarchies wherein complex systems survive and perpetuate as they incorporate other discrete subsystems. Clayton's point is that different laws of emergence characterize what happens at the level of physics and chemistry on the one hand, and at the level of biology on the other. Even within the biological domain, there are weaker or stronger forms of emergence across the spectrum, depending on whether we're talking about the emergence of microphysical cell states or of macrophysical organisms (cf. p. 108).

Hence, fifth, the emergence hypothesis *links together disparate processes of complexity* in natural history via broadly similar patterns of creativity. Clayton proposes that observations across the sciences reveal a family resemblance of shared traits that characterize the pattern of emergence across levels. Level 2 emerges from Level 1, he suggests, if $L1$ is chronologically and historically prior to $L2$ and $L2$ *both* does not exist apart from $L1$ but emerges unpredictably (in terms of the rules governing what emerges and in terms of the qualities or properties of the emergent level) from "a sufficient degree of complexity in $L1$" (p. 61) *and* is finally irreducible causally, explanatorily, metaphysically, or ontologically to $L1$. Insofar as this is empirically derivative from scientific data, "emergence is just that pattern that recurs across a wide range of scientific (and non-scientific) fields" (p. 49).

Sixth, *downward causation* is exercised by higher levels on lower levels. The clearest evidence for this is found at the level of biological creatures, especially in the emergent properties of entities that exercise agency at various levels. There are, of course, materialists or reductive physicalists who treat mind or consciousness epiphenomenally, as explicable finally in terms of brain states. There are also nonreductive physicalists who may advocate a theory of the mind as *strongly supervenient* upon brain states: in this case, while admitting that mental states do constrain brain activity, they believe that mental states are finally determined by the physical or neural substrate, resulting in the real explanation being provided by the processes that characterize the subvenient level of brain functions. Alternatively, there is the *weak supervenience* theory that Clayton himself (and others) subscribe to: in this case, the mind is dependent on but irreducible to the neurobiological processes of the brain-body, even while the mind not only constrains but also exercises causal agency that affects brain and body activity. Note here that those who favor *strong supervenience* are like those who advocate *weak emergence*: both groups are likely to suggest that explanation is in principle reducible to the lower level, given further scientific discovery. By contrast, Clayton favors (with others) *weak supervenience* together with *strong emergence*, arguing that brain and mind and lower- and higher-levels are in principle irreducible because they concern qualitatively and ontologically distinct realities. The difference, then, is that strong supervenience finally allows only for "upward causation" wherein brain states affect mind states, whereas weak supervenience accounts for "downward causation" as well.

Seventh is what Clayton calls *emergentist pluralism*. This combines the hierarchical complexity and ontological pluralism of his second thesis with the temporal and emergent monism of his third, resulting in the claim that new levels of ontologically primitive realities appear over time that are not just aggregates of lower-level entities and cannot be reduced to them. Further, Clayton also wishes to emphasize the pluralism of levels spanning the entirety of natural history (to date) and the broad spectrum of the scientific disciplines. If there were only two levels — that is, physical and mental — then Clayton's emergence theory would collapse to a dualist metaphysics. However, if there are three or more levels — and Clayton often refers to Harold Morowitz's study that identifies at least twenty-eight distinct levels[5] — then identification of similar patterns of activity across these multiple levels sustains a more comprehensive philosophy of emergence that goes beyond reductionistic materialism or dualism.

Finally, Clayton proposes to understand *mind as emergent*. More accurately, rather than claiming to understand "mind" fully, Clayton prefers to talk about "mental properties" (e.g., p. 169) as dependent upon, interactive with, and irreducible to physical properties. The driving force behind Clayton's theory of mind is the "hard problem of consciousness" (pp. 120-23): self-conscious and personal states of experience. The options, generally speaking, remain: (1) materialism or epiphenomenalism; (2) dualism; (3) strong supervenience/weak emergence; or (4) weak supervenience/strong emergence. (1) fails to account for either the hard problem or human moral agency; (2) fails to account for the neuroscientific data that shows mental states to be dependent upon brain states; and (3) is finally reductionist, allowing only "upward causation" but not the reverse. Only (4) preserves human agency, acknowledges that the mind is dependent on but irreducible to the brain, and provides an account of consciousness that can deal with the hard problem. Mind as emergent is therefore a way between reductionism on the one side and dualism on the other. Generalizing from the neuroscientific data toward an ontology of part-whole relations (with neither being reducible to the other) and a theory of downward causation leads Clayton to his theory of emergence.

It is important to note that Clayton recognizes that the perspective of science will endorse the weak emergence thesis if attracted to emergence theory at all. This is because the weak emergence thesis privileges the physical domain and presupposes a kind of ontological closure to the world that not only enables its final reductionistic move but also fits with the strict demands of empirical science. In this sense, Clayton acknowledges that weak emergence is the position to beat (p. 32). On the other hand, Clayton advocates the strong emergence thesis — as defined by the preceding eight characteristics — because of its greater explanatory power, especially with regard to human consciousness and causation. Further, insofar as emergence theory passes initial plausibility conditions, it provides a theoretical framework for a scientific research program that can invigorate

5. See H. Morowitz, *The Emergence of Everything: How the World Became Complex* (New York: Oxford University Press, 2002).

scientific inquiry. Finally, inasmuch as emergence is presented as a metaphysical hypothesis, it is in principle falsifiable by the empirical data that is culled from such a wide-ranging scientific research program. In any case, throughout, Clayton attempts to find a *via media* between attention to empirical detail and philosophical generalization (in terms of scientific and philosophical method), between physicalism and dualism (with regard to the neurology and philosophy of mind), and between reductionism and supernaturalistic emergence (with regard to naturalism and materialism versus supernaturalistic theism).[6]

I have not so far said anything about where theism fits into Clayton's hypothesis. While Clayton's discussion of theism occupies only part of the final chapter of his book, some comments need to be made in light of what follows. That Clayton is led to theism seems to follow naturally from his working to find a more complete metaphysical account which goes beyond simply rejecting physicalism, postulating "persons as self-conscious agents" (p. 175), advocating for the causal openness of the world (against weak emergentists), and presuming an inexplicable rationality to the world. Clayton's suggestion to "conceive mind (or spirit or deity) not merely as an emergent quality of the natural world, but also as a source of agency in its own right" (p. 182) signals his shift from an immanentist theism to a transcendent divine mind. As a fairly traditional theist who rejects the idea that God is dependent upon the world, Clayton recognizes that he is trading in the mind-body dualism for "theological dualism" (pp. 185-87). While Clayton can talk about the emergence of mind or consciousness and, in that sense, about the emergence of (human) spirit, he cannot talk about the emergence of the divine Spirit within these same processes of natural and biological history without compromising the otherness of God.

What then does Clayton think about the God-world relation? While God may be at work at the quantum level, this is empirically untestable. Further, surely God can influence human minds even as human beings influence one another, but we need to be wary lest the divine mind be anthropomorphized and reduced to just another consciousness at work in

---

6. To appreciate the deftness with which Clayton navigates between the Scylla and Charybdis of these various poles, see the essay by M. Silberstein, "Reduction, Emergence, and Explanation," in P. Machamer and M. Silberstein, *The Blackwell Guide to the Philosophy of Science* (Malden, Mass., and Oxford, U.K.: Blackwell, 2002), pp. 80-107.

the world. In the end, Clayton generalizes from the human experience of personal and purposeful activity leading to the conclusion that divine activity is similarly personal and purposeful. The cost, of course, is that divine activity is not amenable to scientific investigation even as the language of purpose, intention, and desire we know at the human level escapes the scope of scientific inquiry. Yet this theistic account, Clayton suggests, is not incompatible with the data of science, and in fact adds substantially to a more complete metaphysical vision.

A Canonical-Pneumatological Reading of the Creation Narratives

At this point I turn to provide what I would call a "pneumatological assist" to Clayton's project, and do so through a rereading of the creation narratives. While I am in no position to dispute Clayton's interpretation of scientific data (members of the scientific community will have to assess those details of Clayton's argument), as a theologian I am interested in further securing the theological credentials of emergence theory without undercutting its appeal to the sciences. I am optimistic that a pneumatological reading of the creation narratives will contribute to a more robust theological vision both in terms of correlating aspects of emergence theory with the biblical witness and in terms of the mutual illumination that I believe can occur between a metaphysic of emergence and a pneumatological theology. In the concluding section, I will also briefly suggest reasons why the following pneumatological theology of creation sustains rather than undermines scientific inquiry.

At this point, however, the question may arise: why Genesis 1–2? This is not unimportant since few biblical scholars and theology-and-science researchers today would be willing to read these chapters as contributing to a scientific understanding of the world. From a strictly exegetical and historical perspective, I believe that the authors of the Priestly and Yahwist portrayals were intent on combating ancient Near Eastern cosmogonies rather than either the Big Bang theory or neo-Darwinism, just to name two contemporary scientific orthodoxies.[7] From a canonical-pneumatological per-

---

7. Hence a literary-theological interpretation of Genesis 1–2 would emphasize its contrasts with other ancient Near Eastern cosmogonies, the biblical account being less, if

spective, however, I suggest that the creation narratives contain key insights that would complement and even enrich the (rather anemic) theological component of Clayton's emergence metaphysic as presented in *Mind and Emergence*. By "canonical-pneumatological," I am referring to the broader biblical witness and its thematic contributions to a Christian understanding of the Holy Spirit.

Having made this claim, however, I would also insist that there are grounds within the creation narratives themselves that justify such a pneumatological interpretation. These grounds are twofold. First, the Priestly account of the *ruach Elohim* (breath, wind, even storm of God) that "swept over the face of the waters" (Gen. 1:2)[8] continues with the breath *(nephesh)* given to *all* living creatures (1:30). The Yahwist account also adds that the LORD breathed *(naphash)* specifically into *ha-'adam* "the breath [*nishmah*] of life" (Gen. 2:7). I suggest that references to the wind and breath of God at the beginning and end of the Priestly narrative — not to mention the further specification in the Yahwist text — together serve as "bookends" of an account regarding divine creativity that not only allows but also solicits a more specifically pneumatological understanding.[9]

---

not completely, nonpolitical, noncultic, and nonmythological. For developed arguments, see N. M. Sarna, *Understanding Genesis: The Heritage of Biblical Israel* (1966; New York: Schocken Books, 1970), esp. ch. 1; H. Blocher, *In the Beginning: The Opening Chapters of Genesis*, trans. D. G. Preston (Leicester, U.K., and Downers Grove, Ill.: InterVarsity Press, 1984); and S. Niditch, *Chaos to Cosmos: Studies in Biblical Patterns of Creation*, Scholars Press Studies in the Humanities 6 (Chico, Calif.: Scholars Press, 1985).

8. All biblical quotations are from the New Revised Standard Version. "Swept over" has also been translated "hovering over" (NIV) or "moved upon" (KJV), and is from the Hebrew *meraphehet 'al* which means, literally, "flutter," "flap," or "shake." More literally, *ruach Elohim . . . meraphehet 'al* could read "the wind of God . . . shook. . . ." Yet the word occurs elsewhere only in Deut. 32:11 to denote a bird brooding over its young, retaining some of the connotations of the Syriac root, *rahep*, literally, "to brood," "incubate," "shake," or "protect"; see L. Koehler and W. Baumgartner et al., *The Hebrew and Aramaic Lexicon of the Old Testament*, trans. and ed. M. E. J. Richardson, 2 vols. (Leiden, Boston, and Köln: Brill, 2001), 2:1219-20. For this reason, I present a pneumatological-*canonical* perspective on the creation narrative, since the warrant to see *ruach Elohim* as referring to the Spirit of God comes not explicitly from the Priestly account but can be derived implicitly from the text if read within the broader framework. My thanks to G. A. Long for pointing me to the Syriac background.

9. For another attempt to read the creation narratives from a pneumatological vantage point, see D. L. Dabney, "The Nature of the Spirit: Creation as a Premonition of God," in G. Preece and S. Pickard (eds.), *Starting with the Spirit: Task of Theology Today* (Adelaide: Australia Theological Forum, Inc., and Openbook Publishers, 2001), 2:83-110.

From this, second, a canonical reading of the creation narrative justifies connecting the breath given to all creatures in general and to *ha-'adam* in particular with the *ruach Elohim* especially in light of Qohelet's affirmation that "the dust returns to the earth as it was, and the spirit [*ruach*] returns to God who gave it" (Eccles. 12:7). There is no need to read the divine *ruach* here as referring to the third person of the Trinity since that would certainly be an anachronistic imposition upon this text. At the same time, given the Christian testament witness to God as spirit (cf. John 4:24), a pneumatological rereading of Genesis 1–2 can proceed at least on this basis. Within this framework, I agree with Jay McDaniel that creation can be understood to be "en-spirited by God."[10] Not only does God create all things through Word — "Let there be . . ." — by the Spirit, but all things are what they are as creations of God precisely because they originate in the divine Word spoken and uttered by the *ruach Elohim*.[11]

Gerhard von Rad claims that Genesis 1:2 with its reference to the divine breath stands on its own concerning God's activity over the chaotic elements, and that the Spirit "takes no more active part in creation."[12] In response, while verse 1 certainly introduces the entire creation narrative, verse 2 equally certainly belongs at least to the activities of God on the first day.[13] But, further, from a canonical perspective, the psalmist also warrants a pneumatological reading of the creation story: "By the word of the LORD the heavens were made, and all their host by the breath of his mouth" (Ps. 33:6), and "When you hide your face, they [the animals] are dismayed; when you take away their breath, they die and return to their dust. When you send forth your spirit, they are created; and you renew the face of the ground" (Ps. 104:29-30). Again, of course, this pneumato-theological account should then be understood

10. See J. McDaniel, "'Where Is the Holy Spirit Anyway?' Response to a Sceptic Environmentalist," *Ecumenical Review* 42:2 (1990): 162-74.

11. See W. Pannenberg's discussion on "Cooperation of Son and Spirit in the Work of Creation," in his *Systematic Theology*, vol. 2, trans. G. W. Bromiley (Grand Rapids: Eerdmans, 1994), pp. 109-15.

12. Von Rad continues, "The Old Testament nowhere knows of such a cosmological significance for the concept of the spirit of God"; G. von Rad, *Genesis: A Commentary*, rev. ed., trans. J. H. Marks (Philadelphia: Westminster, 1972), pp. 49-50.

13. U. Cassuto, *A Commentary on the Book of Genesis, Part I: From Adam to Noah, Genesis I-VI8*, trans. I. Abrahams (1961; reprint, Jerusalem: Magnes Press, The Hebrew University, 1989), pp. 19-20; and C. Westermann, *Genesis 1–11: A Commentary*, trans. J. J. Scullion, S.J. (Minneapolis: Augsburg, 1984), pp. 94-97 and 102-10.

not primarily as a scientific treatise about the history of creation (notice the creation of light, day and night and the appearance of terrestrial vegetation before the calling forth of the sun and moon), but rather as a statement against polytheism, astrological practices, and the pantheistic worship of nature in its variations, all prevalent in the surrounding ancient Near Eastern cultures.[14]

First, creation in all its complexity flows from *ruach Elohim* brooding over or moving upon the primeval watery chaos *(tohu wabohu).*[15] For good reason, then, the rabbis since at least the time of Philo have understood the spirit of God as "the element of creative fire, or the divine intellect that gives form to matter."[16] In this case, not only does the *ruach Elohim* restrain and reshape the primeval chaos, but this chaos is itself neither a messy something-or-other nor literal void. Of course, some who affirm the traditional doctrine of *creatio ex nihilo* would understand the void to be purely chaotic and, hence, indeterminate and in that sense indistinguishable from nothing.[17] Yet the Priestly author indicates that the *ruach Elohim* hovered not over pure nothing, but over the waters *(mayim).*[18] On the one hand, then, some have understood the primeval chaos as "a state of maximal plenitude, in which all things are churning, boiling, but without the discrete unities and form that enable the stuff of this world to obey

14. Thus, the Priestly writer's insistence on the creaturely status of the sun and even light itself reflects his concern with the ancient worship of the sun. Later biblical writers, however, would equate light with the divine itself; cf. Ps. 104:1-2; 1 Tim. 6:16; James 1:17; and 1 John 1:5 with Westermann, *Genesis 1–11*, p. 114.

15. If verse 1 is understood as introductory to the entire narrative, then any speculation about a primeval fall of angels, etc., between the first two verses is just that: speculation read into the text rather than emergent from the text; see von Rad, *Genesis*, pp. 50-51.

16. P. Ochs, "Genesis 1–2: Creation as Evolution," *Living Pulpit* 9:2 (April-June 2000): 8-10, quote from 9. See also M. Pulver, "The Experience of the *Pneuma* in Philo," in J. Campbell (ed.), *Spirit and Nature: Papers from the Eranos Yearbooks*, Bollingen Series 30.1, trans. R. Manheim (1954; reprint, Princeton: Princeton University Press, 1982), pp. 107-21, who discusses Philo's view of the *pneuma* as an intelligent cosmic principle.

17. For this view, see R. Cummings Neville, *God the Creator: On the Transcendence and Presence of God* (Albany: SUNY Press, 1992). For a more traditional creation-out-of-nothing reading of Genesis 1, see P. Copan and W. Lane Craig, *Creation Out of Nothing: A Biblical, Philosophical, and Scientific Exploration* (Grand Rapids: Baker Academic, 2004).

18. I agree with Westermann, *Genesis 1–11*, pp. 109-10, when he says that the debate between *creatio ex nihilo* and creation out of chaos cannot be settled from Genesis 1–2. The Priestly writer intended neither of these ideas, which arose in Judaism much later when it wrestled with Greek thought during the Intertestamental period.

laws and enter into networks of relationship."[19] Others, however, suggest that this is to spin the *tohu wabohu* too positively since current cosmological findings view the initial state (at t = 0) as a matter-less chaotic vacuum (entropy near infinity) and the Big Bang explosion as a quantum fluctuation in this vacuum.[20] Taking both viewpoints together, I propose that the link between *tohu wabohu* and *mayim* is suggestive of both the chaos of disorder and randomness (the vacuum) and the primordial plenitude (or *plenum*), arguably combining to anticipate the chaos of modern science with its unpredictable and nonlinear movement from simple perturbations of potentialities and possibilities to complex outcomes.[21] The *ruach Elohim* is here shown to be transcendent to, but also implicated in the stirrings of the primeval chaos.

From this, second, the working of the *ruach Elohim* proceeds to order or divide light from darkness, evening and morning, on the first day (vv. 4-5), and separate the upper and lower waters, and the waters and the dry land, on the second day (vv. 6-7). We therefore see the creation emerging from out of the primordial chaos through processes of division, distinc-

19. See Ochs, "Genesis 1–2," p. 8; cf. A. Lee Chi-Chung, "Creation Narratives and the Movement of the Spirit," in J. C. England and A. J. Torrance (eds.), *Doing Theology with the Spirit's Movement in Asia*, ATESEA Occasional Papers 11 (Singapore: ATESEA, 1991), pp. 15-26, and for full-length theological argumentation, J. E. Huchingson, *Pandemonium Tremendum: Chaos and Mystery in the Life of God* (Cleveland: Pilgrim Press, 2001), esp. chs. 5-6.

20. These would be spontaneous disappearances of a pair of antiparticles, producing a large amount of energy, which can form another pair of antiparticles, and so on. I am grateful to S. L. Bonting for (electronic) conversations helping me to formulate this point. For explication, see Bonting, *Chaos Theology: A Revised Creation Theology* (Ottawa: Novalis and St. Paul University Press, and Mystic, Conn.: Twenty-Third Publications, 2002). Others who argue that Genesis 1:2 supports a creation out of chaos instead of the traditional *creation ex nihilo* include B. Anderson, *Creation versus Chaos: The Reinterpretation of Mythical Symbolism in the Bible* (New York: Association Press, 1967); J. D. Levenson, *Creation and the Persistence of Evil: The Jewish Drama of Divine Omnipotence* (New York: Harper & Row, 1987); R. K. Gnuse, *The Old Testament and Process Theology* (St. Louis: Chalice, 2000), esp. ch. 8; and C. Keller, *Face of the Deep: A Theology of Becoming* (New York: Routledge, 2003). Each of these authors, however, understands the primordial chaos differently. From a scientific perspective, my own view most closely approximates Bonting's, even if this should not be understood as if Bonting agreed with all I say in this essay.

21. See T. Xuan Thuan, *Chaos and Harmony: Perspectives on Scientific Revolutions of the Twentieth Century*, trans. A. Reisinger (Oxford: Oxford University Press, 2001), ch. 3 on chaos.

tion, differentiation, and particularization, beginning with the separation of light from darkness and continuing with the separating out of species of plants and types of animals, each in its own or after its own kind (1:11, 12, 21, 24, 25).[22] These primordial divisions have not only ontological significance, but also epistemological and linguistic implications, thus providing for the possibility of thought (the Logos) and of language (the naming of things and the animals; cf. Gen. 2:19) as well.[23] At this point, we want to stop short of saying that the process of differentiation in the Priestly narrative is equivalent to Clayton's hierarchical, temporal, and emergent pluralism theses; rather, better to suggest that the ancient biblical witness is not incompatible with such a hypothesis, provided that the order of "emergent" levels in the biblical narrative is not taken chronologically as referring to natural history.

At this point it is important to note that in Clayton's emergence hypothesis, the earlier stages of cosmic evolution — for example, that of chemistry and physics, especially — reflect not the intentional and purposive character of God's intervention but rather the autonomic aspect of God's influence in the evolutionary process. Is this aspect of the emergence theory compatible with a pneumatological theology of creation derived from the Priestly narrative? A more complete answer to this question requires comparing and contrasting the emergence theory with the intelligent design hypothesis, a task that would take us too far afield.[24] Two options are available in response. *Either* we say that emergence is compatible with the Spirit's working not personally in the creative process but "imper-

22. L. R. Kass, "Evolution and the Bible: Genesis 1 Revisited," *Commentary* 86 (1988): 29-39. For more on pneumatology and the distinctiveness, concreteness, and particularity of created things, see G. Hendry, *Theology of Nature* (Philadelphia: Westminster, 1980), pp. 169-70; and C. Gunton, *The One, the Three, and the Many: God, Creation and the Culture of Modernity* (Cambridge: Cambridge University Press, 1993), pp. 180-209.

23. This point is made by Westermann, *Genesis 1–11*, p. 123, following F. Delitzsch. See also A. V. Nesteruk, "Design in the Universe and the Logos of Creation: Patristic Synthesis and Modern Cosmology," in N. H. Gregersen and U. Görman, eds., *Design and Disorder: Perspectives from Science and Theology* (London and New York: T&T Clark, 2002), pp. 171-202, esp. 198: "all things are differentiated in creation and at the same time the principle of their unity is that they are differentiated. In particular, it provides a common principle for the unity of intelligible and sensible creation."

24. For more on the intelligent design theory, see my "God and the Evangelical Laboratory: Recent Conservative Protestant Perspectives on the Interface between Theology and Science," *Theology and Science*, forthcoming.

sonally" in empowering the creativity of the creaturely responses to the divine "letting be,"[25] *or*, if we are unhappy about depersonalizing and de-intentionalizing the Spirit's creative work in chemical and physical evolution, we push the analogy between theological and empirical approaches and say that the Priestly "faith perspective" allows us to see divine intentionality unfolding in the creaturely domain on the one hand even as the scientific and "naturalistic perspective" allows us only to identify the causal trajectories of emergent processes on the other. The former would in effect be a metaphysical claim about the modality of the Spirit's "working" in natural history, while the latter allows only for an analogy between the two "languages" of science and faith so long as the "faith perspective" is not taken literally. Either response addresses Clayton's concern so long as we assume not a literal (read: historical-scientific) correlation between the seven days of creation and the evolution of the world, but a literary-theological reading of the Priestly narrative somewhat like the one I am providing here.[26]

This leads, third, to our observation regarding the interactivity and co-creativity between the divine and the creation.[27] There is not only the commandment breathed out by and from God and the responsive performance of the created order throughout the creation narrative, but at a few points God even seems to allow the creation to take the initiative. So, while in each case God "lets be" or allows the creation to organize and produce,

25. This could then be understood either in terms of the more hidden work of the Spirit (see J. Polkinghorne's essay in this volume) or in terms of the Spirit's creative working as mediated (albeit ambiguously) through the processes of nature (e.g., K. Tanner, also in this volume).

26. In doing so, however, we must not bifurcate theology and science as if they were completely demarcated arenas. The languages are distinct, but their references *may* overlap, and it requires patient translation to determine if indeed such overlap occurs. And the problem is not only on the theological side but also on the scientific: scientists have reached no consensus on the various theories of evolution. So, any theology in dialogue with science works best when neutral with regard to which scientific theory is finally decided to provide a better ultimate explanation of how things are. Here I follow M. Heller, *Creative Tension: Essays on Science and Religion* (Philadelphia and London: Templeton Foundation Press, 2003), esp. the very helpful ch. 2, "On Theological Interpretations of Physical Creation Theories" (esp. 13-15), where he suggests that this is the route to go rather than to univocally equate a theological idea with a specific scientific theory.

27. Here I have been greatly helped by M. Welker, "What Is Creation? Rereading Genesis 1 and 2," *Theology Today* 48 (1991): 56-71; and Welker, *Creation and Reality*, trans. J. F. Hoffmeyer (Minneapolis: Fortress, 1999).

not in all cases is the "let there be . . ." followed by the statement that God then acted. Thus God actively makes the dome and separates the waters (1:6); God makes the great lights and sets them in the skies (1:16-17); God creates the great sea monsters and the birds of the sky (1:21); and God makes the animals on the ground (1:25). But in some cases, it should not be overlooked that God creates and makes by saying (emphases mine): "Let the earth *put forth* vegetation: plants *yielding* seed, and fruit trees . . . that *bear* fruit . . ." (1:11); "Let the waters *bring forth* swarms of living creatures . . ." (1:20); and "Let the earth *bring forth* living creatures of every kind . . ." (1:24). In the first and third case (but not the second), God's command is followed by an "And it was so" before indicating God's response and activity. Further, on the third day the dry land is allowed to appear, and God proceeds only then to call it Earth (1:9-10). Subsequently, the earth itself is said explicitly to bring forth vegetation (plants, fruits, and trees), and God responds evaluatively, seeing this to be good (1:11-12).

Hence the text emphasizes, on the one hand, God as reactive, seeing, naming, and responding to creation, and, on the other, creation's own environmental activity and agency in bringing forth and (re)producing various heterogeneous forms of life-processes. The Creator-creature distinction certainly should not be blurred — that is, in large part, the main point of the creation account. At the same time, it is also the case that God creates by calling forth the orders of creation as co-creators and enabling the various levels of creation, to use Clayton's language, to participate in the processes of production and reproduction. That the narrative indicates some domains to be more active and others more passive in the creative process may correlate with the observation in emergence theory that there is no monolithic law of causality operative throughout the various levels of creation. Some would suggest that in this reading the debate over evolution shifts to a different plane since the created order may be considered not only to be fully gifted with evolutionary capacities from the beginning, but also to be equipped to make whatever adjustments are needed along the way.[28] While this would reflect the unfathomable creativity and resourcefulness of the divine wisdom, it would also be open to the charge of deism unless (as I suggest here) creation's work is set within a robust pneumatological frame-

---

28. E.g., H. Van Til, "The Fully Gifted Creation ('Theistic Evolution')," in J. P. Moreland and J. M. Reynolds (eds.), *Three Views on Creation and Evolution* (Grand Rapids: Zondervan, 1999), pp. 159-218.

work that preserves the ongoing creative activity of God *(creatio continua)*. The pneumatological hypothesis I am proposing is that the processes of separation, differentiation, division, and distinction seen in the creation narrative reflect the character of *ruach Elohim* clearly articulated elsewhere in scripture as the dynamic, particularizing, relational, and life-giving presence and activity of the Spirit of God.[29]

Even as Clayton acknowledges that the emergence of mind provides the kind of data for strong emergence lacking in physical, chemical, and biological processes, so also, I contend, the creation of living creatures and *ha-'adam* on days five and six provides insights into a more robust pneumatological theology of creation consonant with emergence theory than that which is described about the previous days. For starters, the biblical narrative acknowledges the dependence and interconnectedness between the human spirit and its material substrate in a way that is consistent with the emergent monist thesis. In the Jahwist account (2:7), *ha-'adam* is said explicitly to be formed out of and thereby emergent from the dust of the ground.[30] *Ha-'adam*, however, becomes a living being only with the breath of the LORD. This is certainly consistent with the rest of the biblical witness (e.g., Job 34:14-15; Ps. 104:28-29; Eccles. 12:7; Ezek. 37:1-14; Luke 23:46; Rom. 8:11, 18-23). A canonical hermeneutic enables a combined reading of the Priestly and Jahwist creation accounts, which in turn sustains a robust pneumatological theology with regard to the creation of human beings, but one that does not minimize the physical and embodied aspect of what it means to be human. That other creatures are also said to have the breath of life (1:30), but are yet not of the same order as *ha-'adam,* is also suggestive of the fact that there are increasingly complex levels of the emergence of life within the biological domain, each interacting with its environments in various ways.

Further, "en-spirited" creatures are empowered as having lesser or

29. These categories are not, of course, entirely absent from the creation narrative. I develop the biblical background in *Spirit-Word-Community: Theological Hermeneutics in Trinitarian Perspective* (Aldershot, U.K., and Burlington, Vt.: Ashgate, 2002), ch. 1.

30. So C. Westermann's conclusion — "The person as a living being is to be understood as a whole and any idea that one is made up of body and soul is ruled out" (*Genesis 1–11,* p. 207) — effectively undercuts the dominant dualistic reading of the tradition that defines human nature in terms of material bodies plus eternal souls. I further develop the details of this philosophical anthropology elsewhere; see Yong, "*Pneuma* and *Pratityas-amutpada*: Neuropsychology, the Christian-Buddhist Dialogue and the Human Person," *Zygon: Journal of Religion and Science* 40:1 (2005): 143-65.

greater capacity to act as causal agents. This is most clear in the case of *ha-'adam,* who is commanded to take responsibility for the creation and is hence considered to be under personal and purposive obligation. Further, that the fish of the sea and the birds of the air are also blessed and commanded to be fruitful and multiply (1:22) points to a certain impersonal but yet causal capacity they possess to respond to the divine mandate.[31] In this sense, living creatures in general and human beings in particular represent the unfinished dimension of the creation, with the potential to fulfill creation's reason for being, but also with the potential, given the greater dimension of freedom humans are endowed with, to perhaps sabotage the divine intentions. It is noteworthy that the phrase "And it was so" does not follow the creation of *ha-'adam* as it does elsewhere (vv. 7, 9, 11, 15, 24, and 30). While this may dovetail with Clayton's rejection of the causal closure of the world on the one hand, it certainly implies the open-endedness rather than definiteness of the human path or way to be.[32] This ambiguous nature of what it means to be human may be the reason why God does not specifically see and immediately pronounce *ha-'adam* as good, as God had done with the work of days three through six.[33] The later narrative of the "fall" (Gen. 3) reflects human freedom exercised *against,* rather than in harmony with, the nature of things, thereby breaking the relationships among human beings with God, creation, and each another.

Finally, *ha-'adam* is created as a relational creature, representing the divine image and likeness. Of course, the divine relationality in the creation narratives derives not from the allegedly proto-Trinitarian "Let *us* make . . ." (1:26) but from the God-world and God-humankind relationships. More specifically, the divine image is revealed in the creation of *ha-'adam* as male and female. Here the testimony of the later biblical traditions that the Spirit makes present the divine love within human hearts (Rom. 5:5) and repli-

---

31. I suggest, building on the observation of L. Stone, that the fish and the birds are also addressable by God because they also have the breath of life in them (1:30); see L. G. Stone, "The Soul: Possession, Part, or Person? The Genesis of Human Nature in Genesis 2:7," in J. B. Green (ed.), *What about the Soul? Neuroscience and Christian Anthropology* (Nashville: Abingdon, 2004), pp. 47-61, esp. 51-52.

32. See R. Sacks, "The Lion and the Ass: A Commentary on the Book of Genesis (Chapters 1-10)," *Interpretation: A Journal of Political Philosophy* 8:2-3 (1980): 29-101, esp. 38-39.

33. See L. Strauss, "On the Interpretation of Genesis," *L'Homme* 21:1 (1981): 5-20, esp. 18-19.

cates the fellowship of the triune God amidst the people of God (2 Cor. 13:13) fills out the pneumatological content of *ha-'adam* given the breath of life to embrace each other as well as the Creator. And of course, human relationality does not stop with God and human beings. Rather, as a close reading of 1:26b-30 reveals, the sexual differentiation of *ha-'adam* points both to interpersonal sociality and to inter-creaturely relationality. *Ha-'adam* as male and female are told not only to multiply and fill the earth, but also to subdue and care for the created order.[34] This clear relationship among human beings, the animals, and the earth itself, not to mention the formation of *ha-'adam* from the dust of the ground, reflects the symbiotic and ecological character of what it means to be human. In this re-portrayal of the doctrine of creation, the interdependence of the physical, environmental, biological, mental, and (even) spiritual realms of creation can be seen as suggestive of the hierarchically and pluralistically ordered but yet complexly interconnected vision of the world enunciated in emergence theory that is open, in Clayton's terms, to transcendence. A pneumatological perspective on the creation narratives is thus consistent with contemporary perspectives that go beyond traditional dualist definitions of humans as "embodied souls" toward ontological holist understandings of human beings as emergent, interpersonal, interrelational, and cosmologically and environmentally situated creatures.[35]

Whither Spirit in the Science-Religion Conversation?

This final section is devoted to accomplishing two objectives: identifying more explicitly how the preceding pneumatological reading of the creation

34. This point is clearly argued by Welker, *Creation and Reality*, pp. 64-69. See also J. McIntyre, *The Shape of Pneumatology: Studies in the Doctrine of the Holy Spirit* (Edinburgh: T&T Clark, 1997), pp. 190-93, for the thesis that "The Holy Spirit is God the Creator himself setting us in a right and responsible relation to the animal and natural order" (quote from 93).

35. E.g., J. B. Green, "'Bodies — That Is, Human Lives': A Re-examination of Human Nature in the Bible," in W. S. Brown, N. Murphy, and H. Newton Malony (eds.), *Whatever Happened to the Soul? Scientific and Theological Portraits of Human Nature* (Minneapolis: Fortress, 1998), pp. 149-73, and Green, "What Does It Mean to Be Human? Another Chapter in the Ongoing Interaction of Science and Scripture," in M. Jeeves (ed.), *From Cells to Souls — and Beyond: Changing Portraits of Human Nature* (Grand Rapids: Eerdmans, 2004), pp. 179-98.

narratives contributes toward the formulation of a more robust theological concept of emergence theory, and specifying how a pneumatological theology of creation nevertheless justifies the scientific research program called for in Clayton's emergence hypothesis.

I have already suggested that I agree with Clayton's reticence to say too much about theology, given his desire to make as strong a philosophical argument as possible to the scientific community. As a theologian, however, I am also concerned that Clayton's theory pass muster from a biblical and theological point of view. Hence I propose that the pneumatological theology of creation presented here contributes to emergence theory at three levels.

First, it brings philosophical theory and biblical text together in mutually beneficial ways: on the one hand, the scriptures are illuminated against the backdrop of the emergentist hypothesis; on the other hand, a specific instantiation of an abstract theory is provided by way of an analogical reading of the ancient creation narratives.

Second, the much richer detail of a pneumatological theology of creation can supplement and in that sense fill out the theological content of Clayton's emergence metaphysics. While this may be risky within the broader theology-and-science dialogue, it is nevertheless true that the theologians in the conversation need to find ways of speaking more theologically without undermining the discussion with the scientists. I trust that the merits of a pneumatological perspective for this interchange are clear.

Most importantly, I believe that a pneumatological approach provides some relief to the strain imposed by the acknowledged theological dualism in Clayton's theory of emergence. Recall that Clayton was led to this position in order to avoid an immanentist construal of God as finally dependent on the world similar to how human consciousness is dependent on its material substrate. From the angle of the *ruach Elohim* hovering *over* or moving *upon* the primordial chaos, this transcendent aspect of divine presence and activity is certainly justified. On the other hand, from the angle of the breath of life given to and operative *in* creatures and *ha adam*, the Spirit is also present and at work from within the creaturely domain. A pneumatologically informed metaphysic, in other words, requires us to hold the immanent and transcendent aspects of divine presence and activity together, regardless of how tempted we are to privilege one over the other. This way forward, I suggest, enables the theistic dimension of Clayton's metaphysic to fit more coherently within his hypothesis since the final conceptualization requires, not a one-sided theological dualism, but rather a theological *non-dualism* whereby God is neither merely immanent nor merely transcendent on the one hand, and neither merely emergent nor merely purposive and personal on the other.[36]

But what about Clayton's concern that too much theological discourse will wreck the theory of emergence in terms of its dependence upon scientific data and its intention to more coherently explain and in that sense empower scientific inquiry? This is an important matter which needs to be attended to. At one level, if we assumed the category of "spirit" to be metaphysically opposed to "matter" (as is the case with most natural scientists, but not so much with social scientists), then it may be difficult to advance the theology-and-science conversation by impulses of pneumatological theology. On the other hand, if we agree that ontologically distinct and ontological plural realities do not necessarily require a dualistic metaphysic — witness Clayton's emergent monism thesis — then there is no a priori reason why the inclusion of a nuanced pneumatological theology of creation need sabotage the theology and science dialogue. On the contrary, in conclusion, I suggest three ways in which a pneumatological perspective actually further legitimates what Clayton wishes his theory to do, namely, to undergird a sufficiently robust research program that would enhance scientific inquiry.

First, the creation narrative read in pneumatological perspective sees the *ruach Elohim* as both presiding over and empowering from within the processes of differentiation, separation, and particularization that constitute the days of creation. I suggest that this denotes the differentiation-in-unity of Spirit. Elsewhere in the biblical narrative, we find this feature of the Spirit even more emphatically pronounced, as in the multiplicity of

---

36. At one point, I found curious Clayton's suggestion that he has explored a "view of the God-world relation that radicalizes the immanence of God" (p. 187). I wondered if he did not mean "transcendence" of God since I did see where he had proposed a radical account of divine immanence in his book. Elsewhere, Clayton has developed a panentheistic theology, which details have been left out of *Mind and Emergence*, no doubt given his focused attempt to convince scientists of the emergence hypothesis. Whether or not one agrees with a panentheistic construal of the God-world relationship, this enables recognition of God's responsiveness and relatedness to the world. On Clayton's panentheism, see Clayton, *The Problem of God in Modern Thought* (Grand Rapids: Eerdmans, 2002), and P. Clayton and A. Peacocke, eds., *In Whom We Live and Move and Have Our Being: Panentheistic Reflections on God's Presence in a Scientific World* (Grand Rapids: Eerdmans, 2004).

tongues somehow harmoniously giving glory to God and as in the plurality of members each playing a distinctive and indispensable role in the edifying of the one body.[37] Transposed into a metaphysical key, I suggest that a pneumatological theology of creation further secures the ontological pluralism articulated in Clayton's theory of emergence. This provides theological legitimacy for the plurality of disciplines in the sciences, even while it holds forth a kind of complementarity principle which anticipates the various disciplines each providing distinctive but essential perspectives on reality. From an epistemological vantage point, such multidisciplinarity would neither break down reductionistically (so that any one discipline could claim a final word) nor result in disciplinary isolation (because each discipline supposedly deals with methods and realities incommensurable with the others); rather, the *ruach Elohim* that hovers over the waters and is the breath of life brings about an inter- and trans-disciplinary convergence directed toward the revelation of truth in the long run.[38]

Second, a pneumatological theology of creation would reaccentuate the biological and especially psychological and humanistic sciences that risk being neglected in the theology-and-science conversation, which agenda is often dictated by those engaged in the natural sciences. Clayton does acknowledge that "theists have traditionally claimed that there are analogies between human persons, and in particular human minds, on the one hand, and God, understood as divine mind of Spirit, on the other" (p. 183). Of course, this is in part the reason why the status of the psychosocial sciences has been perennially devalued by those who equate true science with the natural sciences. But only a dogmatic scientism would arbitrarily terminate this conversation and reject the possibility of the human sciences' contributing to what truly counts as knowledge. Further, the fascinating strides made in the biological sciences in the last generation and the recognition and articulation of the "hard problem" of consciousness both also provide clues, I suggest, to the mystery of *psyche* and spirit in cre-

37. See M. Welker's chapter herein on the Spirit as a multicontextual and polyphonic presence; cf. also Welker, *God the Spirit*, trans. J. F. Hoffmeyer (Minneapolis: Fortress, 1994).

38. See Yong, "Academic Glossolalia? Pentecostal Scholarship, Multi-disciplinarity, and the Science-Religion Conversation," *Journal of Pentecostal Theology*, forthcoming. My reference to the "long run" is inspired by C. S. Peirce's theory of truth; see Yong, "The Demise of Foundationalism and the Retention of Truth: What Evangelicals Can Learn from C. S. Peirce," *Christian Scholar's Review* 29:3 (Spring 2000): 563-88.

ation. Not surprisingly, the category of spirit cannot be exorcised from this conversation since it will often reappear under another name.[39]

Last, I propose that spirit serves as a limit category that continually calls the scientific enterprise forward beyond itself. For science to fulfill its promise, it has to go where the trail of discovery leads. The fertility of spirit as a philosophical and even empirical category points to both the problem and the promise of a pneumatological contribution to the theology and science conversation.[40] On the one side, the challenge is how to engage spirit conceptually and empirically, since something that can mean so many things may result in its meaning nothing. On the other side, the human spirit of curiosity and inquiry continues to respond to the wondrous Spirit of creation. Philip Clayton's theory of emergence is one attempt to depict the openness of the world to its future. A pneumatological theology of creation would affirm this openness even while it enlists the aid of the sciences and empowers scientists to explore the edges of this world whatever they be and the frontiers of knowledge wherever they are. In this process, who knows if we might catch a whiff of the wind of God that blows where she wills?[41]

39. As suggested in the full title of P. S. MacDonald, *History of the Concept of Mind: Speculations about Soul, Mind and Spirit from Homer to Hume* (Aldershot, U.K., and Burlington, Vt.: Ashgate, 2003).

40. In another place, I have identified fifteen ways in which "spirit" has been worked into the religion-science conversation: "'The Spirit Hovers over the World': Toward a Typology of 'Spirit' in the Religion and Science Dialogue," The Digest: Transdisciplinary approaches to Foundational Questions — *The Metanexus Online Journal* 4:12 (2004) [http://www.metanexus.net/digest/2004_10_27.htm].

41. My thanks to P. Clayton for his feedback on an earlier draft of this essay.

The Spirit in Evidence:
Stories of How Decisions Are Made

DONALD G. YORK AND ANNA YORK

Most walks of life involve evidentiary thinking: daily personal decisions, court cases, government policy, science, academics, religious life, and environmental preservation, to name a few examples. Even so, the more sophisticated we become in these arenas, the less conclusive are the types of evidence that have worked in the past. This is true even in science, which is often considered as being a bastion of evidential purity — if it's scientific, it must be "true." In this chapter we discuss the limitations of evidence, focusing on historical examples from astronomy. The principles we present in astronomy are also applicable in other branches of science.

Good decision-making in science, as well as other arenas of life, involves analysis of evidence with a healthy dose of insight and common sense. While scientists use evidence to change their own minds and the minds of their peers, experience often shows that conclusions reached by rapid peer review turn out to be wrong when one looks over intervals of decades or centuries. In science, it is necessary to make decisions and move forward without waiting that long to get at the truth. Thus, what may eventually be proven to be inadequate evidence must always be weighed with a healthy dose of insight and common sense in order to reach conclusions that make sense for the time at hand.

In the light of inadequate evidence, how have individuals in science reached correct conclusions? We speculate that the work of the Spirit of God in the world is what serves to complete the evidence in all walks of life, allowing us to draw conclusions and make decisions that move us forward even when we do not have full information or truth. We connect this idea with the work of some theologians who discuss that the Spirit of God is manifest in *Sophia* wisdom and suggest that *Sophia* wisdom can be discerned in the world and in science by the following criteria: knowledge, discernment, truth, and beneficial fruit.[1]

Historical, Astronomical Examples of the Dilemma of Evidence

Our understanding of the universe has changed in very significant ways in only a few years. In the discussion below, we will cite some historical examples of the way our view of the universe has changed, using the examples of asteroids, planets, stars, and galaxies. The examples illuminate how beliefs can be based on inadequate evidence. The inadequacy is demonstrated as being due to data that one did not even know to seek, on aspects of the technology of measurement that were not understood or on the fact that the evidence did not reveal itself on a fast enough time scale for one human, or even a culture, to put things together and reach a correct conclusion. Nevertheless, opinions and views were developed, and some of them were correct.

Story of Parallax

During the sixteenth century, Copernicus developed an argument that the Earth went around the Sun, in contradiction to the commonly accepted view that the Sun went around the Earth. Galileo, in 1610, used a telescope and discovered the moons of Jupiter, which were obviously moving around the planet. The four satellites he could see changed positions on a nightly basis, so he saw four small dots, all at different distances, moving around the central object, switching sides from night to night. He had the insight that the moons of Jupiter could serve as a smaller-sized analogy to the Copernican system in which the moons of Jupiter were to the planet as the planets of the solar system are to the Sun, though the periods of the

---

1. The astronomical portions of this chapter were written by Donald G. York; the nonastronomical portions were written by Anna York.

planets orbiting the Sun are years, not days. At best, the discovery confirmed that Copernicus's argument might be correct — or, at the very least, that Copernicus's ideas could be used to tell the story of the solar system more smoothly than could be done using the geocentric model of the universe.

The fact that the moons went around Jupiter made Galileo think he had evidence that the Earth might move around the Sun, instead of vice versa. The entire analogy may have taken less than twenty-four hours to develop in Galileo's mind, but this bit of data and deep insight changed the world of science forever, literally overnight. But, even though it was a brilliant idea — and a correct one — the idea that the Earth went around the Sun was not universally accepted at that time. The church was committed philosophically to the geocentric view. Furthermore, no matter how much sense it might make to some, there was no convincing evidence or proof on which all people, educated or not, scientists or clergy, could come to understanding and agreement.

Apart from the famous religious reasons for this controversy over Galileo's ideas, it was thought that if the Earth circles the Sun, there should be a parallax many times larger than the measuring error of the instruments that were available at the time. Parallax is the effect in which the positions of nearby stars appear to wiggle, against the distant, apparently fixed stars, as the Earth moves around the Sun. To see the effect, imagine that your right eye represents a telescope on Earth when the Earth is at a certain part of its annual solar orbit. Your left eye is the same, six months later. Hold up a finger so you can see it against a fixed background object, such as a lamp or a doorpost. Now alternately close one eye and then the other. Your finger represents a nearby star and the distant, fixed object represents the distant fixed stars. The apparent motion of your finger back and forth as you shift from one eye to the other is the wiggle referred to above, and the size of the shift in motion is the parallactic angle. For the experiment just described, the angle is several degrees, but for a distant star, say one 200,000 times more distant than the Sun, the angle is about one arcsecond. (A circle of 360 degrees is divided into 60 arcminutes per degree and 60 arcseconds per arcminute. An arcsecond is about 1/600,000 of a full circle.) The instruments available in Galileo's time were not able to detect such a fine motion, and thus there was no way to get the evidence to prove that his argument was correct. But it was generally believed that the stars were close enough that a measurable parallax should be seen, if Copernicus's ideas were right. No parallax meant the Earth did not go around the Sun.

Several lines of thought led to the conclusion that the stars were close enough to show parallax. If the Sun is like the stars, then the stars might be assumed to have the same physical size as the Sun. Assuming this size, scientists could infer the distance of the stars, by the rule that objects of fixed size look smaller and smaller as they are viewed from greater distances. Stars were judged to be closer than we know they are today because they appeared to be large (astronomers say "resolved") in telescopes. Three effects served to make the stars appear to be over a million times larger than they actually were. First, the size of a stellar image depends on the aperture of the telescope, a consequence of the physics of light. Second, the optics were imperfect and had blurring aberrations. Finally, the atmosphere of the Earth blurs images, because of thermal effects. The true distance of the stars was much greater than inferred, so the failure to prove parallax just showed that the distance was larger than previously thought but did not prove that Galileo was wrong.

The Catholic church used the absence of evidence for parallax to force Galileo to teach his idea as a theory, not as truth. Of course, as noted earlier, the church had other reasons, but since science requires that theories have verifiable consequences, this reason was quite powerful.

The first parallax of a star was not published until 1838: it was 228 years from compelling theory to definite demonstration that the Earth goes around the Sun. The enthusiasm Galileo showed for the new theory was the direct result of the application of a technology developed for another purpose (the eyeglass). The failure to confirm the new theory was the result of inadequate technology and of inadequate understanding of the limited technology available at the time. The final demonstration of the stellar parallax in 1838 was the result of technology specifically built for the particular problem (by Fraunhofer, 1824-1826). Previous technologies were not, in hindsight, adequate to allow the measurement of the parallax. The heliocentric theory was not provable in the seventeenth century, and it had to be let alone, accepted but not proven for many years. We dwell a bit on this point, because similar situations occur today: theories cannot be fully tested because the technology we have is inadequate to measure the expected effects. Thus, evidence is often lacking.

The Story of Galaxies

We now move from the changes in our worldview brought about by a deeper understanding of planets and stars to the galaxies, aggregates of billions of stars, evidently the building blocks of the universe, in our modern view.

Aristotle thought the stars were located on the celestial sphere, as small dots painted on the inside of a dome. He thought the size of the universe was the size of the orbit of the moon. This view was disrupted, rather severely, by the idea that the stars must be very far away. By 1750, despite the absence of parallax, the expansiveness of the realm of the stars was becoming evident, for reasons we will not go into here. Suffice it to say that the Greeks left the world with competing views: Aristotle's view (ca. 300 B.C.E.) and a second view, attributed, among others, to Democritus (ca. 450 B.C.E.), that the universe of stars stretched unendingly in all directions. It took almost two thousand years to get a resolution as to which was the right view.

Following Galileo's startling discoveries (the moons of Jupiter, sunspots, shadows on the moon, to name a few), telescopes were improved and new catalogs of the heavens were made. A critical step in any science is the construction of catalogs of physical objects of interest in the relevant field, by unbiased observers whose only goal is to assemble a description of "what is out there." Catalogs of stars were in existence, based on naked eye observations, for 1,600 years prior to the time of Galileo. As the much-improved astronomical catalogs were assembled using better and better telescopes, the artificially enlarged images of stars seen by Galileo, which were discussed earlier, were reduced by a factor of eight or so in apparent size. As most of the universe came into focus, a few objects persisted in looking fuzzy, being extended with a variety of shapes, but generally in the form of disks and circles.

It was Thomas Wright (1750) who explained the Milky Way as an aggregate of faint, distant stars so close together that they could not be resolved. He considered that this aggregate might be a dish-like assemblage of stars and that we on the Earth might be sitting in the dish. In this case, when we are outside observing the stars at night, we would see a band of light all around us when we look in the plane of the dish. If we look in the perpendicular plane to the dish, we would see only a few random stars.[2]

2. D. Layzer, *Constructing the Universe* (New York: Scientific American Library, 1984), p. 110.

Immanuel Kant used Wright's insight to make the intellectual break-through that the fuzzy patches (called nebulae) that were being seen through improved telescopes could be large aggregates of faint stars, so far away that their images were blurred together. We do not know how long it took Kant to make the intellectual leap you are about to see, but perhaps we can think of it as being about twenty-four hours, the same as Galileo's revelation about the moons of Jupiter. It is best to simply tell the story in Kant's own words.

> I come now to that part of my theory that gives it its greatest charm, by the sublime idea which it presents of the plan of creation. The train of thought which has led me to it is short and natural; it consists of the following ideas. If a system of fixed stars which are related in their positions to a common plane, as we have delineated the Milky Way to be, be so far removed from us that the individual stars of which it consists are no longer sensibly distinguishable even by the telescope; if its distance has the same ratio to the distance of the stars of the Milky Way as that of the latter has to the distance of the Sun; in short, if such a world of fixed stars is beheld at such an immense distance from the eye of the spectator situated outside of it, then this world will appear under a small angle as a patch of space whose figure will be circular if its plane is presented directly to the eye, and elliptical if it is seen from the side or obliquely. The feebleness of its light, its figure, and the apparent size of its diameter will clearly distinguish such a phenomenon, when it is presented, from all stars that are seen single.
>
> We do not need to look long for this phenomenon among the observations of the astronomers. They have been astonished at its strangeness; and it has given occasion for conjectures, sometimes to strange hypotheses, and at other times to probable conceptions which, however, were just as groundless as the former. It is the "nebulous stars" which we refer to, or rather a species of them, which M. de Maupertuis (*Discours sur la Figure des Astres*, Paris, 1742) thus describes: "They are," he says, "small luminous patches, only a little more brilliant than the dark background of the heavens; they are presented in all quarters; they present the figure of ellipses more or less open; and their light is much feebler than that of any other object we can perceive in the heavens."[3]

3. I. Kant, *Universal Natural History and Theory of the Heavens*, 1755, as printed in translation by D. Layzer, *Constructing the Universe* (New York: W. H. Freeman, 1984).

The perception of the size of the universe "grew" by a factor of over a million million in linear scale, if Kant was correct in his inference from the evidence available, compared to the relatively tiny world of Copernicus and Galileo, which was itself larger than Aristotle's universe. Of course, the exact factors could not have been known at that time, because the scale of Kant's ruler, the Milky Way galaxy, was itself not known, though one could have made an intelligent guess.

There was no way to prove Kant's speculation. Kant was postulating distances which were five thousand times larger than the Milky Way, which is itself larger than the likely distance to the nearest star by a factor of 20,000. This was a vastly larger universe than anyone had imagined up to that time, even though it was still a tiny fraction of what we think of as the size of the universe today. It is a wonder that he even had the nerve to publish the idea. It is doubtful if any astronomer was asked to do a peer review of the book in which it appeared.

Perhaps the most famous attempt to prove Kant right was that of the independently wealthy Sir William Herschel, who built a telescope so big that a man could walk inside it, an enormous instrument for its day. With this telescope, a more manageable twenty-inch telescope, and his own leisure to observe, Herschel created catalogs that are still used today, mapping the heavens, cataloguing star clusters, galaxies, and even dark patches of sky, which turned out later to be the outlines of dust clouds projected onto the sky. Herschel worked with that telescope for most of his life, and his son, Sir John, spent most of his life making further catalogues. But, working between 1780 and 1850, they could not fulfill Sir William's dream of proving that Kant was right. By the end of the nineteenth century, virtually all textbooks in astronomy assured their readers that the universe was bigger than that of Copernicus, possibly by a factor of a million, but was nowhere near what Kant would have estimated.

There were many times in the years between 1850 and 1930 at which new evidence was brought to bear on the problem of the distance of what Kant called "island universes," but each discovery brought with it new surprises that did not fit into what was known. The period between the Civil War and World War I was the time of the recording of the first stellar spectra, the filling out of the periodic table, the discovery of radioactivity, the development of the concept of the quantum, the revelations of the rudiments of quantum mechanics, and the development of special and general relativity. Finally, in 1921, a wonderful argument was developed that Kant was right: the case was made that Herschel's dust clouds caused the massive rift in Cygnus that splits the Milky Way as it passes overhead in the summer sky. It was known by this time that similar dark lines appeared in the images of the distant galaxies. By analogy, the distant nebulae must be like the Milky Way. When Hubble discovered the expansion of the universe (1929), the cloak fell away from the eyes of astronomers and the true size of the universe became manifest. The immediate, quantitative evidence still underestimated the size of the visible universe by a factor of 10 in linear scale, but most of Kant's ideas were by then confirmed. The current estimate of the size of the universe was essentially fixed to within a factor of two by 1960.

Of course, the expanse of the reach of galaxies in the universe is only one aspect of the story: we do not know how they form. Their nature is still very much debated. Threads of evidence now relate their origins to primordial density fluctuations in the energy/matter density of the universe. Recently, a new thread has developed relating the formation of stars in galaxies to the presence of relatively tiny black holes that are now found at the centers of galaxies. While the science enterprise is many times larger than it was in 1850, the questions are much more profound. We may not expect that we will have the answers to the deeper questions for a very long time. The evidence is simply very hard to acquire, and each small success leads to even deeper questions, setting us off anew for evidence to support new ideas.

Story of Asteroids

We turn now to a final astronomical story that covers much smaller scales but is much more immediately relevant to our future on Earth. Meteors, comets, and asteroids are all trash from the creation of the solar system. Now we understand that the solar system is "under construction," but that is a relatively recent view.

Recently, a meteor fall occurred in a suburb of south Chicago, a very rare event at any place on Earth. One resident, awakened by his dog at the appearance of a large flash in the sky from the burning meteor, created as the space junk fell through the atmosphere of Earth, got out of bed and went downstairs. When he returned, he found on his pillow a chunk of the meteor, which had come through the roof while he was downstairs and had landed right where his head had been only a few minutes previously. The next day, he was completely confused and unable to comprehend how close he came to death. He called his boss and told him he could not come in that day and explained his state of mind after nearly being killed by the meteor. His boss said, "OK, but don't use that excuse again."

Don was observing the skies in New Mexico that night and was shaken when an e-mail arrived from his friend Roger in Paris. He had checked out the news on CNN that morning and wanted to know if it was true that Chicago had just been destroyed by an asteroid. Don started to call home to Chicago to check, but then thought, "No, Anna would not be amused by a call with such an absurd question at one o'clock in the morning in Chicago." After calming down, he consulted the *Chicago Tribune* website and decided that Chicago was still there.

An asteroid falling on the Earth is extremely rare, as emphasized by these personal stories. Meteor showers have been observable throughout history, but few meteors reached the ground, and most of those that did went undiscovered. There were no known sightings indicating the existence of asteroids, the massive parents of the meteors, before 1807. Now, we have catalogued over 200,000 of these massive parents, which have sizes above 0.5 km; it is believed that a very large version of such space junk was involved in forming the Earth-Moon system, and it is commonly accepted that a massive impact with space junk caused the extinction of the dinosaurs. A few large craters on Earth record past large impacts. Of course, it was asteroids that created the craters on the Moon, which craters were first understood as such by Galileo. Being trained in art, he understood chiaroscuro and realized that the shadows on the Moon were mountains created by the impact of objects from space.

Thus, while the evidence was all around and observed by all, it is a recent insight of scientists that this space junk is the most likely candidate to eventually destroy life as we know it on Earth. In other words, our view of our world and our potential destiny is intimately tied up with objects that were not known even two hundred years ago. There was no evidence of meteors with a high enough rate of occurrence that humans could have noticed it. Scientists are focused on facts that are known, not those that are unknown. Events that are too far apart and that require the right expert to be around to find them and recognize their significance are often outside the ken of scientists. Their significance for our lives and our worldviews may go unnoticed.

DONALD G. YORK AND ANNA YORK

Dark Matter, an Unfolding Story

The scientific "Breakthrough of the Year" in 2003, according to *Science* magazine,[4] is the work done on "dark energy," employing the technology of the Wilkinson Microwave Anisotropy Probe (WMAP) and the Sloan Digital Sky Survey, a telescope for which one of the authors (Don) was the founding director. This research, the work of many scientists, confirms the disturbing information that the universe is only about 5 percent "ordinary matter," the stuff of stars and trees and people, and only about 1 percent can be detected with instruments we have now. The other 4 percent of this "ordinary matter" is only inferred to be there. About 25 percent is some mysterious, undefined stuff called "dark mass" that may be made up of an as yet undetected particle. The remainder of the mass of the universe, an astonishing 70 percent, is "dark energy," which is "dark" partly because scientists do not know what it is or how it has functioned or is functioning in the creation and expansion of the universe. These figures reveal the embarrassing fact that we know only about 5 percent of the universe and that 95 percent of it is "dark," or a mystery, even to the greatest minds who are working on the problem. In our secure world of terra firma, tables and chairs and flesh and blood, it's hard to think about the idea that most of the universe is invisible and unknown, that the universe is infused and propelled by energy we do not understand.

While we do not now have the theory or the technology to unravel this mystery, it is possible that this will be the great opportunity of the future for one or more great minds to have the type of breakthrough insights we have discussed here, insights that will once again transform our understanding of the universe and our place in it.

The Spirit in Evidence

How does one judge that enough is known to reach a conclusion? If an individual or even a whole community or culture holds a certain opinion, what is necessary to change their minds? Is it more evidence? Better

4. C. Seife, "Breakthrough of the Year, #1 Winner: Illuminating the Dark Universe," *Science* 302 (19 December 2003): 2038.

evidence? The examples in this chapter and our experience of life show that we usually seek evidence in order to make decisions; however, evidence that is reliable and that can stand the test of time is elusive, if not impossible to find. Sometimes people get the right answers for the wrong reason; sometimes they get the wrong answers with the right evidence; sometimes they can reinterpret old evidence in a new way. Sometimes answers may appear to be correct and the evidence may be correct as far as it goes, but the answer is incomplete. Sometimes there will be a great insight that yields the truth and that comes suddenly with little or no evidence at all, such as Kant's idea of galaxies or Einstein's theory of relativity. Even Newton's laws of gravity are not final because they do not apply near black holes. In the end, there is little that is final. We can chip away at the facts, but, historically speaking, "understanding" could be centuries away. "Truth," in terms of absolute knowing, may never be in our grasp.

In order to draw conclusions and make decisions in most areas of life, some separate source or agency must be brought to bear. We suggest that this agency is Wisdom. Wisdom can be manifest in many different ways and through many different types of people; it can be manifest suddenly, through a single individual, or through many people in complex ways over long periods of time. In some cases Wisdom calls to us, but we are able to hear only after hard experience of failed attempts and wrong answers. In science, Wisdom sometimes convinces us by making something seem right and reasonable when we don't have enough solid evidence to judge intellectually. Sometimes Wisdom works over decades or even centuries. Wisdom is often manifest in a sudden insight that seems to come from nowhere and that changes the way we view ourselves, our world, and the universe in which we live. Sometimes we are not able to hear the voice of Wisdom at all.

We suggest that the Wisdom to which we are referring is the work of the Spirit of God and that God's Wisdom is always at work in the world. The hallmarks of this wisdom are the following: knowledge, discernment, truth, and beneficial results. We suggest that the Spirit brings forth these qualities not by providing us with perfect evidence or by proliferating more evidence for us to examine but by giving human beings the wisdom to interpret the evidence and make decisions in appropriate ways even when the evidence is insufficient or false.

As you can see, we have tended to personify Wisdom, and in doing so we draw on an ancient tradition. In biblical literature Wisdom is personified as the feminine *Sophia*, *Sophia* being the Greek translation of the Hebrew word *(chokmah)* for wisdom, which is also feminine. Her role is described extensively in the book of Proverbs, especially in chapters 8 and 9, and in other Wisdom literature.[5] In Proverbs *Sophia* speaks, describing herself as being the source of truth and insight. She says she was in the beginning with God before the world was created, and, in fact, that she was the beginning of God's work: "Yahweh created me at the beginning of God's work, the first of God's acts of long ago. Ages ago I was set up, at the first, before the beginning of the earth" (Prov. 8:22-23).

Sophia was active in the creation, describing herself as a "master-worker" who was there when God established the heavens and marked the foundations of the earth. She resides in God's presence and rejoices in the world and the human race. After the work of creation is done, *Sophia* is the one who guards and guides the faithful in every good path of life.[6] We can see here that Sophia's work is the same as that which we usually identify as the work of the Spirit of God in creating and sustaining the world and in guiding and empowering human beings. Some theologians have noted a functional equivalence between *Sophia* and the Spirit of God.[7] Picking up on that theme, we will point out some other characteristics of *Sophia* from the Wisdom literature that are relevant to our point here. Most of these are drawn from Proverbs 1 and 8, but some are from other books in the biblical Wisdom literature:

- *Sophia* is a street preacher, a prophet who cries aloud in the market and at the city gates, saying that she longs to pour out her thoughts and make her words known. Too often her voice is unheeded, and

5. *Sophia*/Wisdom appears in the following scriptures: Job 28; Proverbs 1; 8; and 9; Sirach 51:26; 24:23; Wisdom of Solomon 7; 8; 9; and 10; Baruch 3:37; 1 Enoch 41:1-2. See E. A. Johnson's *She Who Is* (New York: Crossroad, 2001), pp. 86-100 for an extended discussion of *Sophia*, including Johnson's conclusion that *Sophia* is a female personification of God's own being in creative and saving involvement with the world. Johnson includes her analysis of *Sophia*'s field of action as being the same as that of Israel's God under the name YHWH. S. McFague draws the same conclusion in *Models of God* (Philadelphia: Fortress, ³1989), pp. 114-15.

6. See Proverbs 1 and 2. See also M. Borg, *Meeting Jesus Again for the First Time* (San Francisco: Harper, 1995), pp. 98-102, where he describes the attributes of Wisdom in the Intertestamental books of Sirach and the Wisdom of Solomon.

7. Johnson, *She Who Is*, pp. 86-94 and 133-41.

calamity comes on those who refuse her. Those who listen to her will be secure and live at ease, with no fear of disaster (Prov. 1:20-21; 8:1-3).

- From her mouth comes what is right and truth, and there is nothing twisted or crooked in it (Prov. 8:6-9).
- She offers prudence, knowledge, and discretion (Prov. 8:12).
- She hates arrogance and perverted speech (Prov. 8:13).
- Those who seek her find her, but they must watch daily at her gates and wait beside her doors (Prov. 8:17, 34).
- *Sophia* is a giver of life (Prov. 8:35).
- *Sophia* provides good advice, sound wisdom, insight, and strength (Prov. 8:14).
- She reaches mightily from one end of the earth to the other, and she orders all things well (Wis. of Sol. 8:1).
- She has the power to enlighten, to teach skills and crafts, to provide knowledge of the structure of the world and the activity of its elements, the cycles of the seasons and the stars, the varieties of animals, plants and roots, and human reasoning (Wis. of Sol. 7:17-22).

All of these things that are said about *Sophia*/Wisdom are found elsewhere in the biblical tradition to be the work of the Spirit of God in creating and sustaining the world and all that dwells in it. What qualities of Spirit/Wisdom are relevant for our subject of evidence? We suggest the following: knowledge, discernment, truth, and beneficial results. The first and most basic, knowledge, comes through experience with objects and circumstances encountered in the world.[8] In any particular field of study, knowledge may be connected with the collection of basic information and data acquired through physical apprehension by the senses of sight, sound, hearing, and other means.[9] This is what we refer to in this paper as "evidence," and it is the most fundamental component of Wisdom.

The second quality is discernment,[10] which goes beyond merely

8. A. Yong, *Beyond the Impasse* (Grand Rapids: Baker Academic, 2003), p. 148.

9. See Yong's discussion of the Hebrew verb *nakar*, translated as "discern" or "recognize," and the Hebrew word *yada'*, translated as "knowledge," in *Beyond the Impasse*, pp. 145-48.

10. Discernment is connected more with the Hebrew word *bina*, which includes discernment, insight, perception, and understanding. Yong discusses *bina* as being both a gift

gathering data and involves judgments and assessments of how to use the knowledge one possesses. It is a skill developed over time that helps one to be attuned to the features of the historical and social world and allows one to move beyond external forms to perceive the inner workings of things. Discernment is described in the New Testament as a "gift" for spiritual discernment, but the biblical data indicates that it applies on a much broader scale to physical, cognitive, and affective qualities and skills that help one perceive features of the natural world and the socio-cultural phenomena and interpersonal relationships that are in the world.[11] Development of such skills may require comprehensive training and years of discipline and study, such as that which is required for advanced accomplishment in medicine, law, and science. On the other hand, discernment as a gift suggests the possibility of sudden insight that seems to come from nowhere and that has the capacity to dramatically change the way we view things — as per the examples in our text of the insights by Galileo and Kant.[12] Further, discernment enables one to guide actions in a responsible manner. Thus, we see that the discernment of Spirit/Wisdom is manifest in a great variety of ways in the spiritual, physical, and cultural dimensions.

The third quality of Spirit/Wisdom is truth, which is an advanced derivative of both knowledge and discernment. In many, perhaps most, arenas of life, truth is very difficult to identify, as we have seen in the examples in this chapter. Truth cannot be equated with "facts" because, as we have seen, facts (or knowledge) are only the most basic aspects of wisdom and are subject to discernment in order to be meaningful. What we perceive as "true" often changes over time as we discover new information or reinterpret old information. Indeed, truth is the gold that comes forth from the crucible in which knowledge and discernment are tried by the fires of time. We may hope that the gold comes forth pure enough that it allows us to function as though it is true, at least for certain practical purposes. It is noteworthy that gold in its most common, functional forms is usually an alloy.

---

of God and a human capacity (*Beyond the Impasse*, p. 147). It is a power of judgment and perceptive insight and is demonstrated in the use of knowledge (p. 148).

11. Yong, *Beyond the Impasse*, p. 149.

12. The connection in some biblical passages of the word *bina* with the word *leb* (heart) indicates a dimension of emotion and intuition that may be brought to bear in the process of discernment (Exod. 35:26, 36:1; Job 9:4; Prov. 10:8; 16:21).

The final quality of Spirit/Wisdom we will discuss here is beneficial results. A scientific program may be regarded as being beneficial or successful when it asks questions and offers answers that allow continued progress of investigation and insight. Thus, even though no final conclusion may be drawn and the ultimate "truth" may not be discovered, a beneficial program will open the way to further work and insight in the future. On a broader scale, questions of whether anything is beneficial to the world and its peoples cannot be answered except over very long time spans. The assessment of what is beneficial may change over time. While we assume that science and technology are beneficial, we may discover that the results are ambiguous, as we have with atomic energy and a host of other scientific and technological innovations. Perhaps the key to Spirit/Wisdom is that it is never set in stone but is dynamic, actively seeking to bring forth as much fullness of its qualities as is possible in particular times and settings and also over very long periods of time in a great variety of contexts.

Who is able to receive this Spirit/Wisdom and do her work? Is it only the holy people, the overtly godly people, the people in churches and temples and synagogues and mosques? The fact that the Spirit of God is present and active in creation[13] indicates that knowledge penetrates all aspects of the created order and that wisdom is available to all those who seek it.[14] In Proverbs, *Sophia* is crying in the street for anyone who will hear her call, suggesting that the Spirit's voice of Wisdom is always seeking a channel through whom it can move and a voice through whom it can speak. The Spirit is like the wind and blows where it will. Anyone can be the recipient of Wisdom. Even so, the biblical texts make it clear that Wisdom is not achieved lightly nor cheaply and that there are few who attain it. Those who want Wisdom must cultivate certain qualities; they must be willing to listen, humble, honest, just, persevering, and committed to waiting and watching at *Sophia*'s doors. Where and when can this Spirit/Wisdom come forth? It can come forth any place and at any time. Perhaps, as in our example of parallax, it takes a long time for it to work through history, or

13. Genesis 1:1-2.

14. In Yong's *Beyond the Impasse,* he articulates and discusses the following axioms: "God is universally present and active in the Spirit" and "God's Spirit is the life-breath of the *imago Dei* in every human being and the presupposition of all human relationships and communities" (pp. 44-45). See his discussion of "The Hermeneutics of Discernment: The Biblical Materials" (pp. 39-49).

perhaps it dawns on one individual, such as an Einstein or Galileo or Kant, in a brilliant moment that changes the world. Even when there is insufficient evidence, we will know her by the hallmarks: knowledge, discernment, truth, beneficial results.

The Spirit in Philosophical, Theological, and Interdisciplinary Perspectives

MICHAEL WELKER

This chapter starts with the question, Does the strong theological and philosophical interest in the personhood of the Spirit conflict with the interest in making the Spirit a worthwhile topic in the science-and-theology dialogue? My answer is that it depends on the notion of personhood used in theological and philosophical inquiries. I will show that great philosophers such as Aristotle and Hegel cultivated a notion of the personhood of the spirit that is not adequate for an understanding of the Spirit of God as grasped and reflected in the Jewish and Christian normative texts of the biblical traditions. The core of the philosophical concepts of personhood and spirit is a cognitive self-referentiality. The biblical traditions, however, require a more demanding concept of personhood (which in the current culture is possibly still counterintuitive). The discourse with the sciences, but also the ecumenical discourse between different faith-traditions, might be of help in the interpretation of, and the operation with, this more complex understanding of the personhood of the Spirit.

The Self-Referential Spirit in Aristotle's and Hegel's Philosophies

One of the most famous philosophical texts in human history is Book XII of Aristotle's *Metaphysics*.[1] With this text, Aristotle shaped Western intel-

1. *The Works of Aristotle,* vol. 8: *Metaphysica,* trans. W. D. Ross (Oxford: Clarendon, 1928).

lectual religiosity in general (beyond specific religious traditions) by proposing a notion of "the Divine" or "the Divinity." He also shaped a notion of "the spirit" that was adopted by Western elites inside and outside of religious communities. This notion of "the spirit" was used in religious and anthropological theories, in epistemologies, and in theories of cultures. It provided a key concept to orient religious and cultural developments. Although the term *nous,* which he uses, has been translated not only as "spirit" but also as "reason" and "thought," the activity described by Aristotle appeared to many thinkers to be a convincing candidate for "the ultimate" and even "the Divine." Book XII of the *Metaphysics* implicitly equates God and this spirit (reason, [ultimate] thought). A fragment by Aristotle *On Prayer* explicitly says, "God is *nous.*"[2]

Aristotle describes the spirit as a creative and living thinking power, which takes part in and becomes part of what is being thought: "Spirit becomes itself an object of thought by grasping and thinking that which is thought, so that spirit and that which is thought are identical."[3] It is characteristic of the spirit that it connects a thinking relation to itself and a relation to another content of thought. Aristotle says that the spirit should not be reduced to the mere potentiality of thinking. The point is the self-actualization of the spirit in which — without losing itself — it can identify itself with the content of thought and can differentiate itself from the content of thought. "For that which is capable of receiving that which is thought and which is, is also spirit, to be sure, but it is in actual activity only when it has (that which is thought). Thus actually active thought, more so than the capacity to think, is the divine element that the spirit seems to have."

Aristotle does not only differentiate the lower level of the potentiality to think from the higher level of the actualized activity of the spirit. He also differentiates between levels of actualization. The thinking spirit can deal with more or less trivial or important contents. What is it that allows us to make gradations within the contents and the activities of the spirit? For Aristotle it is the fuller and stronger self-awareness in the activity of thinking that qualifies "higher" activities of the spirit from lower ones. The self-experience of the spirit (which cannot be achieved by resting on the

2. *Aristoteles Fragmenta Selecta,* in W. D. Ross (ed.), *Scriptorum Classicorum Bibliotheca Oxoniensis,* 3rd ed. (Oxford: Oxford University Press, 1964), p. 57.

3. This and the following quotations are from Aristotle's *Metaphysics* 1072b, 19-32.

level of mere potentiality of thinking!) is that which is best and which is the high point of all imaginable pleasure. Philosophical thinking, *theoria*, comes closest to this pleasure, which Aristotle understands as divine. "Intellectual contemplation (philosophic thought) is what is most pleasant and best. If, then, the Divinity is always doing as well as we sometimes (are), this compels our wonder. If the Divinity is doing still better, this compels our wonder still more. And the Divinity indeed is doing better."

Aristotle's remark with respect to the Divinity that enjoys "eternal life" in its self-referential actual spiritual activity is not a pious gloss. It marks a problem of human aspiration towards higher and higher "spiritual" activities. The stronger the self-actualization and the self-awareness, the closer the human spirit gets to the Divine. The mere relation to the potentiality of thinking, however, will not be the solution, no matter how intellectually sophisticated it may be. The highest potentiation of the self-relation is a self-actualization that disengages itself from the mere potentiality of thinking.

It was Hegel who most clearly noticed this complicated core of Aristotle's theory. He admired the depth of Aristotle's insight and closed his *Enzyklopädie der philosophischen Wissenschaften* with a long citation of the text inspected above.[4] Hegel sees that in the spirit thus conceived there is a dramatic tension. In order to reach the higher and highest level of self-referentiality, the spirit has to wrest itself loose from itself, to release itself. A self-bifurcation and a self-acquisition have to go hand in hand. This "life of the spirit" includes a moment of self-alienation. The greater and the richer the intensity of the full self-awareness that is intended, the harder the breaking away from itself must be. It is at this point that Hegel could include his "death of God" theory in his reading of Aristotle's theory of the spirit.

Hegel has no problem with the final goal of a self-referential spirit in Aristotle's theory. "As spirit I am only insofar as I know myself. . . . Know thyself, the inscription above the temple of the knowing God at Delphi, is the absolute commandment that expresses the nature of the spirit."[5] His complaint, however, is that Aristotle's theory of the spirit conceptualizes the working of the spirit in terms too intellectual. Aristotle's theory re-

---

4. *Enzyklopädie der philosophischen Wissenschaften im Grundrisse* (1830), ed. F. Nicolin and O. Pöggeler (Hamburg: Meiner, 1968), p. 463.

5. Hegel, *Vorlesungen über die Geschichte der Philosophie* 3, *Werke*, 20:480-81.

mains abstract, fixated on a highest principle. He fails to grasp the spirit in its true reality, that is, as a world-shaping activity. According to Hegel, Aristotle ingeniously sees the ultimate principle of the spirit. "But this element of thought itself is abstract. It is the activity of an individual consciousness. Spirit, though, is not only understood as individual, finite consciousness, but as spirit that is universal and concrete in itself."[6] Spirit is thus not only a thinking relation to itself. It is a power in which individuals, communities, cultures, indeed, a whole world not only captures itself in thoughts, not only comes to an understanding of itself, but also presents and manifests itself, shapes and transforms itself. Spirit is much more than just a contemplative creativity.

In all this, however, the spirit does not lose its goal of self-referentiality. Although the spirit enters into the finite and perishable, in its union with what is finite and perishable, the spirit is only "in itself and at home with itself." Hegel can say: "spirit is being-at-home-with-self" or spirit is the "reconciled return to itself out of its other."[7] Although this return to itself includes an element of self-differentiation, even of self-estrangement, this element is only a "moment" in the life of the spirit. The self-referentiality embraces the activity of the spirit in the same way that is described by Aristotle in his *Metaphysics* Book XII, 7.

The Spirit and Its Personhood in the Biblical Traditions

The cognitive self-referentiality, so central to Aristotle's notion of the *nous* and the divine life, is no topic in the biblical references to the Spirit. There is no indication that they are interested in a "reconciled return" of the Spirit "to itself out of its other" in Hegel's sense. This does not mean that the Spirit is without cognitive dimensions. Quite on the contrary, the messianic traditions of the *Tanach*/Old Testament declare that the messianic bearer of the Spirit will bring not only justice and mercy to Jews and Gentiles but also a universal knowledge and cognition of God (Isa. 11:2, 9; 42:6-7; 61:6). And the "pouring of the Spirit" is clearly connected to a new cognition of God and a renewal of spiritual insight and proclamation

---

6. Hegel, *Vorlesungen*, p. 481.

7. Cf. Hegel, *Philosophy of Fine Art*, vol. 2, trans. F. P. B. Osmaston (New York: Hacker Art, 1975), p. 309.

(Ezek. 39:28-29; Joel 3:1; Zech. 12:10 with 13:4-5; Acts 2:11, 17ff.). Throughout the New Testament traditions we find a close association of "Spirit" and "truth."

Paul says that the Spirit teaches and "interprets spiritual truths to those who possess the Spirit" (1 Cor. 2:12-13) and connects sanctification by the Spirit and belief in the truth (2 Thess. 2:13). John also speaks of the "Spirit of truth" (14:17) and declares that God "must be worshipped in Spirit and truth" (4:23-24). 1 John 5:7 states: "the Spirit is the witness, because the Spirit is the truth," and 2 Timothy 1:14 refers to "the truth that has been entrusted to you by the Holy Spirit who dwells within us."

However this relation of Spirit and truth is understood, it is most important to notice that self-referentiality is not its basis. John 16:13 says: "When the Spirit of truth comes, it will guide you into all the truth, *for it will not speak on its own authority,* but whatever it hears it will speak, and it will declare to you the things that are to come." The "Spirit of truth" will bear witness to Christ and will not speak on its own authority (cf. John 15:26).

Although the New Testament traditions insist on the fact that insight and proclamation in the power of the Spirit are stronger than mere human words and wisdom (cf. Rom. 15:19; 1 Cor. 2:4; 1 Thess. 1:5), they clearly emphasize the revelatory and enlightening power of the Spirit in the lives and minds of human beings. First Corinthians 2:10 speaks of God's revelation through the Spirit and says: "For the Spirit searches everything, even the depth of God." The Spirit provides a depth of insight and circumspection that leads to Paul's claim: "The spiritual person judges all things, but is itself to be judged by no one" (1 Cor. 2:15).

Is this all self-congratulating rhetoric, or can we gain a picture of the activity of the Spirit that allows not only understanding but also an academic defense of these claims? In Romans 8:26-27 Paul speaks about the Spirit, who intercedes "for us with sighs too deep for words."[8] Why and how does the Spirit reach these depths of pre-cognitive insight and preverbal expression? The answer to this question is that the Spirit of the New Testament traditions is not a self-referential personality but an utterly empathetic personality with a multi-contextual presence.

John Polkinghorne has argued that the personhood of the Holy

---

8. Cf. also Romans 8:27: "He who searches the hearts of men knows what is the mind of the Spirit, because the Spirit intercedes for the saints according to the will of God."

Spirit should be understood in relation to its context-sensitivity and encounter-sensitivity.[9] The Holy Spirit is not a power that acts and operates in every context in "the same way." First Corinthians 12:11 speaks of the "one Spirit, who apportions to each one individually as it wills," and Hebrews 2:4 says that God acts "by various gifts and miracles of the Holy Spirit distributed according to its own will." This might be compatible with the affirmation in John 3:34 that God "gives the Spirit without measure." All associations of uniformity and homogeneity, however, must be corrected associations, which might be evoked by some "oneness statements" such as 1 Corinthians 12:13: "by one Spirit we were all baptized into one body," or Philippians 1:27: "you stand firm in one spirit," or that according to Philippians 2:1, by participation in the Spirit we have the "same mind, the same love." According to the biblical traditions, the Spirit is context-sensitive and individuality-sensitive. This is perfectly compatible with the assurance in 2 Corinthians 3:17: "Now the Lord is the Spirit, and where the Spirit of the Lord is, there is freedom."

But how, then, can we avoid the conclusion that the Spirit is an amorphic and only so-called "personality," a chameleon that changes with each encounter and each context? The personal identity of the Spirit, its faithfulness and its trustworthiness, is guaranteed by the dual relation to God the creator and to the Lordship of Jesus Christ. Second Corinthians 3:18 states: "The Lord who is the Spirit changes us into his likeness from one degree of glory to another." The text oscillates between the Lordship of the Spirit and the Lordship of Christ.

As we have shown in several research projects with scientists, biblical scholars, and theologians, we have to correct reductionistic biologistic and scientistic modes of thought when we want to deal with the "new creation" and the reality of the resurrected Christ.[10] We need not abandon all rationalities and modes of academic and scientific inquiry when we deal with the reality of the resurrection. However, we have to face, and to think, the edifying "wholeness" of the person and life of Christ who encounters us in

9. John Polkinghorne, *Faith in the Living God: A Dialogue* (London: SPCK/Philadelphia: Fortress, 2001), pp. 71ff., 97; and cf. his essay herein.

10. John Polkinghorne and Michael Welker, eds., *The End of the World and the Ends of God: Science and Theology on Eschatology* (Harrisburg: Trinity, 2000); Ted Peters, Robert Russell, and Michael Welker, eds., *Resurrection: Theological and Scientific Assessments* (Grand Rapids: Eerdmans, 2002); Hans-Joachim Eckstein and Michael Welker, eds., *Die Wirklichkeit der Auferstehung* (Neukirchen-Vluyn: Neukirchener, 2002; 2nd ed. 2004).

the resurrection. The resurrection is not a resuscitation, but the presence of the wholeness of Christ's life and person in "Spirit and faith," a "spiritual body," so difficult to grasp for a conventional biologistic and natural-scientistic way of thinking. This wholeness can draw human beings poly-individually into this life. Different spiritual gifts make possible different relations to the eternal life of God. In different individual ways we are changed "into his likeness from one degree of glory to another."

This requires the "tolerant" but by no means indifferent forms of faith, hope, and love to deal with a spiritual reality that gives time and space for such different accesses to the same complex reality. It is remarkable that the working of the Spirit is continuously associated with "joy and peace,"[11] a constellation in which the individual member of the community of faith is not only affirmed but elevated and elated and at the same time reconciled even with those who seemed to endanger this person's very existence. Differences are transformed into contrasts; conflicting differences are transformed into creative ones.

The context-sensitivity and encounter-sensitivity of the Spirit is also correlated with its vulnerability. Statements such as 1 Thessalonians 5:19, "do not quench the Spirit"; Ephesians 4:30, "do not grieve the Spirit of God, in whom you were sealed for the day of redemption"; Acts 5:9, "do not tempt the Spirit"; and Hebrews 10:29 about "outraging the Spirit of grace" would be impossible if the Spirit were merely an irresistible force. The power of the Spirit and the subtlety and sensitivity of its working do not contradict each other.

The intrinsic richness of the Spirit is acknowledged, when its definite givenness to human beings is expressed by the terms of "pouring" the Spirit and the mode of "filling" them with the Spirit.[12] The Spirit enables people to gain an immediacy to God, even a unity not only with one another but above all with Christ himself and with the divine Creator.[13] This unity becomes manifest in the intimate address to God. "God sent the Spirit of his Son into your heart, crying Abba!" (Gal. 4:6; cf. Rom. 8:15). On the other hand, this unity, intimacy, and immediacy does not mean simplicity and uniformity. A rich personality in faith and a complex and lively community

---

11. Cf. Rom. 8:6; 14:17; 15:13; Gal. 5:16ff.; Eph. 4:3; 1 Thess. 1:6.
12. Cf. the notion of the "temple of the Holy Spirit" in 1 Cor. 3:16 and 6:19 and the frequent talk about human beings "filled" by the Spirit in Acts.
13. Rom. 8:9; 1 Cor. 6:17.

are constituted by the Holy Spirit. The Spirit gives the power to human beings to host in themselves the fullness of Christ and the creativity of God.

The ability to host the Spirit even in our bodies and to unite with God in Christ "in the Spirit" is a simply breathtaking elevation, an extension of the real human existence. The ability to be present "in the spirit" even when we cannot be bodily present (1 Cor. 5:3; Col. 2:5) mirrors this anthropologically and realistically. Visions, experiences of theophany and revelation, and the power to proclaim the gospel in a convincing way are related to the workings of the Spirit. Various New Testament texts emphasize the access to eschatological realities experienced by people "who have tasted the heavenly gift and have become partakers of the Holy Spirit" (Heb. 6:4) — eschatological realities such as the participation in the resurrection, the entrance into the reign of God, a share in eternal life (Gal. 6:8). Paul even speaks of salvific repercussions on the bodily existence and the whole creation that let those "who have the first fruit of the Spirit, wait for the redemption of our bodies . . . with patience" (Rom. 8:23).

The multicontextual and polyphonic presence of the Spirit accounts for the connection of various very different phenomena addressed by biblical traditions:

- the canonic coherence of the biblical traditions provided by the Spirit, who speaks as the one voice in and through the different voices of the canon;[14]
- the fact that different ways of access are possible for Jews and Gentiles, related to the working of the Spirit or of the Messianic bearer and dispenser of the Spirit, respectively;[15]
- the trust that the Spirit is present in different contexts of trial and danger and that it gives voice to the persecuted and oppressed;[16]
- the figure of the "pouring" of the Spirit and the insistence that "male and female, young and old, masters and slaves" and people of different nations, languages, and cultures will be endowed with prophetic insight and power.[17]

---

14. Cf. Mark 12:36 par.; Acts 1:16; 4:25; 11:28; 20:25. See also Michael Welker, *God the Spirit* (Minneapolis: Fortress, 1994), ch. 5.5.

15. Cf. Isa. 11; 42; 61; Rom. 15:16; Eph. 2:18. See also Welker, *God the Spirit,* chs. 1 and 6.2.

16. Cf. Mark 13:11 par.

17. Joel 3:1ff. and Acts 2:17ff.; cf. Welker, *God the Spirit,* chs. 3.3-4 and 5.1.

The multicontextual and polyphonic presence of the Spirit requires us to question simple one-on-one relations and monohierarchical forms of social interaction in their ability to express basic religious experiences and interactions. Theories of "emergence" have to be used to explain the multicontextual and polyphonic character of the Spirit and its working.[18]

The pouring out of the Spirit brings about a pluralistic striving for God's righteousness and truth. The complex multicontextual and polyphonic unity brought forth by the Spirit is not a luxury or a "postmodern" invention. The pluralistic unity of the Spirit is the divine power by which God works through frail and finite human creatures against the powers of sin and distortion. Not only the pouring of the Spirit, but also the resurrection of Christ, the constitution of the post-Easterly body of Christ and the coming of God's reign are of such an emergent pluralistic structure. They all have in common that they work among human beings in complex instead of in monolinear ways. They work in emergent ways — that is, they alter a complex constellation with a multiplicity of internal relationships by reconfiguring the internal relations and clusters of relations, be it gradually or at once.[19] The new relationships and constellations do not only modify each other; they also have unforeseen effects and joint effects on "the whole" constellation.

The powers of God that counter evil and the forces of sin, freeing creation from self-jeopardy and self-destruction, often come in most astounding modesty. This is very clear with respect to the "coming reign of God." According to the parables used in Jesus Christ's proclamation, this reign does not come like a storm and not even like a train or a bus.[20] It comes like green leaves out of a branch or like grass out of the ground. While for some they are still invisible, for others they predict a good harvest. God's reign comes like the early morning light, which some see as the beginning day and others still call night and darkness. Jesus' parables speak of this emergent reality brought forth in numerous experiences of mercy, of forgiveness, and of free and unexpected deeds of justice and love.

18. Cf. Amos Yong's essay herein.
19. Cf. the essay by Donald and Anna York herein.
20. Cf. Michael Welker, "The 'Reign' of God," *Theology Today* 49 (1993): 500-515, and "Theological Realism and Eschatological Symbol Systems: Resurrection, the Reign of God, and the Presence in Faith and in the Spirit," in Ted Peters, Robert Russell, and Michael Welker (eds.), *Resurrection: Theological and Scientific Assessments* (Grand Rapids: Eerdmans, 2002), pp. 31-42.

Similar observations can be made with respect to the resurrection of Christ. It happens in a much less triumphalistic mode than often depicted. In his many different appearances and revelations, in the midst of uncertainty and doubts, the insight emerges that Jesus has risen from the dead. Out of a multitude of witnesses, mingled with skepticism and uncertainties, grows the post-Easter body of Christ that bears Christ's new presence. It is this complex spiritual reality that overcomes the powers of death and destruction: a reality that guides the search for truth in the midst of uncertainty and doubts.[21]

Consequences for the Ecumenical and Interdisciplinary Dialogue about the Spirit

Deep, ecstatic experiences of an awesome power are characteristic of the experience of the Spirit. This holds true for the biblical witnesses and the Pentecostal and Charismatic theologies.[22] This also holds true for philosophical and scientific processes of discovery in which most amazing truths are found and revealed and most astonishing truth-claims are encouraged in the midst of uncertainties and open questions.[23] The power that conditions these experiences both in natural reality and in human minds is identified as "the Spirit." The Spirit has the dual character of a personal, namely, context-sensitive and intentional instance — and of a structuring force-field, which operates in polycontextual and polyphonic forms.[24] The notion of the "pouring" of the Spirit seems to combine both characters and modes.

The biblical traditions know about good and evil spirits, salvific and demonic powers. The New Testament traditions identify the divine Spirit, the Holy Spirit, as the Spirit of the merciful creator and the Spirit of Jesus Christ, which is the divine living and loving power that unites the self-revealing God and connects God and creation in sustaining, saving, and ennobling ways. In science and philosophy, too, we know about deceiving

21. Cf. Michael Welker, "Resurrection and Eternal Life: The Canonic Memory of the Resurrected Christ, His Reality, and His Glory," in Polkinghorne and Welker (eds.), *The End of the World and the Ends of God,* pp. 279-90.

22. Cf. the contributions by James Dunn and by Frank Macchia herein.

23. See the essays by John Polkinghorne and by the Yorks herein.

24. Cf. the contribution by Bernd Oberdorfer herein.

spirits, we know about individual and shared certainties that prove to be wrong, misleading, and distortive. We know devastating forms of consensus that breed dangerous ideologies or stale theories that block insight over ages. Thus the discernment of the spirits is a most important task in all named fields of experience, knowledge, and conviction.

One of the most pressing questions in the dialogue within and between the different traditions of faith that gave rise to this volume was the role of individual excitement and its public resonance in valid experiences of the Spirit.[25] Does the Spirit primarily work in exceptional events on the interior depth of the individual person or persons? Or does it work in more hidden ways through historical and social processes in ordinary life, as a patient comforter, enabler, and teacher?[26] There was no pressure for an abstract "either/or" in the dialogue. But there were questions concerning the standards to discern the spirits in religious and academic contexts. The connection of Spirit and truth was affirmed by all members of the discourse. The related question was how truth-seeking communities were to be understood both in religious and academic environments.

Most members from the Pentecostal and Charismatic traditions have insisted on the importance of "Spirit baptism" for their own faith tradition.[27] The interpretation of this symbol in the framework of the polycontextual and polyphonic dwelling of the Spirit opened a way to mediate between the insistence on dramatic and sensational individual experiences as "initiation events" of faith and the insistence that the "Spirit of truth" is characterized by its connection to Jesus Christ and to a Wisdom that operates in astounding, though not necessarily spectacular ways.

The unfolding of multidimensional anthropology as proposed by the sciences, over against transcendental and existentialist theories of the human being, and theories of pluralistic configurations in current societies, cultures, and ecumenical communications will help us to develop our ability to handle emergent processes with greater ease. Methodologically, it will be crucial to understand the inner texture of truth-seeking communities in order to make clear that the multicontextual and polyphonic presence of the Spirit does not create chaos or lead to the loss of clear orientation.

25. Cf. the essay by Margaret Poloma herein.

26. Cf. the contributions of Kathryn Tanner, John Polkinghorne, and Lyle Dabney herein.

27. See especially the contribution by Frank Macchia.

Truth-seeking communities are not groups of people who look around to somehow find some kind of truth. Nor do they claim to possess the full truth and to speak it with the expectation that everybody else just has to listen, to agree, and to obey. Truth-seeking communities are willing to formulate truth-claims, to express an utmost certainty similar to the famous words of Luther before the Reichstag at Worms: "If I am not overwhelmed by clear arguments of reason or arguments from Scripture, then I am already overwhelmed and my conscience is bound in God's Word." In formulating truth-claims, truth-seeking communities express not only utmost certainty, but also topical insight. In addition, they develop standards of argumentation for the challenge of their truth-claims and certainties and for the improvement of their insights.[28]

Truth-seeking communities do not affirm the same certainties in repetitive ways. Rather, they search for growth in certainty, they strive for a strengthening of their conviction and consensus. At the same time they search for growth in insight. Neither correct insight without personal and communal certainty nor personal and communal certainty without topical insight is sufficient. The mutual challenge and possible growth of certainty and insight bring individuals and communities on the road towards truth.

28. Cf. Polkinghorne and Welker, *Faith in the Living God*, ch. 9, and Michael Welker, "Theology in Public Discourse outside Communities of Faith?" in Luis E. Lego (ed.), *Religion, Pluralism, and Public Life: Abraham Kuyper's Legacy for the Twenty-first Century* (Grand Rapids: Eerdmans, 2000), pp. 110-22.

Contributors

D. Lyle Dabney teaches Protestant systematic theology at the Roman Catholic Marquette University in Milwaukee. He is the author of a number of articles on pneumatology in scholarly journals as well as a work in German on the Holy Spirit, *Die Kenosis des Geistes: Kontinuität zwischen Schöpfung und Erlösung in Werk des Heiligen Geistes* (1997), and published in the volume *Starting with the Spirit: The Task of Theology Today II* (2001). He is currently working on pneumatology as a field of discourse and on theological anthropology.

The New Testament scholar James D. G. Dunn is emeritus Lightfoot Professor of Divinity at the University of Durham. His writings on the Holy Spirit, St. Paul, and Jesus and his studies of the evolution of the historical-critical method are widely known. Having chaired several academic associations, he was founding chairman of the Association of University Departments of Theology and Religion and Religious Studies in the U.K. and president of both the British New Testament Conference and the *Studiorum Novi Testamenti Societas*. He is the editor of the Cambridge University Press series, Theology of the New Testament, as well as of three journals. As author or co-author he has published some 180 articles and about twenty-four books, from the early *Baptism in the Holy Spirit* (1970) to the recent *Jesus Remembered* (2003), the first volume of Christianity in the Making.

Veli-Matti Kärkkäinen is professor of systematic theology at Fuller Theological Seminary. He also holds a visiting professorship in Theology and Missiology at Iso Kirja College, teaches ecumenics at the University of Helsinki, and serves as a member of the advisory council of the International Charismatic Consultation on World Evangelisation, the advisory group for Church and Ecumenical Relations of the World Council of Churches and the World Council of Churches Consultation on Healing and Faith. He has published about sixty journal articles and ten books, including the latest, *One with God: Salvation as Deification and Justification* (2004).

The Pentecostal theologian and Assemblies of God minister **Frank D. Macchia** is professor of theology and director of graduate programs in Religion at Vanguard University in Costa Mesa, California. The former president of the Society for Pentecostal Studies serves as co-chair of the Justification/Sanctification/Ethics Study Group of the Faith and Order Commission of the U.S. National Council of Christian Churches. He is editor of *Pneuma: The Journal of the Society for Pentecostal Studies* and of the *Journal of Pentecostal Theology* and has published some twenty-five journal articles and essays, as well as his book *Spirituality and Social Liberation: The Message of the Blumhardts in the Light of Wuerttemberg Pietism* (1993).

Bernd Oberdorfer is professor of systematic theology at the University of Augsburg and has specialized in Trinitarian theology and pneumatology. He worked on topics in the history of Christian doctrine, Ecumenical theology and interdenominational dialogue, Orthodox theology and theological theories of culture. He has published about thirty articles and two books in German, including *Filioque: Geschichte und Theologie eines ökumenischen Problems* (2001).

John C. Polkinghorne, a distinguished particle physicist, started a second career as a theologian and was named president of Queens' College in 1989. He is a Knight of the British Empire and a Fellow of the Royal Society, a member of the Society of Ordained Scientists, and a Fellow of Queens' College as well as Canon Theologian of Liverpool. He is also the founding president of the International Society for Science and Religion and the winner of the 2002 Templeton Prize for Progress toward Research or Discoveries about Spiritual Realities. In addition to writing on theoretical elementary particle physics, he is editor and author of seventeen books on the interrelationship of science and theology, including most recently *Science and Trinity* (2003).

Margaret M. Poloma is *professor emerita* of sociology at the University of Akron and has specialized in analyzing the Pentecostal charismatic movement. She was a council member of various academic associations and is still a member of the steering committee of the Christian Sociological Society and of the advisory board of the Lewis Wilson Institute for Pentecostal Studies. She has been editor or co-editor of seven journals and is currently an editor of *Pneuma: The Journal for the Society of Pentecostal Studies* and of the *Journal of Psychology and Theology*. She has been author or co-author of eight books, including the latest, *Main Street Mystics: The Toronto Blessing and Reviving Pentecostalism* (2003).

Kathryn Tanner is professor of theology at the University of Chicago Divinity School and relates past theological traditions to areas of contemporary concern by using critical, social, and feminist theory. She currently serves on the Theology Committee of the Episcopal House of Bishops and on the editorial boards of the *International Journal of Systematic Theology, Modern Theology,* and the *Scottish Journal of Theology*. She was co-editor of *Converging on Culture: Theologians in Dialogue with Cultural Analysis and Criticism* (2001) and is the author of a number of journal articles and four books, including the latest, *The Economy of Grace* (2005), and is the editor of *The Oxford Handbook of Systematic Theology.*

Grant Wacker is professor of church history at the Duke University Divinity School and specializes in American Pentecostalism. Formerly president of the Society for Pentecostal Studies, he currently serves as editor or co-editor of five journals, including *Pneuma: Journal of the Society for Pentecostal Studies*. He is the author of more than twenty journal articles and essays and three books, including *Heaven Below: Early Pentecostals and American Culture* (2001), for which he has received several awards among them the 2002 Award for Excellence from the American Academy of Religion. He is an advisory editor of the *Encyclopedia of Protestantism,* which will be published in six volumes.

Michael Welker is professor and chair of systematic theology in the Theological Faculty of the University of Heidelberg and has focused on the interplay among religious, legal, moral, scientific, and other cultural codes that shape the ethos of the postmodern world. He has been director of Heidelberg University's *Internationales Wissenschaftsforum* since 1996 and still is a member of the editorial boards of eight journals, such as the *Jahrbuch für Biblische Theologie*. He has published some two hundred journal articles and has written or edited more than twenty books, including *What Happens in Holy Communion?* (2000) and (with John Polkinghorne) *Faith in the Living God: A Dialogue for Troubled Friends and Educated Despisers of Christianity* (2001).

Amos Yong is associate professor of theology at Bethel College in St. Paul, Minnesota, and a minister in the General Council of the Assemblies of God, and his research focuses on pneumatology and the theology of religions. He has authored some thirty-five articles in journals and volumes of collected works, as well as four books, including most recently *The Spirit Poured Out on All Flesh: Pentecostalism and the Possibility of Global Theology* (2005). He presently serves on the steering committee of the Evangelical Theology Group of the American Academy of Religion and is an editor of two journals, including *Pneuma: Journal of the Society for Pentecostal Studies*.

Anna York is the former associate pastor of the Ellis Avenue Church in Chicago. She currently does educational consulting and tutoring and is the author of *RisingUp! A Story of Hope, Power and Transformation*, which will be published by HarperCollins in 2007. The book is an account of her forty-year struggle with multiple sclerosis and recovery from severe disability through traditional Chinese healing arts.

Donald G. York is the Horace B. Horton Professor of Astronomy and Astrophysics at the University of Chicago. His research has focused on the gas and dust between galaxies for the clues they provide to the formation and evolution of the universe. He was the founding director of the Apache Point Observatory in Sunspot, New Mexico, and of the Sloan Digital Sky Survey. He is also the founder and co-director of the Chicago Public Schools/University of Chicago Internet Project and the author of some 330 scientific papers.